NIGELLA CHRISTMAS

NIGELLA COLLECTION
BY NIGELLA LAWSON

HOW TO EAT
THE PLEASURES AND PRINCIPLES OF GOOD FOOD

HOW TO BE A DOMESTIC GODDESS
BAKING AND THE ART OF COMFORT COOKING

NIGELLA BITES

NIGELLA SUMMER
EASY COOKING, EASY EATING

FEAST
FOOD THAT CELEBRATES LIFE

NIGELLA EXPRESS
GOOD FOOD FAST

NIGELLA CHRISTMAS

NIGELLA KITCHEN
RECIPES FROM THE HEART OF THE HOME

NIGELLISSIMA
INSTANT ITALIAN INSPIRATION

'THE PERFECT PRACTICAL SURVIVAL GUIDE
TO THE FESTIVE SEASON, NIGELLA-STYLE'

MARIE CLAIRE

NIGELLA CHRISTMAS

FOOD ❄ FAMILY ❄ FRIENDS ❄ FESTIVITIES

NIGELLA LAWSON

PHOTOGRAPHS BY LIS PARSONS

Chatto & Windus
LONDON

Published by Chatto & Windus 2014

2 4 6 8 10 9 7 5 3 1

First published in Great Britain in 2008 by
Chatto & Windus
Random House, 20 Vauxhall Bridge Road,
London SW1V 2SA

www.randomhouse.co.uk

A CIP catalogue record for this book
is available from the British Library

ISBN 978 0 701 189167

The Random House Group Limited supports the Forest Stewardship Council® (FSC®),
the leading international forest-certification organisation. Our books carrying the FSC
label are printed on FSC®-certified paper. FSC is the only forest-certification scheme
supported by the leading environmental organisations, including Greenpeace. Our
paper procurement policy can be found at
www.randomhouse.co.uk/environment

Design and Art Direction: Caz Hildebrand
Cookery Assistant: Hettie Potter
Editorial Assistant: Zoe Wales
Props: Rose Murray
Layout/Design: Julie Martin
Home Economics adviser: Moyra Fraser
Index: Vicki Robinson

Printed and bound by C&C Offset Printing Co., Ltd., China

CONTENTS

INTRODUCTION

I'LL BE HONEST: I NEVER THOUGHT I'D WRITE A CHRISTMAS BOOK. But then, not so long ago, I never actually thought I'd become a food writer. I hadn't rejected either idea; it just never occurred to me. That's how life works, and so much the better for it. I accept – with gratitude – that what makes one happiest cannot be planned.

This is not to say I have anything against Christmas. Far from it: almost every book I've written has a chapter on Christmas. I wallow in it; I relish it. Everything I believe in – essentially, that warmth and contentment and welcome and friendship emanate from and are celebrated in the kitchen – finds most cogent expression for me at Christmas. But I can't deny that I am, simply put, a heathen. Although I have not been able to stop myself from writing piecemeal about the joys – and the stresses, I don't dispute – of cooking for Christmas, I felt a certain reserve at interjecting myself a little too presumptuously into other people's feast and faith.

But truth is, the Christmas we celebrate in our kitchens is not the Christmas that is celebrated in Church. Yes, of course, they coincide, and, for many, the latter corroborates and gives meaning to the former, but the Christmas feasting, the Christmas lights, the carousing and the gift-giving, these come from much further back than the birth of Christianity. Indeed, one of the great geniuses of Christianity has been its sage piggybacking of pre-existing feasts and festivals. If you want to encourage the heathens to adopt your faith, how very sensible to reassure them that their fun is not going to be taken away. This, anyway, is the frank explanation of what is more eruditely tagged syncretism. Biblical scholars generally tend to believe that Christ's birth probably fell about six months after Passover, which would make it nearer September than

December. However, the Roman Festival of Saturnalia – a time of merry-making, excess and misrule, precursor to the office party and much else besides – fell around the middle of December, and led up to the Sol Invictus – or unconquered sun – festival. Around this time mummers would go about carousing and entertaining people in their homes, which is what has led to our carol-singing now. The idea of the unconquered sun, or the rebirth of the sun, has been linked by Catholics to the notion of the birth of Christ, and links, too, with the pagan notion, the one I cling to most affectionately, of the winter solstice being about the promise of the return of light in the depth of the dark winter.

This isn't a history lesson, nor would I be qualified to give one, but this mesh, or rather mish-mash, of traditions and festivities, enthrals me as it speaks so pointedly to our customs now. Saturnalia – in other words, the celebration of Saturn, the Roman god of agriculture and plenty – began the tradition of gift-giving, in the sense that the rich were encouraged to give food and money to the poor, at what was an inhospitable time of year. And, taking advantage of all that,

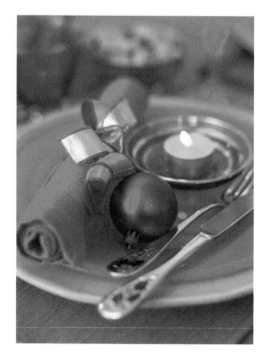

it was Pope Julius I who decreed that the birth of Christ be celebrated on December 25th, the better to bring recalcitrant Romans, still very much in the majority, into the fold. The day itself had other advantages, being as well, in Ancient Babylon, the Feast of the Son of Isis, Goddess of Nature, and a time, too, of hedonistic mayhem, gluttony, inebriation and the bestowing of monies and presents. Or so I believe, and want to believe. It's obvious that the day is intended to have pan-significance, and I embrace that joyfully. I like the sense of enjoying the legacy of partying down the ages.

But my greatest love, my deepest feelings, are for the pagan rituals that underpin the contemporary Christmas. In fact, I'd go further and say that my approach to the festival is ultimately pagan. We all know that the tree is a remnant (or adoption, if you wish) of the pagan celebration of the winter solstice, when a green bough would be brought into the house to serve as a reminder that the earth would renew itself again, and that the crops would return. But there is so much more to it than that. Christmas in my home really is about bringing light and fire and warmth into the chill darkness. I love the reminder of the cycle of the seasons, the belief in the beneficence of Mother Nature and the sense that the hearth and the home keep the light alive and provide sustenance and hope. For me, Christmas is not just a time when the Domestic Goddess comes into her own but a moment to conjure up the Domestic Druid as well. There are those within the fantastically named Pagan Federation, who still call the winter solstice, not Yule, as the Scandinavians did, but in the style of the Anglo-Saxons, Mother Night. When I was once on a radio programme discussing Christmas rituals, a high priestess of a Wiccan coven and I discovered we celebrated the festival in much the same way; she felt that the lighting of the oven, the creating of the feast, was the human way of understanding, celebrating and enshrining the sustenance of Mother Nature. How could I object to that?

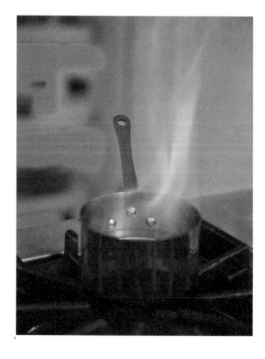

I feel the Christmas rituals of the home are, even if not based around faith, essentially an act of good faith. I see the argument against: the world is starving and we overeat and celebrate overeating; the world is poor and we spend money to give presents to people who don't truly need anything. I know how it seems – crassly commercial, tawdry, tacky and insincere. But I defend the exuberance and the lurch of excess as a kind act in a cruel world. It is about shining a light in the darkness, providing warmth in the coldness. I make no distinction between the glow from the fairy lights, the warmth of the oven, and the welcome in the home. And this is probably best symbolized by the act of bringing the flaming Christmas pudding to the table.

So, if I've found myself having written a Christmas book, it is all this – the belief in hearth and home, the fervent adherence to ritual and tradition when everything else in the world can make one feel unmoored, a faith in hospitality and fellow-feeling – that the book is about. And yes, it is also about indulgence, although I see festive indulgence not as a bad thing or an act of weakness, but a celebration of being alive – a positive source, if not for good, then for happiness. The book's subtitle – food, family, friends, festivities – is not just a frenetic exercise in alliteration but an affirmation of what I believe is important in life, and all – praise be – that Christmas celebrates.

That is my inspiration, but I aim, too, to mop up some of the perspiration. I am not by nature a calm person, and, much as I love Christmas, I can be kyboshed by it. I know from experience how easy it is to be overwhelmed by the sheer workload and the burden of expectations, one's own above all. Christmas has to be about plenty, and the last thing I'd ever advocate is a miserly, pared-down version, but there is abundant sense in finding a workable, enjoyable way through it. This, I hope, my book does. It is certainly the way I have found to save my own seasonal sanity.

I should, though, admit that my own shortcomings and temperamental failings ensure that there are many things this book is not. I have learnt how to get maximum pleasure with minimum stress, but I am never going to be the sort of person who has cake and pudding made and presents bought before November, and this book does not presume that you are, either. If you want to get ahead, and really can pull that micro-management and super-organization off, then this book gives you plenty of scope for that, as there are make-ahead and freeze-ahead tips throughout; if you are not that way inclined, then I have a couple of Christmas cakes you can make at the very last minute and a pudding that is luscious enough without having the traditional year in which to mature. I do indeed own a book – Fanny and Johnnie Cradock's *Coping with Christmas* – that begins: "January 1st: Make Christmas pudding for next year". I don't find such an injunction inspiring; I find it discouraging.

Likewise, although I know that it is in the tradition of Christmas manuals to suggest clever ideas for making table decorations and suchlike, I just couldn't. I'd love to be able to, but I am the living embodiment of the term cack-handed. I can wrap up a book and it looks as though I'm giving a bottle of wine. Still, I did want to share some of my enthusiasms, and thus I give you these presents here (overleaf). Although I have a weakness for bulk-buying giftwrap online, I have a contrary addiction to recycling. I'm afraid my recycling doesn't take the form of good bin management or anything as civic minded as that, but I am always happier to wrap a present in brown paper and string, with a couple of cinnamon sticks, or old newspaper and ribbon, than hand over the sheeniest, shiniest beribboned and rosetted parcel. My prompt is aesthetic rather more than ecological, though you could argue the effect is the same.

But if I can't fashion wreaths or fold napkins, I am happy to say that there is a Christmas craft for the clumsy, and it has an important place in this book. I make chutney. Chutney is jam-making for the time-pressed. When I say that you don't have to do anything except put all the ingredients needed into a pan, bring to a boil and cook for about 40 minutes, untended, I mean it. Moreover, I have quite a few recipes here, if such they can be called, for edible presents that involve no cooking whatsoever. And it is not some post-ironic, post-industrial, make-do-and-mend mentality (though there is every reason for heeding that) that makes me implore you to make your own presents, but a belief that what comes out of your kitchen means more than anything from a shop ever will, and that the satisfactions of the season can stem from the stove.

NOTE FOR THE READER

- all eggs are large, organic
- all butter is unsalted
- all herbs are fresh, unless stated
- all chocolate is dark (min. 70% cocoa solids), unless stated
- all olive oil is regular (not extra virgin), unless stated

THE MORE THE MERRIER

COCKTAILS, CANAPÉS AND MANAGEABLE MASS CATERING

THIS IS PROBABLY THE ONE TIME OF YEAR when people who aren't party-givers give parties. Sometimes, this is due to an uncharacteristic but nevertheless welcome burst of bonhomie and seasonal spirit; as often, it's a duty-date, the product of habit, pressure or other presumed or existing obligations. For as many people who feel a blood-rushing joyousness at the prospect of having their home overrun with people out to have a good time, there are perhaps more who are filled rather with dread, and lacerated by the anxiety that a good time will be neither provided nor had.

This may be a strange thing to say at the beginning of a cookbook, but if it's the cooking that makes you not enjoy giving a party, don't cook. Buy salame, get cheese (all chic Italians hand round roughly chunked shards of fresh Parmesan), put grissini in jars, and regular French breadsticks in vases. But know that, sometimes, the act of preparing for a feast, by cooking simple, low-effort food, can make you look forward to the party more. I love to wallow in the Christmas spirit as I get it all underway. I'm always happy in the kitchen with Christmas songs – Elvis singing "Silent Night", Wham with "Last Christmas" – a-playing, fairy lights a-twinkling, platters of food slowly covering every surface.

And, actually, I think that a Christmas party is the best sort to give. For one thing, everyone is predisposed to have a good time. They're out to enjoy themselves:

they're not coming to carp at your canapés.

Of course, there are ways of making things easier on yourself. It is indeed my hope, my very aim to make things easier on you: I am too clumsy and time-squeezed to do anything elaborate, so I don't expect you to, either. You can make a lot of different bits and pieces, or keep the choice restricted. This is up to you, though I have always, with food, had my mantra: Better a lot of a few things, than a little of many. That's my own rule, but you should also bear in mind the professional caterer's rule, which is that the more people there are, the less they eat per head.

Not that it helps, I find, to get too mathematical about it. A certain amount of clipboard briskness is all well and good, but the only formula that really works is that the less stressed you are, the better the party will be. (I know that the two most irritating things someone can say to you are "Relax!" or "Calm down", but I am trying to help.) So: make sure all drinks that need to be are chilled on time; don't wear new or uncomfortable shoes; and invite everyone you can think of, as worrying about people being cross with you for not being invited is more anxiety-provoking than having too many people in the house.

"The more the merrier" might not be something you believe now, but the only way to enjoy Christmas fully is to act as if you do. And then you will.

COCKTAILS

Believe me, you don't have to turn mixologist to throw a good party. I am more than happy to provide nothing but wine, for all that Kingsley Amis once said that the three most depressing words in the English language were "Red or White?". And fizz doesn't have to be champagne, either: my preference here is for Prosecco, which (and I think I have told you this before) is known in casa mia as "Prozacco", for its mood-enhancing qualities.

But a cocktail can be a wonderful thing – exuberant, extravagant, humdingingly uplifting – and a Christmas party is a good excuse for one.

POINSETTIA

This is probably the most serviceable, all-round Christmas drink: eminently refreshing; satisfyingly quaffable. Think of it as a juicily seasonal Buck's Fizz (a drink I normally find too acidically challenging at best and downright depressing at worst). This prettily pink – rather than authentically red – Poinsettia can be knocked back without a moment's thought. Whether this is entirely a good thing is another matter . . .

Makes 8–9 glasses

1 x 75cl bottle Prosecco or other fizzy dry wine, chilled
125ml Cointreau or Grand Marnier or Triple sec, chilled
500ml cranberry juice, chilled

❄ Mix the Prosecco or other fizzy wine with the Cointreau (or Grand Marnier or Triple sec) and cranberry juice in a large pitcher.

❄ Pour into wine glasses or champagne flutes.

MAKE AHEAD TIP:
Mix together the Cointreau and cranberry juice in a large pitcher, cover with clingfilm and keep chilled for up to 24 hours. Just before serving, top up with the chilled fizz.

POMEGRANATE MARTINI

ice cubes

2 parts vodka

1 part Pama pomegranate liqueur

1/2 part Grenadine

I must confess, upfront, that I don't make a martini like a bartender, and don't expect you to either. Of course, if you're throwing an intimate party for two, a quick shimmy with a cocktail shaker is entirely possible, but it is inconceivable for a crowd so I don't bother. And not being a really proper drinker (despite the evidence of these pages) I don't mind diluting hard liqueur with ice.

I find the simplest way to give measures for this sort of drink is by ratio, but if you prefer amounts, think of "1 part" as equivalent to a barman's 25ml shot. And a shot measure is easy enough to buy.

Although I keep my vodka in the freezer, I cannot overestimate how important extra ice is here. A martini has to be temple-achingly cold, and I can't be faffing about with straining, so let those cubes chink, and just drink up before the martini is turned to water.

If a gin martini is more to your taste, proceed and pour accordingly.

❋ To make 1 drink, put at least 3 ice cubes into a martini glass and pour the alcohol over, using a 25ml measure per part. I like a small (130ml) martini glass rather than one of those vast, gaping upended triangles on stems.

❋ To make a pitcher, chill a jug and cram with ice, then use a 250ml measure per part, to make 875ml, enough for 10 drinks, or maybe 8 if each waiting martini glass hasn't got ice to bulk up the drink.

If you'd prefer to stick to my pomegranate theme, but dispense with the vodka (or bear this in mind as an add-on rather than a substitution), make my Christmas Fizz by adding a glug or two of the Pama pomegranate liqueur to a glass of champagne or fizzy wine. Or you can branch out and add viscous, fragrant drops of flavoured Monin syrups – think gingerbread, cranberry, spiced winter fruits (see Stockists p.267) – to fizzy wine for party pizazz.

MAKE AHEAD TIP:

Make in a pitcher just before guests arrive and keep chilled by sitting the pitcher in a large bowl of ice and water, or stash in the fridge.

LYCHEENI

After a pomegranate, the lychee feels the most seasonally celebratory of fruits, and it didn't seem fair to leave it out of the Christmas canon, just because of its unfestive pallor. Plus, I stumbled across *the* most beautiful bottle, in the form of a French crème de lychee (see Stockists p.267) that begged to bought. I couldn't resist, and I love this lychee martini it was born to make.

And it's not just for the party scene that it gives seasonal succour: even a never-ending school concert is a little more manageable with a hit of this inside you; I have been known to empty out a small water bottle and pour in some of this clear and precious liquid instead. But then, I come to the conclusion that my motto has to be All Life Looks Up With a Lycheeni.

I can't peel a lychee without savaging it, so I feel fine about suggesting canned ones for adornment and a hint of pearly sweetness.

ice cubes
1 part white rum
1 part vodka
2 parts crème de lychee
1/2–1 part syrup from canned lychees
canned lychees to garnish

❅ Chunk up a martini glass with ice, and add the rum, vodka and lychee liqueur, using a 25ml measure per part. If you want this a little sweeter, which all but real firewater-drinkers will, add some of the syrup from the can of lychees to taste.

❅ If in garnishing mood, pierce a lychee on a cocktail stick, and drop into the martini.

❅ To make a pitcher, cram ice into a jug, and add the alcohol (and syrup, to taste), using a 250ml measure per part. You will have about 1 litre, more than enough for 10 drinks. This is strong stuff!

As with the Pomegranate Martini, opposite, you can simply add a splosh of this creamily fruity liqueur straight into a glass of fizzy wine – my Lychee Fizz. Or, for those who like sweeter drinks with less kick, look out for lychee purée in foil pouches and add it to sparkling wine, about 1 part purée to 2 parts wine.

MAKE AHEAD TIP:
Make in a pitcher just before guests arrive and keep chilled by sitting the pitcher in a large bowl of ice and water, or stash in the fridge.

BLACK FOREST MARTINI

ice cubes

1 part vodka

1 part cherry brandy (the red stuff, not kirsch)

1/2 part crème de cacao

rosemary sprigs

Humour me here. I couldn't help myself, and I'm not sure I'd have wanted to. There is something undeniably Germanic and kitsch in the evolution of the contemporary Christmas and this drink recognizes and marries the two in a fabulous fusion. And the taste – well, it's heaven. Not too sweet, not at all sickly, but with a rounded, hint of puddingyness that makes it a perfect after-dinner cocktail as well as a bolstering early evening mood-lifter.

The rosemary, flavourwise, is a tiny deviation from our walk through the Black Forest, but its scent is beautiful, and the sprig, peeking out from the martini glass, has the right hint of festive fir and woodsy warmth about it.

❊ To make 1 drink, put at least 3 ice cubes in a martini glass and build your drink over them, using a 25ml measure per part.

❊ To make a party pitcher, use a 250ml measure per part; you will have 625ml, enough for 10 drinks, but cram the pitcher with ice, and lay a rosemary sprig in each waiting martini glass.

MAKE AHEAD TIP:

Make in a pitcher just before guests arrive and keep chilled by sitting the pitcher in a large bowl of ice and water, or stash in the fridge.

SANTA'S LITTLE HELPER

ice cubes (optional)

1 part brandy

1/2 part amaretto liqueur

1/2 part Cointreau, Grand Marnier or Triple sec

I'm not even going to broach the possibility of a pitcher of this; it would be irresponsible in the extreme. But it's probably just what you need on Christmas Eve, when you've got to fill the stockings, wrap the presents, get out the Christmas china and do everything else on your overburdened plate. Bottoms up!

❊ To make 1 stiffener, over ice (my choice) or straight up if preferred, pour the alcohol into your glass, using a 25ml measure per part.

AMARETTO SOUR

I was once a whiskey sour drinker, inasmuch as I – an eater rather more than a bevver – drank any spirits at all, but that was a lifetime ago when I felt I had to come up with a request in bars and knew that a Brandy Alexander was probably best avoided, on grounds of coolth and calories. Now, what do I care? But whereas I'd be happy to order something naff and creamy, I wouldn't honestly want to drink it. This is my perfect compromise: sweet, sharp, rich and seasonally aromatic. It gives you the warmth of a mulled something or other, without having to go near a stove.

ice cubes (optional)

3 parts amaretto liqueur

2 parts lemon juice

FOR THE GARNISH:

1 orange for peeling

maraschino cherries

❄To make 1 drink, part-fill a tumbler with ice (unless you prefer to drink this straight up) and build your drink over this, using a 25ml measure per part.

❄Mix together with a twizzle stick or your finger, then plop in a maraschino cherry and, using a vegetable peeler, shave off a curl of orange peel.

❄To make a pitcher, use a 250ml measure per part; you'll have 1.2 litres of amaretto sour. I'd chill the pitcher in the fridge and have a cherry and some orange peel in each waiting glass. Since it's chilled, you won't need ice, so I'd serve in small, squat tumblers, nothing too roomy.

MAKE AHEAD TIP:
If you have no space in the fridge to chill the pitcher, drop a couple of handfuls of ice into the empty pitcher about half an hour before guests are due to arrive. When ready to serve, empty the (now chilled) jug of any remaining ice and water and mix the cocktail.

CORNISH CHAMPAGNE COCKTAIL

Serving: Each 75cl bottle of champagne should require 6 sugar lumps and approx. 90ml liqueur to make 6 cocktails

approx. 6 x 15ml tablespoons from 1 x 35cl bottle Bramley and Gage quince liqueur (see Stockists p.267), or other quince brandy or liqueur of your choice

6 La Perruche pure cane rough-cut cubes, or other sugar lumps of your choice

1 x 75cl bottle Camel Valley sparkling wine, or other fizzy dry white wine of your choice, chilled

MAKE AHEAD TIP:
About half an hour before your guests are due to arrive, pop the sugar lumps in the glasses and pour the liqueur over. Just before serving, top up with the chilled fizz.

A champagne cocktail is a classic that needs no fiddling with, so I should defend my apparent lack of reverence here. When my friend Justine Picardie launched her book *Daphne* recently, I wanted to give her a pre-party party featuring a drink made in her and du Maurier's honour. Justine is a champagne cocktail girl, so replacing the champagne with Cornish fizz, and drenching the sugar lump with a gorgeous West Country quince liqueur instead of cognac seemed right all round. And I am now a convert to the Cornish sparkle even for occasions without the geo-literary justification. (See Stockists on p.267, but since you could substitute any fizzy wine or liqueur, those far away from the wilder shores of Cornwall need not worry.)

I also make a version – my **Tuscan Champagne Cocktail** – redolent of Panettone and Italian Christmases which is simply Prosecco with a shot of Tuaca (and see Stockists again), a liqueur that also merits solo attention.

❋ Put 1 sugar lump into each champagne glass; I like a saucer not a flute and I reckon one bottle of fizz provides enough for 6 glasses.

❋ Pour the quince liqueur or brandy (probably no more than 1x 15ml tablespoon) over each sugar lump to soak it, and then top up with sparkling wine.

❋ For my Tuscan Champagne Cocktail, dispense with the sugar lumps.

YULE MULE

ice cubes
2 parts chilled vodka
1 part chilled cranberry juice
Angostura bitters or lime juice (optional)
5 parts chilled ginger beer

MAKE AHEAD TIP:
Measure the vodka, bitters (if using), and cranberry juice into a large pitcher. Keep chilled over ice, then top up with ginger beer to serve.

OPPOSITE:
Cornish Champagne Cocktail (back left); Yule Mule (back right); Amaretto Sour (front), next to a bowl of Seasonally Spiced Nuts (p.21)

I've always loved a Moscow Mule – vodka, bitters, lime juice and savagely peppery ginger beer – and this is no more than my seasonal slant on that. Very joyous it is, too. I find the tooth-roughening sharpness of the cranberry juice replaces not only the need for lime juice, but also the bitters, but if you wish to squirt in a little lime or drop in some Angostura, then I won't stop you.

❋ To make 1 drink, plonk some ice in a highball glass then build your drink over it, using a 25ml measure per part. Add 3 drops of Angostura bitters (or lime juice), if using.

❋ To make a pitcher, use a 250ml measure per part and you will have 2 litres (about 10 glasses), so it may be wiser to have 2 pitchers crammed with ice.

A SEASONAL MEDLEY OF MOCKTAILS

Before the pile up of over-the-top drinks recipes begins to look like the diary entries of a déclassé dipsomaniac – or have we passed that stage? – I offer a bar-man's splayed handful of cocktails for those who might not want alcohol, but still want to join the party. As a self-confessed, pronounced aquaholic, I feel that any non-alcoholic drink must be well-balanced, finely tuned perfection in order to beat the simple perfection of water. Still, I concede that a night that offers no more drinking choice than still or sparkling could seem slightly lacking in festive spirit. And I certainly wouldn't want that. So the following, I hope, will allow the abstemious to raise a garish glass with the rest of us.

LEFT TO RIGHT:
Seasonal Breeze, Pussyfoot,
Blissful Blueberry, Mistletoe, Xmas Xinger

SEASONAL BREEZE

I've written a recipe with this title before, I admit, but it seems fair to plagiarize oneself. Besides, the title conveys what the drink is about: a Christmassy hit of cranberry in a long drink that is vaguely reminiscent of a sea breeze. You could take the "vaguely" away by squeezing in pink grapefruit juice in place of the orange juice. And while you could use carton orange juice, as I have done in the Pussyfoot, overleaf (and I would if making a big pitcher), I like the pure sharpness that comes from squeezing the fruit proper. Look out, when shopping, for a clear, pressed apple juice – which tends to have a better modulated, less sugary appleyness, whether from a bottle or a carton.

1 part chilled cranberry juice
1 part chilled clear apple juice
1 part chilled freshly squeezed orange juice
ice cubes (optional)

❄ To make 1 drink, pour all the juices (over ice if desired) into a glass, using a 75ml measure per part.

❄ To make a pitcher, chill a jug and cram with ice, then use a 750ml measure per part to make 2.2 litres, enough for 10 drinks.

MAKE AHEAD TIP:
Mix all the juices together in a large pitcher and keep covered in a cool place, or in a bucket of ice, if space allows, for up to 3 hours. Stir in 2 or 3 handfuls of ice when ready to serve.

PUSSYFOOT

FOR 1 GLASS:
150ml chilled pink grapefruit juice
150ml chilled freshly squeezed orange juice
1/2 teaspoon fresh lime juice
1–2 drops Grenadine
ice cubes (optional)

FOR A PITCHER:
750ml chilled pink grapefruit juice
750ml chilled freshly squeezed orange juice
30ml Grenadine
30ml fresh lime juice
ice cubes

MAKE AHEAD TIP:
Mix all the liquids together in a large pitcher and
keep covered in cool place, or in a bucket of ice, if
space allows, for up to 3 hours. Stir in 2 or 3
handfuls of ice when ready to serve.

I wish I could lay claim to this title, but it is the brainchild of a presumably hard-drinking bartender with as much condescension as goodwill towards his abstemious clientele. I have added some lime juice to the sweeter original; a more generous squeeze of lemon would also add a note of necessary, balancing, sharpness. There is nothing fancy about this, which is part of its charm, but a colourful pitcherful of the stuff gives a party a cheery boost, and it tends to be gulped down with brio. (And there is nothing to stop you leaving a bottle of vodka nearby for those who don't want to pussyfoot around.)

The basic ratio is 1 part pink grapefruit juice to 1 part orange juice, but my maths isn't good enough to work out what fraction of a part the Grenadine and lime constitute, which is why I write the quantities out twice.

❋ To make 1 drink, pour the grapefruit and orange juices into a tall glass (with ice if you like), add the lime juice and Grenadine and watch it fire up like a tequila sunrise and – if you can bear to – stir to mix.

❋ To make a pitcher, chill a jug and fill with ice, then proceed as above, to make enough for approx. 10 drinks.

BLISSFUL BLUEBERRY

1 part chilled blueberry juice (sometimes
    labelled blueberry juice drink)
1 part chilled bitter lemon, or other
    sparkling lemony drink
fresh lemon juice
ice cubes (optional)

I'm not sure I could mount a convincing case for the essential Christmassyness of a blueberry, but the festive spirit is supplied by the treat of the, relatively speaking, exotic. It seems strange to me that you can actually buy cartons of blueberry juice at the supermarket now; I am showing my age, but I can remember when we couldn't even buy blueberries. So this, for me, has the out-of-the-ordinariness that is what makes a feast. Plus, there is something regally celebratory about its gorgeous hue. If you'd prefer to use Sprite in place of the bitter lemon do, but squeeze in a little fresh lemon juice at the same time.

❋ To make 1 drink, pour the juices into a glass (with ice if desired), using a 75ml measure per part. Stir gently to combine, adding a spritz of fresh lemon juice to taste.

❋ To make a pitcher, chill a jug, then load it with ice and proceed as above, using a 750ml measure per part; this should make enough for 10 drinks.

MISTLETOE

I love the mixture here of sweet lime cordial, peppery ginger beer and the uplifting sharpness of fresh lime. It's cool but warming at the same time, which makes it an entirely fitting drink for a fabulous Christmas party. (You could also, of course, consider a **Virgin Version of the Yule Mule** on p.8, by simply mixing ginger beer with cranberry juice.)

Again, as with the Pussyfoot, opposite, to avoid mind-numbing fractions, I am giving quantities for the Mistletoe twice, to cover glass and pitcher options. But, essentially, the drink is 1 part lime cordial to 3 parts ginger beer with a squeeze or so of fresh lime.

FOR 1 DRINK:

1 x 25ml shot chilled lime cordial

75ml chilled ginger beer

1/2 teaspoon fresh lime juice

FOR A PITCHER:

250ml chilled lime cordial

750ml chilled ginger beer

1 x 25ml shot fresh lime juice

❅ To make 1 drink, pour the lime cordial and ginger beer into a glass (over ice if required), spritz with fresh lime and stir gently.

❅ To make a pitcher, chill a jug, cram with ice, and proceed as above; this makes enough for 10 drinks.

XMAS XINGER

This is simple and yet special, and a way of making those who have foresworn alcohol feel rewarded rather than punished. I've mentioned it before, a year or so ago, in an aside to a cocktail made with pomegranate liqueur, but this really does deserve stand-alone status.

The pomegranate juice (read the label and check it is pure pomegranate juice) is lusciously Christmassy and the ginger ale brings its own seasonal spiciness and sprightliness.

2 parts chilled pure pomegranate juice

1 part chilled ginger ale

ice cubes (optional)

❅ To make 1 drink, using a 75ml measure per part, pour the pomegranate juice into a glass (with ice if required), top up with ginger ale, and give a gentle stir just to combine.

❅ To make a pitcher, chill a jug and cram with ice, then proceed as above, using a 750ml measure per part, to make enough for 10 drinks.

CANAPÉS

I am never going to be a canapé queen. I lack dexterity and patience and there is some small part of me that feels canapés really belong to the repertoire of the professional caterer, though I suspect the greater part of my reluctance is down to straightforward greed: small portions, little bites, make me panic. I can get over it: I simply produce a lot, but of only a few; in life as on the page, everything is in the edit. Choose about three you want to make for each party, and make plenty of each. It's not rocket science, but it works: your stress is lessened and your guests plentifully welcomed; now you've got a party . . .

DOUBLE-BLUE CROSTINI

I spent the year before last in a haze of Roquamole – my rich, dense and creamy blue cheese and avocado dip. And although I do, on occasion and out of greedy self-interest, bring it out for pre-dinner pickings at Christmas dinner parties, it is, alas, too volatile for canapés; once the avocados start turning dark they may taste fine but, believe me, they lack plate appeal. So this is my seasonal substitute: a gorgeous, tangy blue cheese dip or spread, to be anointed – and here's the second of the two blues of my title – on thick, gritty, blue corn tortilla chips. I've mentioned before the joyous discovery that my favoured canapé, a plate of crostini, can be made with tortilla chips instead of toasted French stick slices, and in many ways the blue corn chip is the finest example of this labour-saving practice, as the chip itself is thicker (and so resists sog for longer) than its yellow corn counterparts, and the taste blander (an advantage in a canapé). Don't worry if some of the chips are broken; I use shards of chips just as happily as whole, perfectly triangular ones. And by all means use the blue cheese spread as a dip, if you like, and simply provide the chips (or some crudités) as scooping tools.

Makes approx. 65 tortilla-chip crostini

125g St Agur or other blue cheese

100g cream cheese, at room temperature

125ml sour cream

35g sliced green jalapeños, from a jar (jars of sliced, pickled jalapeños, green or red, are found with the Mexican foods in supermarkets)

good grinding of white pepper

approx. 100g (1/2 packet) blue corn tortilla chips

1 teaspoon very finely chopped chives

❋ Crumble or mash the blue cheese with the cream cheese and sour cream in a bowl; this is easier if the cream cheese has been out of the fridge for a while.

❋ Finely chop the sliced jalapeños and stir them in with the white pepper.

❋ Using a teaspoon, dollop the blue cheese mixture onto the chips.

❋ Delicately drop the chives over and serve.

MAKE AHEAD TIP:
Make the blue cheese mixture up to 6 hours ahead. Cover tightly with clingfilm and store in the fridge. Remove from the fridge about 20 minutes before using to allow it to soften, then dollop over the tortilla chips just before the party.

CRAB CROSTINI

I can eat crab meat pretty much any way – as a fresh, chillified and garlicky scattering over semolina-sweet linguine, mounded into a lightly but spicily dressed salad, wodged into cakes (and see p.24) – but this is probably the speediest and most effortless incarnation.

It's not so hard to chop spring onions, coriander and chilli by hand, but by all means get out the processor for the job if you prefer. However, be very cautious if you use it to mix in the crab meat; any more than the most fleeting of pulses and the crab meat loses its delicate shreds and turns to paste. It's not a disaster but neither is it entirely desirable.

I like to put chilli into the crab meat – I adore the Christmassy red flecks peeking out of the tender white flesh along with the green of the coriander here – but if you prefer, leave out the chilli and replace the plain tortilla chips with the fierier chilli-flavoured ones, as in the Chilli Cheese Crostini, below.

�֍ Finely chop the spring onion and the chilli (if using), then mix into the crab meat along with the other ingredients, and dollop onto the tortilla chips.

Makes about 50 crab crostini

1 spring onion
1 fresh red chilli, deseeded (optional)
300g white crab meat
60ml sour cream
small bunch of coriander
1/4 teaspoon dried oregano
1 x 15ml tablespoon lime juice
1 small packet plain tortilla chips

MAKE AHEAD TIP:
About 3 hours before serving, stir the chopped spring onion, chilli, coriander and oregano into the crab meat. Cover with clingfilm and store in the fridge. Just before assembling the crostini, stir in the sour cream and lime juice.

CHILLI CHEESE CROSTINI

Yumbariba! The chilli cheese is really just a lazy person's take on my longstanding family-favourite, liptauer (only with a Latino rather than Mitteleuropa flavour), and I ramp up the paprika punch by smearing it on hot chilli tortilla chips.

I specify organic rather than regular cream cheese, as I like the rich texture and rounded flavour (and buy it easily from the supermarket) and it tastes like proper, old-fashioned homemade stuff, but the more familiar oblong-packaged packs of regular cream cheese would not be out of place here.

✖ Mix together the cream cheese and sour cream.

✖ Add the paprika, chopped jalapeños and Worcestershire sauce, combine well, and see the pale cheese turn a fetching coral.

✖ Just before your guests arrive, using a teaspoon, lightly dab the spread on a pile of chips and arrange on a platter or a couple of flat plates.

Makes about 100 chilli cheese chips

350g cream cheese (preferably organic), at
    room temperature
125ml sour cream
2 teaspoons sweet or mild paprika
30g red sliced jalapeños (from a jar), very
    finely chopped
1/2 teaspoon Worcestershire sauce
1 x 200g packet chilli tortilla chips

MAKE AHEAD TIP:
Make the chilli cheese mixture the day before. Cover tightly with clingfilm and store in the fridge. Remove about 20 minutes before using to allow to soften and spread just before serving.

SMOKED SALMON SODA BREADS

Makes approx. 30 salmon soda bread
canapés

100g crème fraîche
50g hot horseradish sauce
1 x 400g loaf brown soda bread or other
    wholemeal bread, sliced
225g very thinly sliced smoked salmon
approx. 75g pickled red cabbage, from a jar,
    drained
small packet/bunch of fresh dill

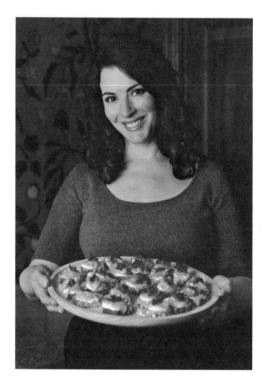

The Irish have long known that the smooth richness of smoked salmon is gloriously partnered with the wheaten roughness of soda bread and I aim to build on that borrowed alliance, drawing on my own Eastern European inheritance. Let me name the guilty parties: horseradish, for tang; pickled red cabbage, ditto, but also for the gloriously seasonal touch of its glistening dark-red tangle; the dill, too, looks fabulously firlike, but most of all, its delicate but resonant scent seals the deal with this flavour-packed mouthful.

Small rounds of pumpernickel, or regular squares of it quartered, can be substituted for the soda bread here.

❋ Mix together the crème fraîche and horseradish.

❋ You will need about 8–10 slices of bread. Cut each slice into 3 or 4 bits; since soda bread comes in rounded loaves, the slices vary in size.

❋ Spread the bread with the horseradish–crème fraîche mixture and top with a snipped ribbon of smoked salmon.

❋ Fork a dark-red tangle of pickled red cabbage on each piece and top with a frond of dill.

MAKE AHEAD TIP:
The day before, cut the soda bread and store in a sealed bag. Make the horseradish–crème fraîche mixture, cover with clingfilm and store in the fridge. Assemble the canapés just before serving.

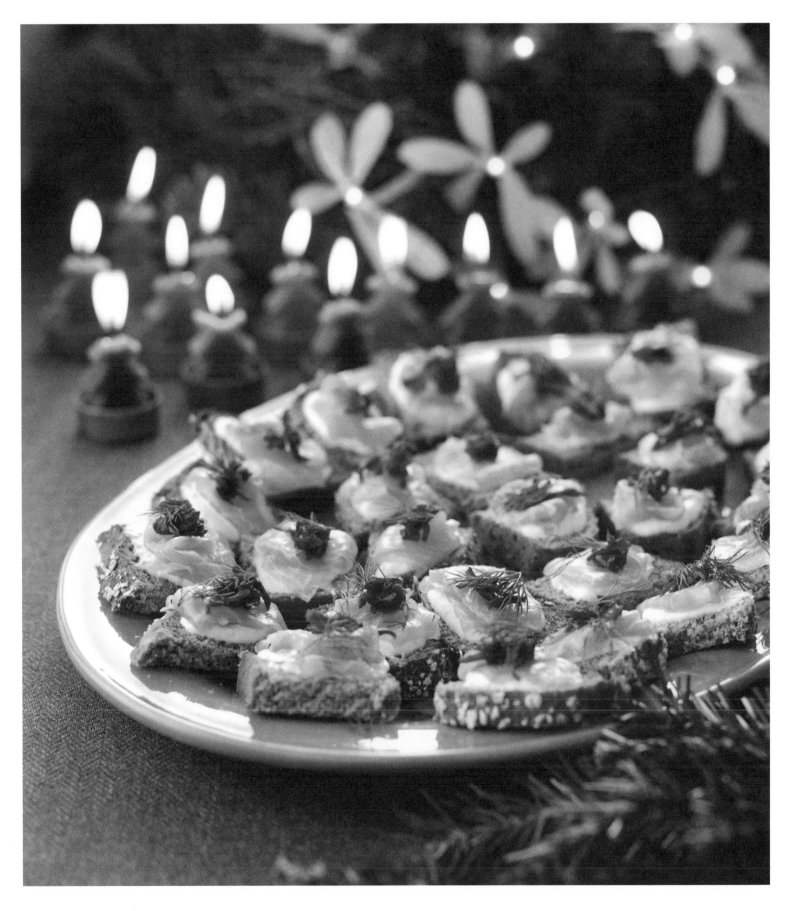

PARTY PARMA HAM BUNDLES

Makes approx. 25 plumptious parcels

**400g sliced Parma ham or other cured
   prosciutto, not sliced ultra-thin**
200g ready-to-eat dried figs
**150g mild soft goat's cheese, such as
   Chavroux**

Since I would find it hard to give a Christmas party without at least one plateful of these feast-time favourites of mine – salty pink prosciutto wrapped around sharp soft goat's cheese and sweet, grainy dried figs – it didn't seem fair to leave them out here, although they have had an outing in print with me before. They are positively *the* party perennial; their omission, for me, not to be countenanced.

✸ Cut or tear each slice of Parma ham into 2 or 3 strips.

✸ Scissor each fig in half or quarters, depending on their size, remove the woody stalks and spread a teaspoon of goat's cheese on the cut half of the fig.

✸ Place the piece of fig cheese-side down on the centre of a strip of ham and then roll or fold up to make a bundle.

✸ Sit each bulging pink parcel so that the darkness of the fig is hidden plate-side.

MAKE AHEAD TIP:
Make the parcels up to 6 hours ahead. Sit in a single layer on a plate and cover with clingfilm. Keep chilled until ready to serve.

SEASONALLY SPICED NUTS

There's something addictive about a bowl of warm, toasted bar nuts, and although I used to bring them out as a starter substitute at dinner parties, I have rejigged my usual seasonings to make these a little more spicily aromatic and find them just the thing to keep a crowd fed without too much commotion.

I don't pay particular attention to how many of each nut I put into the mix, but just go for those packets of mixed, unsalted nuts; my last bag contained (in the order listed on the pack) cashews, almonds, pecans, macadamias and pistachios. If you want to buy nuts in single packets and mix, I'd simply go for pecans, almonds, Brazils and pistacchios. It's the spicing, and the warmth, that's key. Instead of the garam masala, you could use half a teaspoon each of ground ginger and ground cumin, and a pinch each of ground coriander, cloves and cinnamon. Indeed, it's the ginger and cloves in the garam masala that make these taste so Christmassy in the first place.

Makes enough to fill 2 small, not tiny, bowls

500g mixed nuts
1¹/₂ teaspoons garam masala
1 teaspoon celery salt
2 x 15ml tablespoons olive oil
2 x 15ml tablespoons light muscovado or soft light brown sugar
3 sprigs rosemary, finely chopped to make about 3 teaspoons, plus 2 sprigs for garnish
sprinkle of Maldon salt or pinch of table salt

❄ Put a large frying pan on a medium heat.

❄ Line a large baking sheet or swiss roll tin with foil or reusable baking parchment and put at a handy proximity to the stove.

❄ Tip the nuts into the now-warm pan and toss or push about with a spatula for 3 minutes or so until they are lightly toasted.

❄ Add the garam masala and celery salt and push the nuts about in the pan again so that they are evenly coated.

❄ Add the oil, sugar and rosemary and stir about again to mix. When the nuts have darkened a little and are slicked with the sugary spice mix, tip them out briskly (before they burn) onto your prepared, lined sheet, and sprinkle with salt to taste.

❄ Preferably when still warm, arrange in small bowls, and tuck in a sprig of rosemary on top for a seasonal fir-tree flourish!

MAKE AHEAD TIP:
The day before, make the spiced nuts and tip them out onto a foil-lined baking sheet. Sprinkle with salt. Cover with foil and keep in a cool place. About 10 minutes before serving, pop the nuts into a moderate (180°C/gas mark 4) oven to warm through.

DRUNKEN DEVILS ON HORSEBACK

Makes 24

24 ready-to-eat stoneless dried prunes

90ml Armagnac

12 rashers American-style bacon, or 24 thin
    slices pancetta

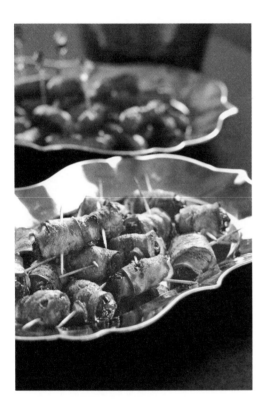

These 24 prunes use up exactly 1 x 200g packet of
Oscar Meyer American-style bacon. If you can't get
American-style bacon, find thin slices of Italian
pancetta, but double the quantity so you use one
whole slice per prune, or use rindless streaky bacon
and roll the slices out between plastic wrap to make
them thinner.

MAKE AHEAD TIP:
Two days ahead, soak the prunes in the Armagnac.
The day before, wrap in bacon and keep, covered,
in the fridge. Allow 20 minutes at room temperature
before cooking.

When I was a child, this is the sort of thing my parents would have eaten at cocktail parties, parties my mother would go to in her white patent boots, angora mini dress and false eyelashes – hairpiece, too – and lips slicked in pale, shimmery colours with names like Moist Madder Pink. It seemed ineffably glamorous – I can smell her wafting scent of face powder mixed with Guerlain's L'Heure Bleue now as I think about it – but also inexplicable: *how* could anyone want to eat a prune (the devil) or oyster (an angel) wrapped in bacon, and why they were on horseback was just as baffling. Now, I know (or think I do) that "on horseback" is a corruption of "hogsback", to indicate the bacon.

Now, too, I'm happy – more than – to eat an angel-on-horseback, though less convinced that I want to make them; someone as clumsy as I am should not be let near an oyster shucker, ever. But a devil, which I like more, anyway – and mine are soused till sticky with Armagnac – is, if not child's food, then certainly child's play to make.

❊The day before your party, soak the prunes in the Armagnac in a covered bowl.

❊On the day of your party, preheat the oven to 200°C/gas mark 6.

❊On a board, spread out a rasher of bacon and cut in half horizontally to give 2 shorter pieces of bacon, or use a whole pancetta slice. Then take a soaked prune from your bowl and roll it up in one of the half pieces of bacon, or a pancetta slice, securing it with a cocktail stick.

❊Repeat this process with the remaining prunes, wrapping each one in bacon, and place them on a lined baking sheet.

❊Cook the drunken devils in the oven for 10–15 minutes, then let them cool a little, to avoid burnt fingers and mouths, before plating them up to serve.

CRANBERRY AND SOY GLAZED COCKTAIL SAUSAGES

I couldn't leave this out, even though you will probably have to follow round after with a packet of babywipes. A party just isn't a party without a sticky sausage or three, and these are joyously seasonal. And nor do I stop here with this sweet, warm, sharp glaze: the ingredients can also be used as a marinade-cum-cook-in sauce for either 30 chicken wings or 20 small spare ribs, with equally lipsmacking results.

Makes 50

125ml Thai or Chinese sweet chilli sauce
60ml cranberry sauce, from a jar
60ml soy sauce
1 x 15ml tablespoon dark brown sugar
juice of 1 clementine/satsuma
juice of 1 lime
50 cocktail sausages

❋ Preheat the oven to 200°C/gas mark 6.

❋ Put the cocktail sausages in a foil-lined roasting tin or, better still, a throw-away foil baking tray.

❋ Mix the chilli, cranberry and soy sauces in a measuring jug and whisk in the sugar along with the clementine (or satsuma) and lime juices.

❋ Pour the glaze over the cocktail sausages and turn them so they are evenly coated, before putting the tin in the oven for 30–40 minutes, with a gentle turnover after 20, by which time they should be hot, burnished and gorgeously sticky. (If you're cooking chicken wings or ribs, having marinated them overnight in the cranberry-chilli-soy goo, you will have to up the cooking time: the wings should need about 45 minutes; the ribs an hour.)

❋ When serving, provide cocktail sticks and napkins, or make sure you have finger bowls or babywipes to hand.

MAKE AHEAD TIP:
Put all the sausages into a large, sealable bag (or glass bowl) and add all the other ingredients. Shake or stir everything together until the sausages are well-coated and leave in the fridge for up to one day. When ready to use, just tip everything into cooking tray and cook as directed.

FREEZE AHEAD TIP:
Make ahead as above and freeze for up to 3 months. Thaw overnight in the fridge.

WASABI CRAB CAKES

Makes approx. 45 crab cakes

500g fresh white crab meat or frozen white
    crab meat, thawed
4 spring onions, very finely chopped
1 clove garlic, peeled and minced
2 teaspoons wasabi (Japanese horseradish)
    powder, or 3 teaspoons wasabi paste
2 teaspoons rice vinegar
3 teaspoons tamari or Japanese soy sauce
100g fresh breadcrumbs
groundnut or other vegetable oil for frying
lemon or lime wedges to serve

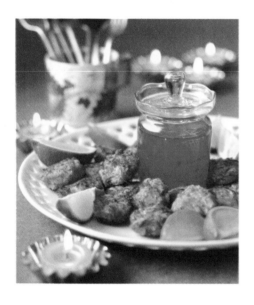

MAKE AHEAD TIP:
For previously frozen crab meat, shape the crab
cakes the day before and arrange on a clingfilm-
lined baking sheet. Cover with clingfilm and keep
chilled overnight. Fry the chilled crab cakes as
directed and keep warm in the oven for 20 minutes.

FREEZE AHEAD TIP:
For fresh, not previously frozen crab meat only,
make the crab cakes and freeze overnight until
solid. Fry from frozen as above and keep warm in
the oven. The crab cakes can also be stored in the
freezer for up to 1 month before cooking.

I cook crab cakes so often, and tinker about with them to suit my mood, that I can offer up any number of variants on the recipe below. I will try and contain myself, though, as too much choice can be paralysing rather than liberating. But feel free, if it suits you, to use 100g brown rice flour in place of the breadcrumbs. If you can't find wasabi, use English mustard (powder or paste) as directed for the Japanese stuff and substitute lemon or lime juice for the rice vinegar.

❉ Press and drain any liquid from the crab meat, and put the crab meat in a large bowl. Add the spring onions, garlic, wasabi, rice vinegar, soy sauce and breadcrumbs, and mix together to combine.

❉ Spoon or pinch out walnut-sized dollops, and press together tightly with wet hands or wearing vinyl disposable gloves, to form bite-sized crab cakes. Arrange the little crab cakes, on a clingfilm-lined sheet that will fit into your fridge or freezer (don't freeze if using frozen crabmeat – see tips, below). You can have a double-decker arrangement if you put another layer of clingfilm on top of the crab cakes. Cover with a final layer of clingfilm and stash in the freezer overnight or for a few hours. If you're using thawed frozen crabmeat, do not refreeze, but just let the patties sit for about 30 minutes in the fridge to firm up.

❉ When party time comes around, preheat your oven to 120°C/gas mark $^{1}/_{2}$. Line a baking sheet large enough to take all the crab cakes with a double layer of kitchen paper.

❉ Heat a frying pan filled with oil about 5mm deep, take the frozen crab cakes out of the freezer, then fry the unthawed crab cakes until golden brown and crisp on both sides, which won't take long.

❉ As they brown, transfer the crab cakes to the paper-lined baking sheet and put in the oven for 20 minutes to heat through, holding them in the oven to keep warm before serving, if required. If you're using thawed crab meat, fry the patties for a few minutes a side only, though you can hold them in the low oven if you want to keep them warm. The crab cakes will not be quite as crisp, but they will be scrumptious.

❉ Remove the crab cakes to a platter or pair of plates, scattering lemon or lime segment wedges among them. They are lovely, too, with sweet chilli sauce. Use a good bottled one or, as I've done, mix a squirt of lime juice (to give extra sharpness and make it runnier) into the Chilli Jam on p.241.

SHORT AND SWEET

The fact that there are a mere trio of recipes for something sweet here is not meant to hint at restraint or austerity on my part. It's because there's a whole chapter you can draw on to strike a sweet note as well as a seasonal one (see Joy to the World, from p.171). You could add a trayful of bite-sized mince pies to hand around, or a nice fat Christmas cake standing proudly on display, with a knife for people to cut their own slices. The picture on p.26 illustrates just this point.

Indeed, add anything you want, or add nothing: the three recipes that follow are simple, no-bake, quick-assembly and low-effort sensations that will keep you, and your guests, sweet.

CHOCOLATE PEANUT-BUTTER CUPS

These are really a homespun version of the famous Reese's confection of the same name, embellished with gold to give a touch of seasonal glitz. I have on occasion used my children – their little fingers are better designed for the job – to press the peanut butter layer into the petit-four cases, but have generally lived to regret it. Anyway, this is not a hard job, just a boring one, and I find once I've accepted that, the mindless, repetitive activity can be positively therapeutic.

❋ Mix together the brown sugar, icing sugar, butter and peanut butter either by hand, using a bowl and wooden spoon, or more easily with a freestanding mixer (my preference) or processor to make a sandy paste.

❋ Use your hands to form scant 1-teaspoon discs to fill the base of about 48 petit-four cases placed in miniature tart tins or mini-muffin tins (each indentation about 4.5cm in diameter). Press the sandy mixture as best you can to form a layer at the bottom of each paper case.

❋ Melt both chocolates very gently, either in a heatproof bowl suspended over a pan of simmering water or, using a suitable bowl, in the microwave, according to the manufacturer's instructions.

❋ Stir the melted chocolates together and allow to cool *a little*, then spoon 1-teaspoonfuls into each petit-four case, covering the sandy base.

❋ Decorate with a gold button or gold star in the middle of each chocolate-covered, peanut-butter cup. Or sprinkle over any other decoration of your choice. Put in the fridge to set for 30 minutes or so before serving.

Makes approx. 48

FOR THE BASE:
50g soft dark brown sugar
200g icing sugar
50g soft butter
200g smooth peanut butter

FOR THE TOPPING:
200g milk chocolate, chopped
100g dark chocolate, chopped
edible gold buttons and stars to decorate (see Stockists p.267) or other decorations, e.g. gold dragées or red, white and green Christmassy sprinkles
48–50 petit-four paper cases (preferably gold, see Stockists p.267)

Don't use wholenut or other virtuous peanut butter here, only the regular sort. For what it's worth, I go for Skippy.

MAKE AHEAD TIP:
Make the cups up to 2 days ahead and keep, loosely covered, in a cool place.

FREEZE AHEAD TIP:
Make the cups and open freeze on a baking sheet. When frozen, pack into a rigid container. Thaw overnight in a cool place on a wire rack.

EGGNOG SYLLABUB

This is, in effect, an Anglo–American union: eggnog is *the* holiday tradition Stateside; and you could hardly get more quintessentially English than a syllabub. And actually, upping the Anglo-ante, I wouldn't mind it one bit in place of the whipped cream in the Boozy British Trifle on p.42. Though, it really would pack a killer punch.

Just as it is here, piled creamily, with celestial lightness into dinky espresso cups or shot glasses, it is, quite simply, exquisite. You can certainly taste the trio of tipples, but you don't feel as if you should avoid stepping near a naked flame after eating it.

❅ In a large bowl, crack the egg and add the vanilla, sugar, bourbon, rum and brandy, and grate in an exuberant amount of fresh nutmeg; you will be grating some more on the top of the syllabubs later, too. If you don't want to use all 3 drinks, then choose your preferred one and triple the single measure given.

❅ Whip together all the ingredients, except the cream, with an electric whisk; I use my freestanding mixer.

❅ Slowly whisk in the cream and continue whisking until the cream is softly whipped but will still hold its shape when the whisk is lifted out of the lightly bulging mass. Be patient: because the alcohol acts as a thinner, the cream will take a while to get desirably, floatily thick; this is why I suggest an electric whisk to do the work.

❅ Dollop moundingly into 15 espresso cups or shot glasses and grate a little more nutmeg over each one.

Makes 15 x 60ml servings
(If you are having a bigger party and want more servings, it would be better to double the ingredients but make it in 2 batches)

1 egg (see note below)
2 teaspoons pure vanilla extract
65g caster sugar
3 x 15ml tablespoons bourbon
3 x 15ml tablespoons dark rum
3 x 15ml tablespoons brandy
500ml double cream
good grating of fresh nutmeg (about a third of a nutmeg)

If you prefer not to give people raw egg to eat then replace the egg and 2 teaspoons of vanilla extract with 2 teaspoons of Bird's custard powder, and reduce the sugar to 50g.

OPPOSITE:
The sweet delights of a dessert-dedicated welcome table.

CHRISTMAS ROCKY ROAD

Makes 24 big-bite-sized bars

250g dark chocolate
150g milk chocolate
175g soft butter
4 x 15ml tablespoons golden syrup
200g amaretti biscuits (not the soft ones)
150g shelled Brazil nuts
150g red glacé cherries
125g mini marshmallows
1 x 15ml tablespoon icing sugar
edible glitter (optional, see Stockists p.267)

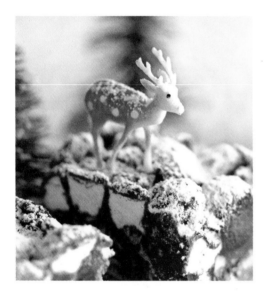

If you want to, there's nothing (except dexterity in my case) to stop you cutting these into tiny, petit-four size pieces, in which case you could almost double the number.

MAKE AHEAD TIP:
Make the Rocky Road and refrigerate to set. Don't add the icing sugar yet, but cut into bars, then store in an airtight container in a cool place for up to 1 week. Decorate with icing sugar and edible glitter about 1–2 hours before serving.

FREEZE AHEAD TIP:
Make the Rocky Road as above and freeze for up to 1 month. Thaw overnight in a cool place. Decorate as above.

It's not that I felt my usual Rocky Road Crunch Bars needed any improvement (though fiddling with recipes is one of life's pleasures) but I thought they would benefit from some seasonal adjustment. So, out go the Rich Tea biscuits and in come amaretti and – in the seasonal spirit – I've crammed in some Brazil nuts and glacé cherries (as red as Rudolph's nose), along with snowy mini marshmallows. The fresh snowfall of icing sugar on top might seem seasonal enough, but not for me. So I add some edible glitter in Disco Hologram White.

❄ Chop both sorts of chocolate small, or use chocolate buttons made for melting, and then put into a heavy-based pan to melt with the butter and syrup over a gentle heat.

❄ Put the biscuits into a freezer bag and bash them with a rolling pin to get big- and little-sized crumbs; you want some pieces to crunch and some sandy rubble.

❄ Put the Brazil nuts into another freezer bag and also bash them so you get different-sized nut rubble.

❄ Take the pan off the heat, and add the crushed biscuits and nuts, whole glacé cherries and mini-marshmallows. Turn carefully to coat everything with syrupy chocolate.

❄ Tip into a foil tray (I use one 236mm x 296mm), smoothing the top as best you can, although it will look bumpy.

❄ Refrigerate until firm enough to cut, which will take about $1^1/_2$–2 hours. Then take the set block of rocky road out of the foil tray ready to cut.

❄ Push the icing sugar through a small sieve to dust the top of the Rocky Road. Then, if you like, add a sprinkling of edible glitter for some festive sparkle.

❄ With the long side in front of you, cut into it 6 slices down and 4 across, so that you have 24 almost-squares.

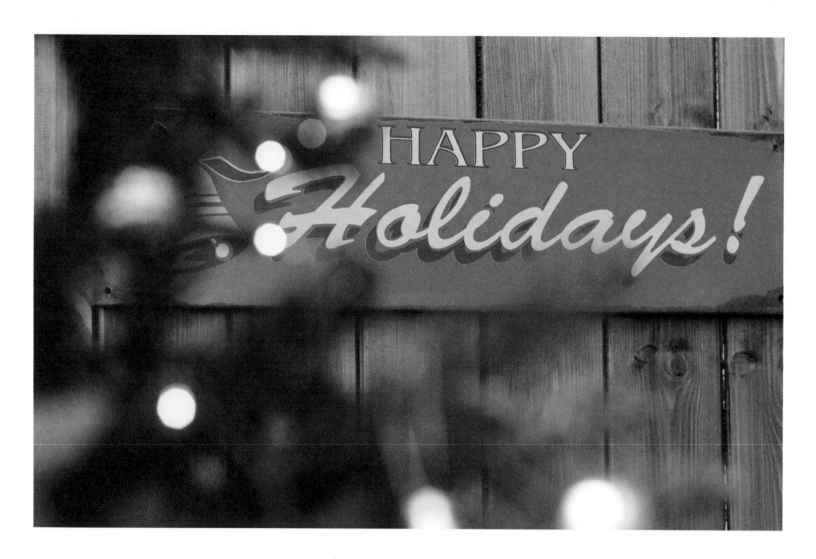

THE WELCOME TABLE

You might be wondering what a "welcome table" is, and you'd be justified. I made it up. When I explain, I think you'll understand: it's the table loaded with food for people to plate up for themselves as they party. It could be called a buffet, I suppose, or a fork supper, but somehow both those terms make me feel I'm throwing a party on a cruise ship.

Besides, the essential element – the prerequisite of a party – is that mood of welcome and abundance, and this is what these recipes are all about. It really doesn't matter if the plates are paper, and there aren't enough chairs: this is food that's easy to make, easy to eat, and makes people know you want them there.

You could make just one or two of the recipes for the hard-core, inner circle who invariably stay behind at the end of a drinks party, but I think of this, my welcome table, as the best way to feed a pile-up of friends at a warmly informal supper party to celebrate the season.

AROMATIC CHRISTMAS HAM

Serves approx. 10

6.5kg smoked gammon, with knuckle bone
250ml red wine
water to cover
1 large onion, halved
2 cloves garlic (unpeeled)
1 head fennel, halved
2 star anise
1 x 15ml tablespoon coriander seed
1 x 15ml tablespoon fennel seed
1 x 15ml tablespoon mixed peppercorns

FOR THE GLAZE:
approx. 20 whole cloves
4 x 15ml tablespoons cranberry or
   redcurrant jelly
$^1/_2$ teaspoon ground cinnamon
1 teaspoon smoked paprika
$^1/_2$ teaspoon red wine vinegar

MAKE AHEAD TIP:
Cook the ham, loosely cover in a "tent" of foil and
keep chilled for up to 1 week.

There's no absolute need to have a cold Christmas ham on a welcome table, but there are few sights more seasonally cheering. I like to have some of the sweet, salty pink meat carved, and some still clove-studded and gorgeously whole, as a joint, on a wooden board. Obviously, it is fabulous hot, too.

If you feel like adding the Christmas Chutney, by all means do (see p.235); I would. Though any number of other condiments in that chapter might also be a good match. Shop-bought mango chutney is certainly not infra dig – or not in my house – and I definitely need English mustard with this. Those who like it less hot could turn to the Redcurrant and Wholegrain Mustard Sauce (a quick stir-up, no cooking) on p.67, perhaps using cranberry jelly (if already using in the glaze) in place of the redcurrant.

❉ Put all the ingredients, except those for the glaze, into a large pan, on the stove but off the heat, adding water until the ham is covered.

❉ Turn on the heat and bring to the boil, then turn down to a simmer and partially cover the pan. Cook for about $3^1/2$ hours. (This may not seem long for a big joint, but as it will carry on cooking as it cools, and this is going to be eaten cold, I don't want it overcooked. Nor do you.)

❉ Preheat the oven to 200°C/gas mark 6. Lift the ham gently out of the hot liquid, sit it on a board and let it cool slightly, not too much but just so that you can touch it without burning yourself.

❉ With a sharp knife, strip off the rind, and a little of the fat layer if it's very thick, but leave a thin layer of fat. I love this work: it is peculiarly gratifying seeing the hot blubbery fat slither off. Use the same knife to score a diamond pattern in the remaining fat on the ham, in lines about 2cm apart. Stud the points of each diamond with a clove.

❉ Put the cranberry or redcurrant jelly, cinnamon, paprika and red wine vinegar into a little saucepan and whisk together over a high heat, bringing it to the boil. Let the pan bubble away, for about 5 minutes, so that the glaze reduces to a syrupy consistency that will coat the fat on the ham.

❉ Now sit the ham in a roasting tin lined with foil, as the sugar in the glaze will burn in the oven as it drips off. Pour the glaze over the diamond-studded ham, then put it in the oven for about 15 minutes, or until the glazed fat has caught and burnished. Take the ham out of the oven and sit it on a wooden board to cool (2–3 hours) before you carve it.

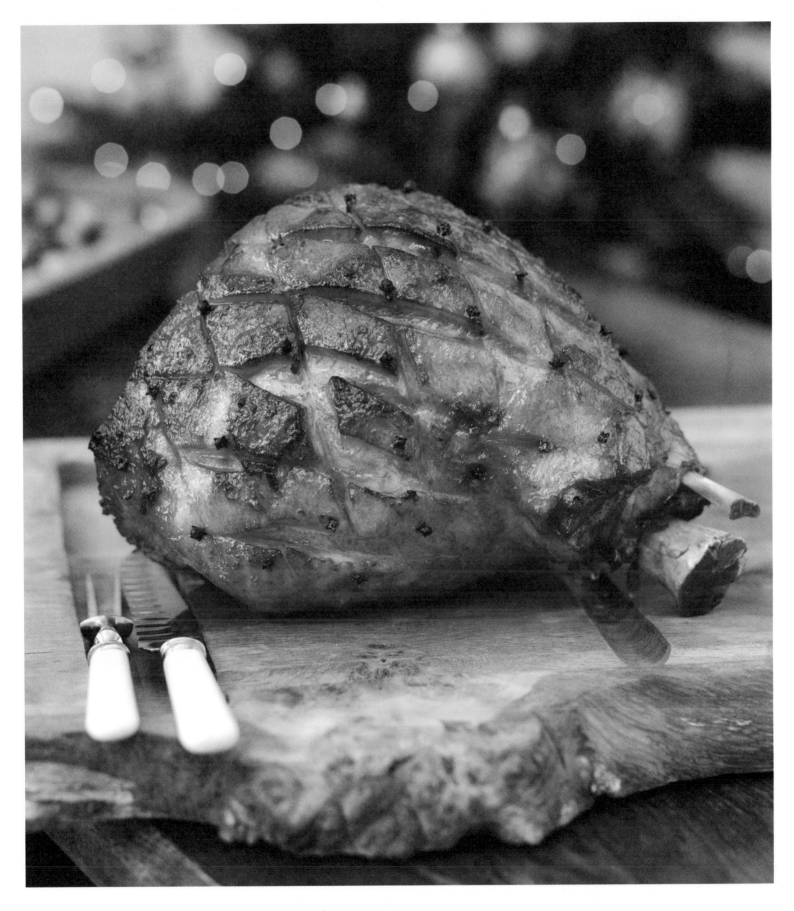

PUMPKIN AND GOAT'S CHEESE LASAGNE

Serves 12–15

FOR THE PUMPKIN FILLING:

2 x 15ml tablespoons olive oil

30g butter

8 sage leaves

2 onions, peeled and finely chopped

3 cloves garlic, peeled and minced

2.2kg pumpkin, peeled, deseeded and cut
   into 3cm rough cubes (this is about half a
   decent-sized pumpkin, a proper eating
   one, not the Hallowe'en kind. When prepared, it yields just under 2 kilos)

75ml vermouth or white wine

60ml water

1 x 400g can chopped tomatoes

salt and pepper

FOR THE TOMATO SAUCE:

1 x 700g (700ml) bottle passata

500ml water

2 x 15ml tablespoons sugar

2 x 15ml tablespoons Maldon salt or
   1 x 15ml tablespoon table salt

good grinding of pepper

FOR THE CHEESE LAYER:

450g soft fresh goat's cheese

500g ricotta cheese

3 eggs

good grating of fresh nutmeg

2 x 300g packets fresh lasagne sheets,
   600g total

2 balls mozzarella

125g pine nuts, toasted in a hot dry pan

salt and pepper

I use a soft goat's cheese log, sold as Chevrissime
blanc, that has no skin and a texture more like that
of a goat's curd cheese.

One of the questions I am asked most often is how do I come up with recipes? The answer is simple: greed. When I'm not eating, I'm thinking about what I might want to eat, and the notion of pumpkin lasagne came into my head when speculo-salivating, and it found its way from my head to my kitchen to my stomach with gratifying ease.

This is an easy lasagne to make in that, unlike a traditional meat one, there are not two sauces to do in advance. I simply cook the pumpkin earlier and layer it up with fresh lasagne sheets (bought in vacuum packs from the supermarket) that don't need pre-cooking and an easy cheese and egg mixture.

Don't be put off by the length of the recipe that follows. It takes longer to explain than to do!

❋ **To make the pumpkin filling:** heat the oil and butter in a shallow casserole and fry the sage leaves over a gentle heat for about 2 minutes.

❋ Add the chopped onion and minced garlic to the pan and fry very gently for another 10 minutes or so.

❋ Add the pumpkin pieces, turn well in the oniony oil and, after about 5 minutes, add the vermouth (or wine), the water and chopped tomatoes. Simmer, covered, for an hour, stirring occasionally so the pumpkin cooks evenly. Taste for seasoning – I tend to add quite a bit of salt here – and leave to cool.

❋ **For the tomato sauce:** simply pour the passata and water into a large jug or bowl, and stir in the sugar, salt and pepper, whisking it all together.

❋ **To make up the cheese layer:** in a separate bowl beat the goat's cheese and ricotta with the eggs, nutmeg, and salt and pepper to taste.

❋ Preheat the oven to 200°C/gas mark 6, slipping in a baking sheet as you do.

❋ To assemble the lasagne, begin by putting 500ml of the cold tomato sauce in the bottom of a roasting tin (measuring approx. 36cm x 26cm x 6cm).

❋ Then layer with a third of the lasagne sheets, overlapping them well (Italians do it with the tin horizontal but the pasta vertical, if that makes sense, but I don't know that it truly matters …). Leave the rest of the tomato sauce aside for the time being.

❋ Layer a third of the pumpkin filling over the lasagne, and dollop on a third

of the cheese mixture, coaxing with a rubber spatula. It won't cover completely; think more of spreading blobs about. Then start again with a layer of lasagne, followed by pumpkin, then the cheese. Repeat once more – lasagne, pumpkin, and the last of the cheese mixture.

❋ Pour the remaining cold tomato sauce over, letting it sink down and be absorbed in the layers.

❋ Slice and chop the mozzarella balls and dot over the top.

❋ Cook in the oven, on the baking sheet, for 1 hour. Once cooked, take out of the oven and let it stand for 15–30 minutes to make cutting and serving easier. (I love this when it's stood for an hour or so, too.) As you cut and slice, you will notice a shallow tomatoey cheesey pool at the bottom of the tin; bread dunked into this is gorgeous.

❋ Sprinkle the toasted pine nuts over the lasagne, and cut into squares to serve.

MAKE AHEAD TIP:
Up to 2 days ahead, make the pumpkin filling, leave to cool and keep, covered, in the fridge. Make the cheese layer and keep, covered, in the fridge. When ready to use, assemble the lasagne and cook as directed.

FREEZE AHEAD TIP:
Cook, cool and freeze the cooked pumpkin for up to 1 week. Thaw overnight in the fridge. When ready to use, assemble the lasagne and cook as directed.

CHRISTMAS COLESLAW

For someone who doesn't consider herself a regular coleslaw eater, I seem to be peculiarly compelled towards this Germerican salad. Generally, I find a way in for myself by leaving out the onion, and throwing in the odd chopped spring onion instead, as earlier recipes of mine will testify. So you have my blessing to leave it out here, but consider this: I am a complete wuss about raw onion and yet I love this coleslaw. Flecks of spring onion look very seasonal alongside the overwhelming rubied redness of the rest of the slaw, so either way, it's a go-er.

❄ Finely shred the red cabbage; it should be very fine, so if you're patient and dextrous use a knife, otherwise use the slicing disc of a processor.

❄ Peel and slice the red onion into fine half-moons.

❄ Peel and cut the beetroot into matchsticks or juliennes. You might want to wear CSI (vinyl disposable) gloves to do this.

❄ Finely slice the fennel, then combine the cabbage, onion, beetroot and fennel in a big bowl.

❄ Mix the chutney, mayonnaise, garam masala and buttermilk (or yogurt) in a bowl. Dress the coleslaw with it, and check the seasoning, adding salt – or whatever you want – to taste.

Serves at least 20 as part of a spread

1 head red cabbage (approx. 1kg)
1 red onion
250g beetroot
1 head fennel

FOR THE DRESSING:
100g Sharwood's Green Label mango
  chutney
75g mayonnaise, preferably organic
1 teaspoon garam masala
60ml buttermilk (see note, below)
salt to taste

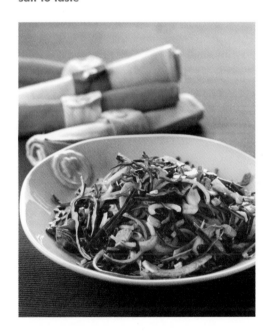

If you can't find buttermilk, use a runny plain yogurt, such as Activia.

MAKE AHEAD TIP:
The day before, mix together the dressing ingredients, cover and store in the fridge. On the day, about 3 hours before serving, mix together the shredded cabbage, sliced onion, beetroot and finely sliced fennel in a sealable bag. Store in the fridge. Toss the salad together about 30 minutes before serving.

CHOC CHIP CHILLI

Serves 12

550g chorizo sausages (not the salami sort),
  to give 10 sausages or 5 linked pairs
1.5kg boneless shin of beef, cut into 1.5cm
  cubes
500g onions (about 3), peeled
3 cloves garlic, peeled
1 fresh long red chilli, deseeded
4 x 15ml tablespoons vegetable oil
seeds from 3 cardamom pods
2 teaspoons ground cumin
1 teaspoon ground coriander
1 teaspoon ground cinnamon
1 teaspoon dried crushed chillies
4x 15ml tablespoons tomato purée
4 x 15ml tablespoons tomato ketchup
4 x 400g cans red kidney beans, drained
3 x 400g cans chopped tomatoes
50g dark chocolate chips
250ml water (swilled out in one of the
  chopped tomato cans)

If you're not buying your meat from a butcher, you can use regular stewing steak from the supermarket, but you'll need to cube it smaller and it is unlikely to get quite as tender as shin. I often buy shin of beef frozen and vacuum-packed online to stash in my own freezer (see Stockists on p.267).

MAKE AHEAD TIP:
Cook the chilli in the oven for 2¹/₂ hours only. Cool, cover and store in the fridge for up to 2 days. When ready to use, tip the chilli into a pan and bring slowly to the boil on the hob, stirring occasionally. Cover tightly and return to the oven for 1 hour until piping hot.

FREEZE AHEAD TIP:
Cook the chilli for 2¹/₂ hours only. Cool and freeze. Thaw overnight in the fridge, then reheat as above.

I've always made chilli with minced meat and added a dash of cocoa to bolster. This time, I wanted to play a little, to achieve something more along the lines of a dark, spicy-sauced cassoulet: that's to say, together with the beans, I use beef cut into fairly small chunks and fiery Spanish sausages. In place of the cocoa there is a sprinkling of dark, dark chocolate chips, which adds real depth and a velvety savouriness. This chilli is not for light eaters but something spicy and substantial is just what you need to soak up seasonal excess.

The Fully Loaded Potato Skins, overleaf, obviously beg to accompany this, but a splodge of the brightly hued Christmas Coleslaw on p.37 goes very well alongside, too. Under normal conditions, I'd also dollop out an **unchillied guacamole** with this, but I worry about having avocados sitting around going grungy, so only make this if you know it won't be hanging around: simply mash 3 ripe avocados with 3 finely chopped spring onions and add the juice of a lime or two and some salt to taste, stir in 3 x 15ml tablespoons of chopped coriander, spoon into 2 or 3 bowls, and sprinkle a little extra coriander over.

❄ Preheat the oven to 150°C/gas mark 2.

❄ Finely chop, or process the onion, garlic and chilli.

❄ Heat the oil in a large ovenproof pan (with lid) or flameproof casserole and fry the onion, garlic and chilli until soft, on low for about 10 minutes, then add the cardamom seeds, cumin, coriander, cinnamon and dried chillies.

❄ Stir the oniony spiced mixture together and then add the chorizo sliced into 5mm coins, letting them ooze their paprika-orange oil.

❄ Drop in the cubes of beef, turning them in the pan with the chorizo and onion mix to brown the meat.

❄ Stir in the tomato purée, ketchup, drained kidney beans and chopped tomatoes. Add the water and bring the chilli to a boil.

❄ Once it's started bubbling, sprinkle the chocolate chips over the chilli and give it a good stir. Put on a lid and transfer to the oven.

❄ Cook at this low heat for 3 hours. Once cooked it is best left overnight to improve the flavour.

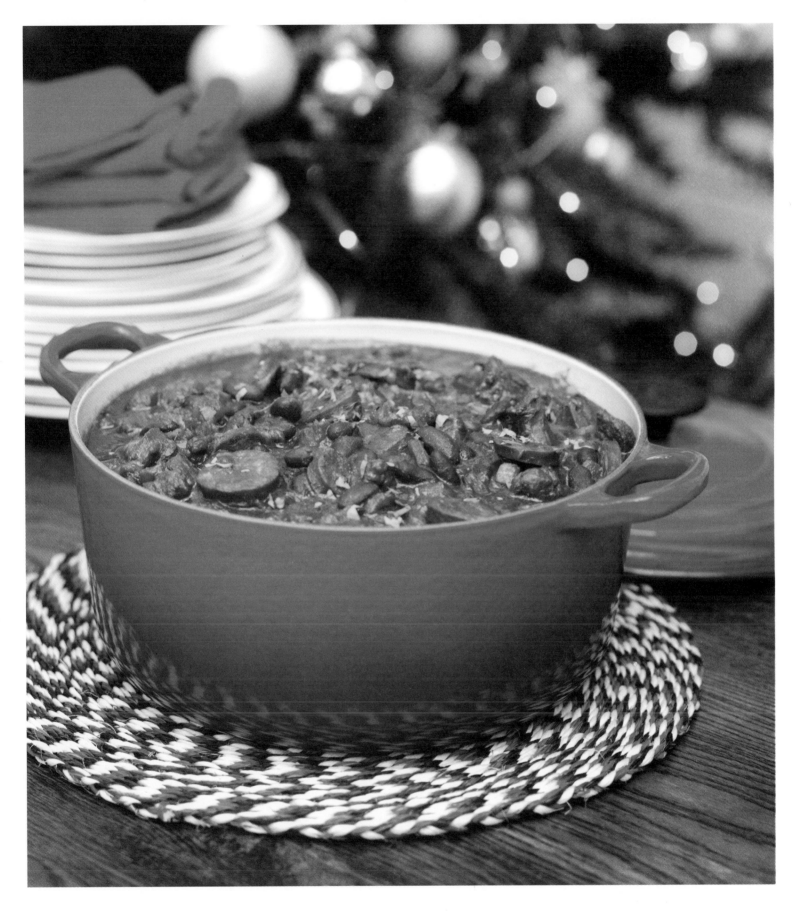

FULLY LOADED POTATO SKINS

Makes 20 stuffed potato skins

10 baking potatoes

225g strong cheddar, or red Leicester

250ml sour cream

4 spring onions

**1 teaspoon Maldon salt or 1/2 teaspoon
table salt (or to taste)**

good grinding of black pepper

1 x 15ml tablespoon Worcestershire sauce

**10 rashers American-style or thin-cut
streaky bacon**

oil for frying

MAKE AHEAD TIP:
Fill the potato skins, as directed, and sprinkle with
the cheese and crispy bacon (or add the crispy
bacon after cooking if preferred). Cover loosely
and keep in the fridge for up to 2 days. Cook as
directed.

FREEZE AHEAD TIP:
Fill the potato skins as above, wrap in clingfilm and
freeze for up to 1 week. To cook, lay the frozen
potato skins on a baking sheet and cover loosely
with foil. Cook in the oven for 35–40 minutes,
removing the foil after the first 15 minutes.

The first time I did these – having longed to write my own recipe for Fully Loaded Skins – I didn't bother with the bacon. I was eating them alongside meat, so it didn't seem necessary. But then I figured, without bacon they're only *partially* loaded, and that wouldn't do at all. So here I've gone, as you can see, the whole hog. However, in the seasonal spirit, you might want to serve them without the bacon, or with the crisp bacon bits in a separate bowl for sprinkling, since it seems unnecessarily antagonistic to make potatoes that your veggie friends can't eat at a party.

❋ The day (or up to 2 days) before you load them, preheat your oven to 200°C/gas mark 6 and bake the potatoes (pricking them first) for about 1¹/₂ hours, or until the skins are crisp and the insides fluffy.

❋ As soon as you can bear to tackle the hot potatoes, cut them in half lengthways and scoop the insides into a bowl.

❋ Put the husk-like skins of the potatoes on a tray and, when cool, cover until you are ready to fill them. Let the potato cool in the bowl, and then cover until needed.

❋ When you are ready to fill the potatoes, preheat your oven to 200°C/gas mark 6. Grate the cheese, and add 200g of it to the cold potato along with the sour cream.

❋ Finely chop the spring onions and add to the potato, with the salt, pepper and Worcestershire sauce.

❋ Spoon the potato filling into the potato skins, and lay each half on a baking tray so they fit snugly together. Sprinkle over the remaining cheese, giving each potato skin a light covering, and cook for 20–30 minutes until golden.

❋ Fry the bacon rashers in oil (or grill them) until crispy, then crumble them and sprinkle half a rasher's worth over each potato skin to make them fully loaded.

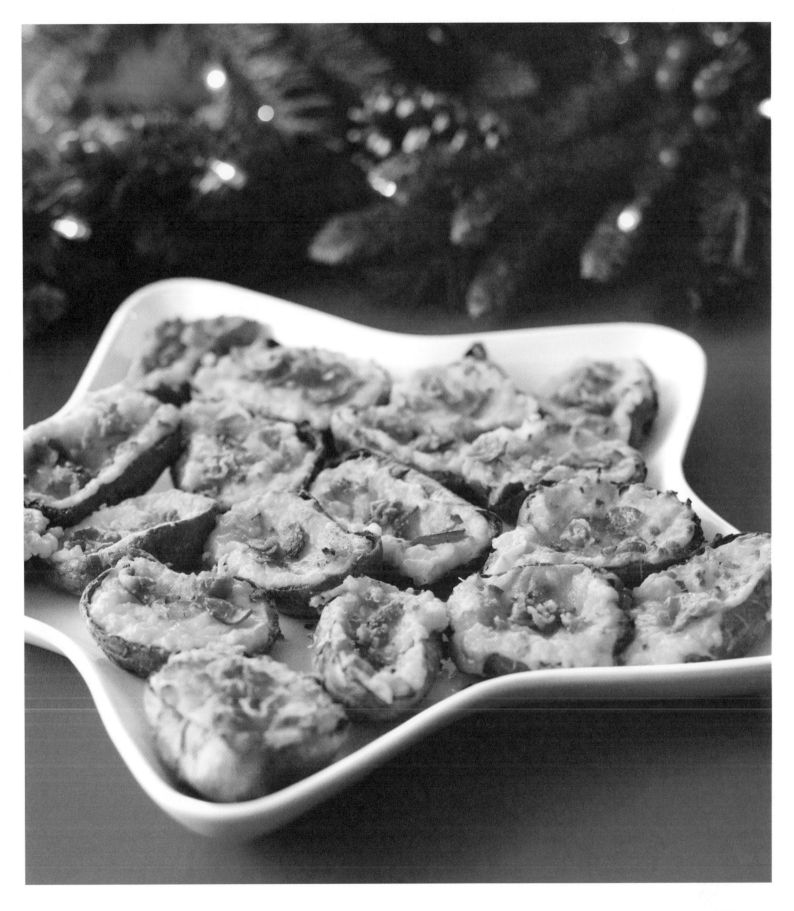

THE BOOZY BRITISH TRIFLE

Enough for 20 portions easily

FOR THE CUSTARD:

1 litre double cream

8 egg yolks (I use the whites to make the
    Prodigious Pavlova on p.45, but you could
    freeze the whites in an airtight freezer
    bag for up to 6 months)

2 whole eggs

50g caster sugar

1 teaspoon vanilla extract

FOR THE BASE:

2 packets trifle sponges (8 sponges in each
    packet)

1 x 340g jar strawberry or blackberry jam

500ml cream sherry

2 x 380g packets frozen summer fruits,
    thawed

zest of 1 orange

25g caster sugar (not needed if using *fresh*
    fruits)

FOR THE TOPPING:

500ml double cream

50g pistachios

1 x 15ml tablespoon crystallized rose petals
    (or crystallized violet petals)

If you really don't want to make custard from
scratch, you can use good shop-bought "fresh"
custard, 2–3 x 500ml (500g) cartons.

Crystallized rose petals or violet petals are easy to
find at specialist cake decoration stores or online
(see Stockists p.267).

MAKE AHEAD TIP:
Make the trifle (without the cream) up to 2 days
ahead. Keep, covered, in the fridge. When ready to
serve, finish with the cream, pistachios and crystallized rose (or violet) petals, as directed.

I think this really says it all. I have written so many recipes for trifle, I scarcely dare reiterate my love for it, but this, perhaps the most traditional of my offerings, shows the sensational, time-honoured pud at its glorious, many-layered best: the jam-slashed and sherry-sodden sponge, the sharp fruity layer of flavour-oozing berries, the eggy custard and the whipped cream. On top, my favourite colour combination: the Victorian pink of crystallized rose petals with the tender green of chopped pistachios. Perfection.

___

❊ To make the custard, heat the cream in a large, wide, heavy-based pan and while it's heating, whisk the egg yolks, whole eggs and caster sugar in a bowl.

❊ When the cream's at boiling point – though *don't actually let it boil* – take it off the heat and pour it over the eggs and sugar, whisking as you go.

❊ Wash out the pan (boring but it does have to be done), then pour the uncooked custard back into it and return to the heat.

❊ Cook over a medium heat (people will tell you it should be low heat but that is just too tedious for words), stirring all the time, until it has thickened. *It must never boil!*

❊ After 10–15 minutes, it should be thick enough, so straightaway pour it into a cold, clean bowl, add the vanilla extract, and whisk a bit to help bring the temperature down.

❊ Cover the very top of the custard, as well as the bowl, with clingfilm and leave to cool, while you start assembling your trifle.

❊ Split the 16 trifle sponges in half and make into sandwiches with the jam. Squidge these into the base of your trifle bowl. A trifle bowl should, I feel, be glass so you can see the layers from the outside. The proportions vary and, since the point of a trifle is the layers, the dimensions of your bowl will determine how these build up and the amount of sponge etc. you will need.

❊ Pour the sherry over the sponge sandwiches and let it soak in.

❊ Now tumble in the thawed summer fruits, with a little of their liquid. (It might seem unseasonal to use "summer" fruits, but I love their tartness against the sweetness of the custard that will drape over them.) Then grate the zest of the orange over the fruit and sprinkle with the caster sugar; if you're not using

frozen fruit (which tends to be sour), don't bother with the sugar. (And you could bake a layer of **pink, forced winter rhubarb**, instead. Use 1kg rhubarb – about 800g trimmed and sliced into 4–5cm pieces. Put the slices in a baking dish, sprinkle with 300g caster sugar, cover tightly with foil and cook, without adding liquid, for 45 minutes in a 190°C/gas mark 5 oven. Once the rhubarb's cold, use that as your fruit layer and boil down the juices to make a syrup for ice cream, or to drizzle – reduced and then chilled – over the cream with the pistachios and roses, later.)

❅ When the custard's cool, remove the clingfilm. Pour and scrape the custard on top of the berries. It will be soft-set: thickened but far from solid. Cover the bowl (not the custard this time) with some fresh clingfilm and refrigerate for at least half a day or up to 2 days – it's this standing time that makes the difference.

❅ When you are ready to serve, take the trifle out of the fridge to stand for about 1 hour. Whisk the cream until softly whipped. You don't want it to merge with the custard, but nor do you want it stiffly peaking.

❅ Remove the clingfilm from the trifle bowl and spread the cream on top of the custard with a rubber spatula.

❅ Finely chop the pistachios, sprinkle over the top of the trifle and adorn with a few, beautiful crystallized rose petals (or crystallized violet petals, if you prefer).

PRODIGIOUS PAVLOVA

This is indeed prodigious: a billowing, regally magnificent mega-meringue, marshmallow within, crisp and almost candied at its sugary edge, dolloped with whipped cream, lychees and passionfruit and drizzled with a vividly red, vibrantly sharp raspberry sauce.

If, like me, you live in the northern hemisphere, this being the deep midwinter, I presume the raspberries will be frozen; and since these berries tend to be sharper, I don't spritz fresh lemon juice into them as I blitz them into a sauce. If you're using fresh raspberries, add a squeeze of lemon as you blend.

I do think the raspberry sauce (coulis to those who remember the 1980s) makes a difference: I love the note of Christmas that the lucent redness brings, and the way, when you cut into it, you get a streak of winter raspberry ripple.

❋ Preheat the oven to 180°C/gas mark 4. Line a baking sheet with baking parchment and draw a rough 25cm diameter circle on it; I pencil round a cake tin that size.

❋ Whisk the egg whites until satiny peaks form, then whisk in the sugar, a tablespoonful at a time, until the meringue is stiff and shiny.

❋ Sprinkle the cornflour, vinegar and vanilla extract over the egg white, and fold in lightly with a metal spoon. Mound the meringue on to the baking parchment within the circle and, using a spatula, flatten the top and smooth the sides.

❋ Put in the oven and immediately reduce the heat to 120°C/gas mark 1/2. Cook for an hour. Then turn off the oven and leave to cool completely. Once it's cool, take the meringue disc out – and you can keep it in an airtight container for a couple of days or freeze for a month.

❋ When you are ready to assemble the pavlova, invert the cooled meringue disc onto a large plate or a stand you can serve it on, and peel off the baking parchment.

❋ Whip the cream until thickened but still soft, and pile onto the meringue – on the squidgy part that was stuck to the baking parchment – spreading it to the edges in a swirly fashion.

❋ Cut the passionfruit in half, and scoop out the seeds, and any pulp and juice, into a bowl. Peel the fresh lychees (if using) over the bowl to catch any juice, then remove the stones, tear the lychees into pieces and let them drop into the passionfruit. Tear the drained, canned lychees (if using) likewise, and drop them in, too.

Makes 14 generous slices

FOR THE BASE:

8 egg whites (reserved, perhaps, from **The Boozy British Trifle** custard on p.42)

500g caster sugar

4 teaspoons cornflour

2 teaspoons white wine vinegar

1/2 teaspoon vanilla extract

FOR THE TOPPING:

650ml double cream

10 passionfruit

10 fresh or canned lychees, drained if canned

300g raspberries (frozen are fine)

25g icing sugar

MAKE AHEAD TIP:
Make the meringue disc and store in a deep, airtight container for up to 2 days. About 3–4 hours before serving, top with whipped cream and keep in the fridge. Just before serving, add the fruits and raspberry sauce.

FREEZE AHEAD TIP:
Make and freeze the meringue disc for up to 1 month. Thaw in a cool room and finish as recipe.

✳Leave the passionfruit and lychees sitting in their bowl for a moment, while you liquidize the raspberries with the icing sugar in a blender.

✳Dollop the cream-topped pavlova with the passionfruit and lychees, and their juices, then zig-zag some red, red, red raspberry sauce over the top, putting the rest in a small jug for people to add to their slices as they eat.

SEASONAL SUPPORT

SOUPS, SALADS, SAUCES AND SERVE-LATER SIDES

THERE IS AN ABSENCE in this book, an absence that is at the heart of this very chapter – and that is a roast chicken. To some extent, its exclusion makes sense. After all, this is the turkey's time; a chicken, puny by comparison, doesn't seem to deserve much of a place in a Christmas book. But, for me, there is no kitchen, no life, without it: no way a roast chicken is not always central. It is the simplest feast: the oven cooks it without interference from you. You just need to be there to put it in the oven, and to take it out. And it's not just lack of time or laziness that makes it crucial: a roast chicken is the taste of home.

Still, there's nothing wrong with laziness or lack of time as motives for cooking particular sorts of food. So long as greed is rewarded at the same time, I am happy. This really is what the recipes in this chapter are all about. Not every meal, even at Christmas, can be a full-on, time-consuming procession of courses. Sometimes I need to know that all I have to do is bung a chicken in the oven and, with one of these salads or soups beforehand or, indeed, the same salad or one of the dishes alongside, a proper dinner can be served. You don't need to make the soup or vegetable dishes in advance, but I find it helpful to do so. For me, cooking in advance is the way of tackling Christmas, and all the meals it involves, express-style. There's too much to do to manage everything at the last minute (though the salads are the work of moments), so what makes life simpler is to stagger tasks, to get food cooked earlier, only to be idly reheated at the last minute.

The salads, too, whether brought out as a first course or side dish to bulk out a dinner, or to add tang and flourish to a tableful of leftovers, are the nearest, neatest thing to a stressbusting, seasonal shortcut.

Maybe it goes without saying – a quick glance at the ingredients list and all is made clear – but my approach at Christmas is "scatter with pomegranate seeds". Their jewelled beauty gives instant Christmas oomph. And I'm unembarrassed about buying the seeds, already popped out into packages, from the supermarket.

So, the roast chicken I mentioned may exist, or may be just the notional main part of the meal you're planning, without a lot of time to fuss over it; the recipes that follow are what make this meal, and others like it, possible.

SOUPS

CHESTNUT SOUP WITH BACON CRUMBLES

Enough to fill 10 soup bowls or 20 cups or small (200ml) mugs

1 onion

1 leek

3 carrots

2 sticks celery

3 x 15ml tablespoons garlic oil

500g red lentils

3 litres vegetable stock (or chicken stock if preferred)

500g vacuum-packed peeled chestnuts

125ml amontillado sherry

salt and pepper

FOR SERVING:

small bunch of parsley (optional)

1 teaspoon garlic oil

10 rashers American-style or other thin-cut streaky bacon

MAKE AHEAD TIP:

Make the soup and liquidize. Cool, cover and keep in the fridge for up to 3 days. Reheat with the sherry, adding more stock/broth if needed. Check the seasoning before serving. Fry the bacon, cool and crumble into a sealable bag. Keep in the fridge for up to 3 days.

FREEZE AHEAD TIP:

Make the soup as above and freeze in an airtight container for up to 2 months. Thaw overnight in the fridge and reheat as above.

This is not a million miles away from the chestnut soup in my first book, *How to Eat*, but the fact that I can't leave it behind tells you not only how good it is, but how important familiarity, tradition and continuity are, especially at this time of year.

I confess, I'd planned a celeriac and chestnut soup to go here: I've cooked it; I've loved it; I'd written the recipe. But as I sit writing, I find it's my older, more basic soup that writes itself into the page. Taste it and you'll see why: a meal in itself with a hunk of warm bread, or a make-ahead starter to bring some cold cuts to party-life, this soup manages to be comforting, elegant and simple all at the same time.

Much as I love the golden intensity of chicken stock (and I'll take mine from concentrate; it doesn't always have to be homemade), I do think when you're catering for groups of people it's wise to make up meat-free soups with vegetable stock, so you can keep the vegetarians happy. Thus the bacon crumbles are, I suggest, better served apart, for those carnivores who might like to sprinkle them over their sweet, grainy soup.

❋ Either by hand, or using a processor, finely chop the onion, leek, carrots and celery.

❋ Heat the oil in a large, heavy-based pan, and add the chopped vegetables, cooking for about 10 minutes on a medium to low heat, until softened a little.

❋ Add the lentils, and turn them in the vegetable mush.

❋ Add the stock and bring to the boil, then, with the heat down a little, let simmer for about 40 minutes or until the lentils are soft.

❋ Add the chestnuts and liquidize the soup in batches, adding more water if it's too thick. However, if you're going to serve this at a later time, I wouldn't bother to add water now, as the soup will inevitably thicken as it stands.

❋ When you want to eat the soup, heat it in the pan along with the sherry, adding more liquid if needed, and season with salt and pepper to taste.

✤ While the soup's getting warm and ready, finely chop the parsley (you will need approx. 3 x 15ml tablespoonfuls), and heat the garlic oil in a large frying pan for the bacon.

✤ Fry the bacon until it is crisp and scorched and remove to some kitchen paper. Crumble the bacon into a bowl or a couple of bowls and put them on the table.

✤ As you serve the hot soup, sprinkle with parsley if wished.

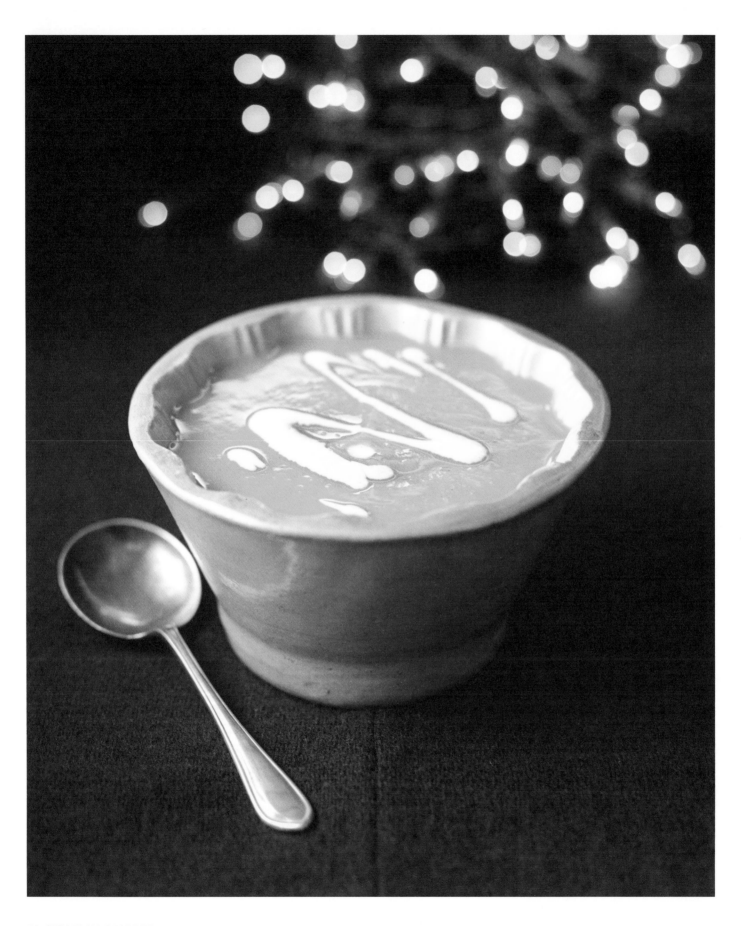

ROAST SQUASH AND SWEET POTATO SOUP WITH BUTTERMILK BLUE CHEESE SWIRL

It may seem a bit fiddly to have a soup prepared in two parts: one in the oven; one in the pan. But I do this not only because I think it intensifies the flavour dramatically, but because it actually makes my life easier.

The thing is this: when you roast a butternut squash, you can go ahead and liquidize it without ever having to peel it (I found this out when I made the Butternut Orzotto on p.134) and when I'm thigh-deep in cooking season, this is a real boon. Plus, I love the slightly flecked look that the spice-sized specks of skin give the soup, as well as the hint of texture.

The robust sweetness of this soup is countered by the buttermilk and blue cheese drizzling-mix that I swirl over the soup as I serve it and, indeed, I think it's the two together that really make it.

❉ Preheat the oven to 200°C/gas mark 6. Put the chopped onion, chopped butternut and sweet potato (again, don't worry that neither of these last two are peeled) onto a baking sheet.

❉ Drizzle the oil over them and sprinkle with the cinnamon and nutmeg, then roast in the oven for about 1–1^1/4 hours, by which time all should be tender. Remove from the oven.

❉ While the vegetables are still warm or at room temperature, liquidize them in 2 batches, adding 500ml of vegetable stock to each batch.

❉ Pour the blended vegetables into a saucepan. Swill another 500ml of vegetable stock in the blender to get out all the remnants of the soup, and pour into the pan. You have now added 1.5 litres of liquid to the vegetables.

❉ On reheating to serve, add the marsala and taste for seasoning. You may need to add up to another 500ml of water if the soup's too thick for your liking.

❉ As the soup warms up, liquidize the blue cheese and buttermilk in a clean blender and spoon into a jug or bowl.

❉ On serving, drizzle some of this mixture over each bowl. Leave the jug on the table for your guests to have more if they wish.

Serves 8–10 as a starter, 6 as a main course

1 onion, peeled and roughly chopped

1 butternut squash (unpeeled), halved, deseeded and sliced into 3cm x 2cm chunks

500g sweet potatoes (unpeeled), cut into 3cm rings

60ml olive oil

teaspoon ground cinnamon

^{1}/2 teaspoon ground nutmeg

1.5 litres vegetable stock, such as Marigold

125ml marsala wine

salt and pepper

FOR SERVING:

125g crumbled blue cheese

250ml buttermilk (if you can't find buttermilk, use a plain, runny – i.e. not set – yogurt, such as Activia)

If you have any buttermilk–blue–cheese mixture left over, put it into a clean jam jar with a fierce squirt of lime juice, and seal. It will keep for a day in the fridge and serve as a good salad dressing with or without an avocado blended into it.

MAKE AHEAD TIP:
Make the soup and liquidize. Cool, cover and keep in the fridge for up to 3 days. Reheat with the marsala, adding more water if needed. Check the seasoning before serving.

FREEZE AHEAD TIP:
Make the soup as above and freeze in an airtight container for up to 2 months. Thaw overnight in the fridge and reheat as above.

TORTILLA SOUP

When I went to Dallas, I became somewhat obsessed with ferreting out this Southwestern speciality and, although I was nominally there to work (under the auspices of Janet McLeod who had, fantastically, been Elvis's publicist), my overwhelming concern was this soup. However, my version is not attempting to ape the various ones I tried on my travels; I don't want to enter into the debate as to what is authentic or not. For one, I lack the credentials. I'm probably about as far from a southern belle as you could get, though I love the twang, adore the manners and could eat tortilla soup until the cows come home.

If you don't know what this is, the name is probably misleading. The tortilla refers to the soft corn tortillas which are cut into shreds and fried to be tossed into a spiced chicken broth, along with some shredded cheese, diced avocado and chopped coriander. Naturally – and it has a particular bearing, given the season – this can be made with turkey in place of chicken.

The chicken stock plays such a part here, it's worth making sure you use a good one. That doesn't have to mean homemade, though it's not difficult to make. Either follow the method on p.265 or cover the fresh carcass and leavings from a roast chicken with about 4.5 litres of water and boil with onion, leek, carrot, bay and salt for about 3 hours. With a turkey carcass you could make double this, easily.

Serves 6 as a main course

3.5 litres chicken stock
2 teaspoons celery salt
2 teaspoons ground cumin
3 bay leaves
1 small clove garlic, peeled and minced
2 fresh red chillies, deseeded and chopped
4 spring onions, finely sliced
300g cooked shredded chicken (or turkey)

FOR SERVING:
2–3 x 15ml tablespoons vegetable oil
1 teaspoon chilli oil
1 packet (8) soft corn tortillas
200g cheddar, or red Leicester, grated
1 avocado, peeled and diced
3 x 15ml tablespoons chopped coriander
3 limes, cut into quarters

❉ Heat the stock in a large pan, and add the celery salt, cumin, bay leaves, garlic, chillies and spring onions.

❉ Let the soup boil gently for about 10 minutes, then take off the heat and add the shredded chicken.

❉ While the soup's bubbling, put about a third of the vegetable and chilli oils into a frying pan to heat. Take a pair of soft corn tortillas, roll them up like a cigar and, with scissors, snip into approx. 1cm strips. Do likewise, in pairs, with the remaining 6 tortillas.

❉ Fry about a third of the tortilla strips in the hot oil and, as they scorch, remove to some waiting kitchen paper. Add and heat another third of your oil and continue like this, with the rest of the tortilla strips and oil. The home-fried tortilla chips may seem disappointingly soft in the pan, but they seem to crisp up as they cool slightly on the kitchen paper and, later, serving plate.

❉ Ladle the hot soup into bowls, and arrange the hot tortilla strips, the cheese, avocado, coriander and lime wedges (for spritzing) in separate dishes on the table to add to the glory of the occasion and to the soup.

MAKE AHEAD TIP:
Make the soup then cool, cover and keep in the fridge for up to 1 day. Bring slowly to the boil to reheat then simmer very gently until piping hot. Avoid too much stirring or the chicken will become stringy.

THREE SEASONAL SALADS

CHRISTMAS SALAD

Serves 6

2 heads red chicory

1 large head radicchio or tardivo

2 red peppers (optional)

seeds from 1 pomegranate, or 75g
    pomegranate seeds from a tub/packet

FOR THE DRESSING:

1 teaspoon Dijon mustard

$^1/_2$ teaspoon honey

juice of 1 clementine/satsuma

1 teaspoon lime juice

pinch of salt

3 x 15ml tablespoons extra virgin olive oil

MAKE AHEAD TIP:
Whisk together all the dressing ingredients, pour
into a clean jar or an airtight container and keep
cool for up to 3 days.

It is predominantly the colour – for all that I have another red salad on p.58 – that makes me think of this as a Christmas salad. But then, the starring role played by *the* Christmas fruit – the pomegranate – would surely be justification enough. This is the salad I bring out time and time again at Christmastime, either to bring a little joy and colour to a quickly gathered together tableful of leftovers, as a side dish when the food really needs no more than a light accompaniment, or even as a starter, so people have something to pick at as I do a little last minute this-or-that.

At this time of year, given my pomegranate-predilection, my fridge is full of those packets of all-done-for-you seeds, and the amount here represents half what I'd expect to find in a packet. If you're going for the whole fruit, use the seeds from a whole pomegranate.

If the salad is a starter, I tend to throw in the red peppers; as a simple side dish it is elegant perfection without.

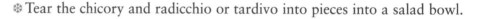

❉ Tear the chicory and radicchio or tardivo into pieces into a salad bowl.

❉ If you are using the red peppers, deseed them and cut into 2cm strips, and add to the salad.

❉ Sprinkle some of the pomegranate seeds over, then whisk together the dressing ingredients to pour over the salad.

❉ Toss everything together, then do a final sprinkling of pomegranate seeds over the top before serving.

OPPOSITE:
Chargrilled Peppers with Pomegranate (back left);
Christmas Salad (back right); Red Salad (front)

RED SALAD

Serves 8

2 x 400g cans red kidney beans

1 red onion, peeled and finely chopped

4 teaspoons good-quality red wine vinegar

250g cherry tomatoes

2 x 15ml tablespoons extra virgin olive oil

a few tablespoons finely chopped parsley
(optional)

MAKE AHEAD TIP:
Make the salad, without adding the tomatoes,
up to 1 day ahead. Cover and keep cool. Add the
tomatoes and parsley (if using), about 1 hour
before serving.

This is a fantastic fall-back not least because it's a speedy, low-effort way to turn something as basic as cold meat or baked potato into a substantial supper. Indeed, you could fork a little best-quality drained, canned tuna straight in and be done. However, even as someone as far from the vegetarian end of the spectrum as could be, I am more than happy to have this, quite simply, as is.

❋Drain and rinse the kidney beans in a colander to get rid of the dark sludge from the tins, then rinse again and put into a serving bowl or dish.

❋Put the chopped onion into a small bowl and pour over the vinegar. Leave to macerate for at least 15 minutes and up to 2 hours.

❋Halve the cherry tomatoes and put them into the serving bowl.

❋Now tip in the macerated onions and toss through the beans and tomatoes. Drizzle over the oil and toss again, sprinkling with some parsley if you want; I like the way its greenness brings out the red.

CHARGRILLED PEPPERS WITH POMEGRANATE

Serves 8

6 peppers (ideally a mix of red, orange and
yellow, but never, ever, ever green; all red
is fine though)

seeds from 2 pomegranates, or 150g
pomegranate seeds from a tub/packet

2 x 15ml tablespoons fresh pomegranate
juice

2 teaspoons lime or lemon juice

60ml extra virgin olive oil

1 x 15ml tablespoon garlic oil

$^1/_2$ teaspoon Maldon salt or $^1/_4$ teaspoon
table salt

3 x 15ml tablespoons drained capers

It was only a matter of time before I came back to the pomegranate. I am relaxed as to how you combine the peppers with the pomegranate. I often make this with frozen bags of chargrilled peppers, which I tip out, unthawed, onto a baking sheet and roast in a hot oven for about 20 minutes. These I often eat warm, with some olive oil and lemon juice (or freshly squeezed pomegranate juice mixed with lime) tossed through, along with a handful of pomegranate seeds. For my cold version I simply use chargrilled peppers from a jar, in place of the roasted packet ones.

Opposite is the method you'll need if you're chargrilling the peppers yourself. It isn't difficult, just fiddly. Sometimes, I like an excuse to busy myself undemandingly in the kitchen. At other times, I unashamedly take the shortcuts above.

This salad is also good if you leave the peppers raw, just deseeded and cut into 1cm-wide strips, all juicy and crunchy, as are the pomegranate seeds, only the peppers are markedly sweeter.

If I know all parties will be agreeable, I make a dressing by blending or whisking 2 anchovy fillets with a tablespoonful of red wine vinegar and three of olive oil. Otherwise, the dressing below is perfect.

To turn this into a first course, simply add some crumbled feta or sharp goat's cheese. And whether I'm using raw, packet, jarred or home-charred peppers, I like to go for a mix of red, orange and yellow, to create an edible flame on the plate.

❋ Preheat the oven to 250°C/gas mark 9.

❋ Cut the peppers in half, remove the stalk and seeds, and sit them cut-side down on an oven tray or a couple of trays. Roast in the hot oven until they blister; about 15 minutes should do it.

❋ Take out of the oven, and quickly tip the blackened peppers into a big bowl. Cover the bowl tightly with clingfilm and leave the peppers to cool enough to handle.

❋ Use your hands to peel off strips of charred skin (don't worry if some is left on) and, as you go, put torn strips of peppers into a serving dish.

❋ When you've done all of them, add most of the pomegranate seeds to the peppers and toss well.

❋ Whisk together the pomegranate and lime juices (or lemon juice, if using), the olive oil, garlic oil and salt. I often just put everything into an old mustard jar with a lid, and shake. Pour the dressing over the salad and toss gently but well.

❋ Add the crocodile-green capers, the perfect salty counterpart to the juicy sweet red peppers, and toss again, taste for seasoning, then add a final scattering of rubied seeds.

MAKE AHEAD TIP:
Make the salad, without the capers, up to 1 day ahead. Cover and keep cool. When ready to serve, add the capers and toss again. Check the seasoning then scatter with extra pomegranate seeds.

SERVE-LATER SIDES

RED CABBAGE WITH POMEGRANATE JUICE

Serves 10

2 x 15ml tablespoons vegetable oil

1 red onion, peeled and halved

scant 15ml tablespoon Maldon salt or 1 tea-
    spoon table salt

2 red apples

1 head red cabbage

3 x 15ml tablespoons soft dark brown sugar

2 teaspoons ground allspice

750ml pomegranate juice

I couldn't have Christmas without red cabbage, and I never veer far from the way my mother cooked it – that's to say, I give it a long, slow stewing with something sharp, something sweet. This recipe takes in my unabating pomegranate pash but, instead of using the seeds, I go for the juice that comes in bottles. Make sure you go for the unadulterated, unsweetened variety; that much is crucial.

I love this with ham (hot or cold), or with turkey or roast pork, but I think it might be at its unsurpassed best (it's a close-run thing) with the Roast Goose on p.149. The important thing to bear in mind is that, as with all stews, this improves as it stands, so not only does it help you to make it in advance, it positively helps the red cabbage and, thus, your dinner, too.

Although as a regular sidedish, this is fine for 10, it stretches easily to half that again as part of a Christmas dinner; when there are so many components, people tend to take relatively small helpings – and I'm talking about my family here, which is really saying something.

❋ Heat the oil in a large, heavy-based saucepan (with a lid) or a flameproof casserole. Finely slice each halved onion into thin half-moons and add to the pan along with the salt. Fry for about 5 minutes until the onion begins to soften but doesn't burn; the salt will help to prevent it from burning.

❋ While this is going on, quarter the apples (no need to peel), cut away the cores and chop them roughly, and add them to the softening onions and cook, stirring occasionally, for another 5 minutes.

❋ Finely shred the cabbage and add it to the onion–apple mixture in the pan, stirring slowly and patiently to mix. Add the brown sugar and allspice and stir, then pour the pomegranate juice into the pan.

❋ Let the mixture come to a bubble, then give another stir, turn down the heat, put on a lid and cook very gently at the lowest possible heat for 2–3 hours, stirring occasionally. It really won't get overcooked. Taste for seasoning only when you're ready to reheat, as the flavours won't have mellowed and come together properly until then.

❋ To reheat, put the pan back on the stove over a medium to low heat, stirring occasionally, for 15–20 minutes.

MAKE AHEAD TIP:
Make the red cabbage up to 3 days ahead. Transfer to a non-metallic dish or bowl then cool, cover and keep in the fridge. Put the cabbage back in the pan, and reheat as directed. Check the seasoning before serving.

FREEZE AHEAD TIP:
Make the red cabbage as above and leave to cool. Spoon into an airtight container and freeze for up to 2 months. Thaw overnight in a cool room and reheat as above.

BOSTON BAKED BEANS

This continues the seasonally warming vegetable theme – here, a pale pulse, after the deep-red cabbage with pomegranate juice – that combines the savoury and the sweet, and although this is less obviously Christmassy than the others, tell me that after you've had a vat wafting its spiced way through the kitchen as you cook. The scent is heady and welcoming as the beans seem to mull in the bacon, mustard, spice and sugar.

These might not be baked beans as a Bostonian (or Messrs Heinz or Campbell for that matter) would cook them, but they work for me – and for anyone I've ever, proudly, fed them to. I warn you now: they are addictive. Must be the salt and sugar, which also – alas – explains why they taste so good.

It may be an obvious pairing, but this begs to be eaten with sausages.

❋ The night (or day) before you want to make this recipe (which could be 2 days before you plan to serve it), soak the beans in plenty of water for 24 hours.

❋ Once the beans are soaked, drain and rinse them and put aside. Preheat the oven to 150°C/gas mark 2 and heat the oil in a large, flameproof casserole or an ovenproof pan with a lid.

❋ Fry the chopped bacon briskly in the hot oil and, after about 5 minutes, turn down the heat and add the chopped onion. Cook alongside the bacon for about another 10 minutes.

❋ Add the mustard, tomato purée and sugar and 500ml of the water, stirring everything together well.

❋ Stir in the rinsed beans, and then add a further 500ml of water. Bring to the boil and let it bubble for 10 minutes.

❋ Put a lid on the casserole or pan and transfer to the oven for 2–2$\frac{1}{2}$ hours or until tender.

❋ Remove from the oven and add the remaining 60ml water along with the vinegar and, after tasting carefully (don't burn your mouth), the salt if wished.

Serves 8

500g haricot beans

2 x 15ml tablespoons garlic oil

125g smoked streaky bacon, chopped somewhere between finely and roughly

1 onion, peeled and chopped

100g grainy mustard

2 x 15ml tablespoons tomato purée

100g dark muscovado sugar

1 litre water, plus 60ml

1 x 15ml tablespoon cider vinegar

2 teaspoons Maldon salt or 1 teaspoon table salt, or to taste

MAKE AHEAD TIP:
Cook the beans for 2 hours then cool and spoon into an airtight container. Keep in the fridge for up to 2 days. To reheat, return to the pan and stir in the extra 60ml water along with the vinegar and salt. Cover with lid and bring slowly to the boil, stirring occasionally. Simmer for 10–15 minutes or until piping hot.

FREEZE AHEAD TIP:
Cook and cool the beans as above. Freeze for up to 3 months. Thaw overnight in the fridge then reheat as above.

PISELLI CON PANNA E PANCETTA

(Peas with Pancetta in Cream All'Italiana)

Even though we constantly read how Italians use olive oil and never butter or cream, of course this is not the case – or certainly not in northern Italy. Yes, it's rich, yes it's got lots of cream, *bla, bla, bla*, as the Italians say, without an "h", but it is Christmas for goodness' sake.

This is good with absolutely everything – plain chicken or fish, or heaped over pasta or rice or *anything*.

❄ Heat the garlic oil in a large, heavy-based pan (with a lid) or a flameproof casserole and tumble in the *cubetti di pancetta* or bacon cubes or lardons (however you like to think of them) and let them cook for about 5 minutes.

❄ Add the spring onions, stir well, and cook for a further 3 minutes.

❄ Add the butter and thyme to the pan or casserole, stir well, then tip in the frozen peas. Cook for a few minutes, stirring, until the frost begins to leave the peas and they start to look a brighter green.

❄ Add the water, give another stir, then stir in the cream. Bring to a bubble, put the lid on and let it cook for 15 minutes.

❄ Take the pan off the heat, and remove the lid while you stir in the Parmesan flakes, then put it back on to let the peas cool in their flavoursome cream. The peas will dull down, losing their bright green colour as they cool and sit. This is as it should be, and don't worry about it; they may look less vibrant but they taste more vivid.

❄ To reheat, put the pan over a low to medium heat and keep it covered – opening it only to stir occasionally – for 5–10 minutes.

Serves 8

1 x 15ml tablespoon garlic oil
200g pancetta cubes (or lardons)
6 spring onions, sliced
15g butter
1 teaspoon dried thyme
900g frozen petits pois
175ml boiling water, from a kettle
250ml double cream
50g Parmesan flakes

MAKE AHEAD TIP:
Complete the recipe but without the Parmesan cheese. Allow to cool, cover and keep in the fridge for up to 1 day. To reheat, put the pan over a low to medium heat and stir in the Parmesan flakes. Cover and reheat gently, stirring occasionally, for about 5–10 minutes.

POTATO, PARSNIP AND PORCINI GRATIN

Serves 8

10g dried porcini, or ceps
150ml boiling water, from a kettle
50g butter
1 x 15ml tablespoon garlic oil
500ml full-fat milk
500ml double cream
3 star anise
1 teaspoon Maldon salt or $^1/_2$ teaspoon
   table salt
good grinding of pepper
900g potatoes
900g parsnips

Cooking potatoes for large numbers of people is not always easy. This gratin makes it so, not least because I don't peel the potatoes (or the parsnips for that matter). Obviously, you don't need to make it ahead, but knowing you can is a help. There is a fabulously musky scent to this gratin, which comes in part from the star anise, in part from the porcini, and also from the culinary alchemy of all the ingredients together. And the thing is, for something so sweetly comforting, it is – I cannot explain why – somehow grand and exquisite, too.

✽ Soak the porcini in the boiling water for about 20–30 minutes.

✽ Preheat the oven to 220°C/gas mark 7. Heat the butter and garlic oil in a large pan.

✽ Drain the porcini, reserving the liquid, then finely chop the mushrooms and add them to the pan to cook for a couple of minutes.

✽ Add the mushroom-liquid, milk, cream, star anise and salt and pepper.

✽ Without peeling the potatoes or parsnips, slice them into 1cm round slices and add to the pan.

✽ Bring the pan to a bubbling simmer and then gently cook, partially covered, for 20 minutes, or until the potato and parsnip are tender but not mushy.

✽ Decant into a gratin-type, ovenproof dish (mine is a round shallow casserole, about 30cm x 7cm deep).

✽ Cook in the oven for about 40 minutes (it will need longer if you have cooked it ahead and left it to cool before putting in the oven) or until the top is coloured in places and the gratin looks bubbly underneath.

MAKE AHEAD TIP:
Decant the vegetables into the gratin dish and leave to cool. Cover tightly with clingfilm and keep in the fridge for up to 1 day. To cook, leave the dish at room temperature for about 40 minutes. Cook in the oven as directed.

FREEZE AHEAD TIP:
Cool and cover the vegetables as above, then freeze for up to 1 week. To use, thaw overnight in the fridge, and cook as above.

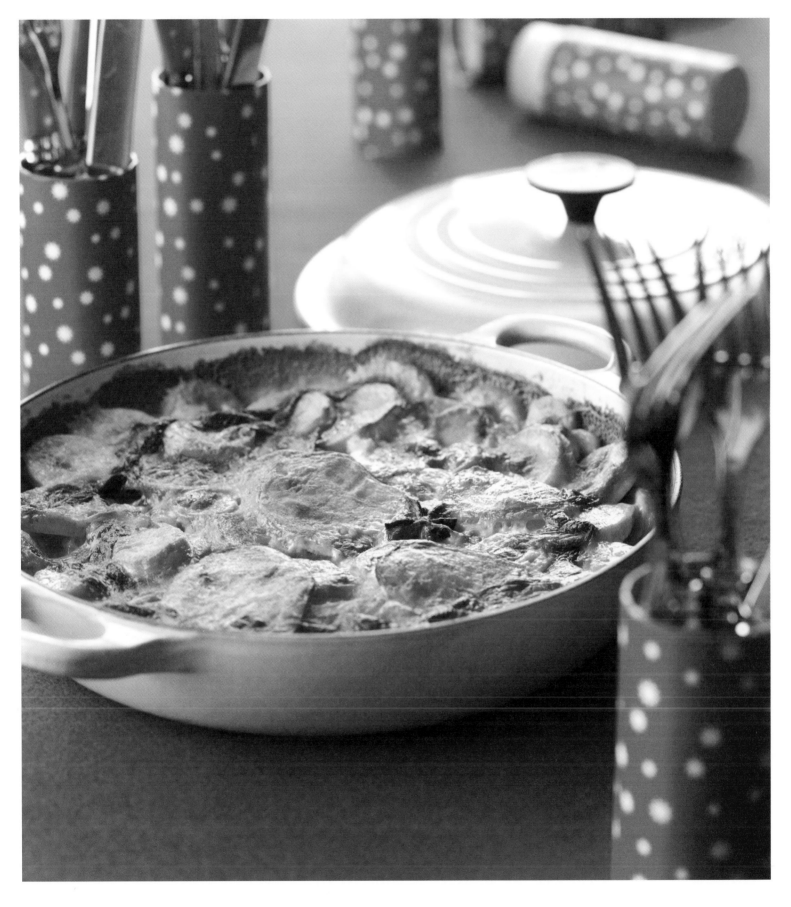

THREE STIR-TOGETHER SAUCES

This trio of sauces is just what you need to be able to prink something into dinner-party fare. And sometimes, it's not so much partifying as adding a crucial touch that makes everything feel complete. There is something about the contrast of components in each whisked-up sauce that offers complexity to the taste while being simple to make: the sweetness of the beetroot plays against the heat of the horseradish; the pepperiness of the mustard counters the fruity sweetness of the jelly; and the sharpness, again of the mustard, undercuts the richness of the mayonnaise.

WHOLEGRAIN HONEY MUSTARD MAYONNAISE

Makes enough to serve as a condiment for 8 people

200g good-quality, shop-bought mayonnaise, preferably organic
75g wholegrain mustard
1 teaspoon runny honey
squeeze of lemon
salt to taste

I love the combination of mustard and mayonnaise, my earliest savour of which was years ago, frightening how many, dolloped alongside some hot skinny chips in Amsterdam. The one here is very different, and different again from the smooth, but equally delicious Dijonnaise I've run into since. This is sweet and nubbly and gorgeous with cold chicken, cold turkey, ham, hot baked potato or in any sandwich.

❋ Put the mayonnaise into a bowl and dollop in the mustard, whisking well to combine.

❋ Add the honey and a spritz of lemon and whisk again, tasting for balance and seasoning.

It may be helpful to think in terms of ratios rather than amounts: in volume (not weight), you have a quarter mustard here to mayo; add honey and lemon juice (and indeed salt) to taste.

MAKE AHEAD TIP:
Cover and keep in the fridge for up to 1 week.

OPPOSITE:
Wholegrain Honey Mustard Mayonnaise (left);
Redcurrant and Wholegrain Mustard Sauce (right))

REDCURRANT AND WHOLEGRAIN MUSTARD SAUCE

This has a distinctly Scandinavian taste, and is the perfect accompaniment to baked ham, eaten hot or cold. It can also make a quick glaze for sausages or, indeed, the ham before you've baked it.

❄There is really nothing to this: you simply put the ingredients together and whisk till they're combined. If you've kept either of them in the fridge and they're too hard to mix, just whisk them in a saucepan over a low heat until they do what they're told.

Makes enough to serve as a condiment for 8 people; it's easy to augment, as you're using equal amounts of each

150g wholegrain mustard
150g redcurrant jelly

MAKE AHEAD TIP:
Cover and keep in a cool place for up to 3 days or longer if in the fridge.

BEETROOT AND HORSERADISH SAUCE

Makes enough to serve as a condiment for 8 eaters

200g hot horseradish sauce

2 x 15ml tablespoons crème fraîche (or sour cream)

1 small, uncooked beetroot

This, in effect, is the Jewish *chrayn*, which makes an unorthodox outing in a Christmas book. I include it here because it enlivens cold turkey and other leftovers, and is particularly wonderful with roast goose or, it must be said, pork.

Because I'm usually pressed for time, I grate the beetroot into hot horseradish sauce from a jar (to which I've added the crème fraîche) but if you have time, you can grate 3 x 15ml tablespoons of horseradish (use a Microplane grater, as for the beetroot) and the small beetroot into a 200ml pot of crème fraîche and add half a teaspoon of Dijon mustard, and salt to taste, stirring well to combine.

❉ Whisk or stir together the hot horseradish sauce with the crème fraîche in a wide bowl (this makes it easier when you grate in the beetroot).

❉ Put on vinyl disposable gloves (if you know what's good for you) and peel the beetroot before pressing it through a fine Microplane grater held over the horseradish bowl. Rap the grater when you've all but finished (don't grate so far that you risk mixing your own blood with the beetroot's) to knock in all the red gunge.

❉ Stir or whisk to combine and decant to a serving bowl or a jar.

MAKE AHEAD TIP:
Cover and keep in the fridge for 1 day.

COME ON OVER...

STRESS-FREE SUPPERS

I DON'T THINK I CAN REMEMBER when I last gave a dinner party. This isn't an admission of regret or guilty confession, but a thankful statement of fact. Friends over for supper is a different matter, though. Around Christmas, I love to pile people in and I don't mind if it's every evening; in fact, that's what I want to happen. From mid December onwards, sometimes even earlier, I want the house to be filled with people sitting around a table, talking and eating.

But this is very much about supper and not dinner. For one thing, I invite people over unfashionably early. I get things ready, but not fussily organized. I plonk cutlery, red napkins in snowflake rings and the shiny multi-coloured tealight holders I bought at one of the children's school Christmas fairs on the bare wood table, along with a pile of plates, add drinks and wait for people to come, sit around and help themselves. I don't go in for serving drinks in one room, with everyone having to get up and shuffle into another to eat. I like to keep the scene of the crime contained. I think it feels cosier, but it makes life easier, too. Besides, I don't like having to act as some sort of MC or white-knuckled party organizer, desperately trying to herd people through the evening. That's not relaxing for anyone.

And, although I'm very happy to have company while I'm pottering stoveside, the food I make for my season of suppers requires so little last-minute attention, I'm never in hostess-meltdown. Most of the menus I suggest here can be prepared largely in advance, or else practically cook themselves. I don't factor in a starter, because I just have never found them necessary. You don't have to agree with me, and the soups and salads in Seasonal Support (from p.50) can help you bump up a two-course supper into a tripartite dinner with gratifying ease. I certainly do, however, put something – most usually one of the Crostini or the Seasonally Spiced Nuts from The More The Merrier (see pp.15–17 and 21) – on the table for people to graze on over drinks as they arrive.

I also feel that, around Christmas, you have to have bowlfuls of lychees and clementines or satsumas to bring out either with pudding or even instead. And, please, the season surely demands a bowl of nuts with a nutcracker nestling in them, as well.

All I want, at this time of year, is to be able to have the people I love round a table with me and the food that follows makes me know I can do this, and enjoy it.

A LUSCIOUS DINNER FOR 6–8

LAMB AND DATE TAGINE
RED ONION AND POMEGRANATE RELISH
GLEAMING MAPLE CHEESECAKE

The symbolic aspect of feast foods has always been an important part of the ritual of celebration; sweet ingredients are there not just to please the palate, but also to bring corresponding harmony to the home. *La douceur du foyer*, that ironic Baudelairean yearning for home, sweet home, and the pleasures of the hearth, is never more keenly felt (or often, indeed, as futilely) as it is at this time of year. I know that good food does not automatically create a good mood, but friends and family gathered around a treat-laden table can make the difference, to both cook and eater. And this indulgent, aromatic menu is the perfect way to begin our season of spirit-lifting suppers.

If the pudding sounds rich after the sweet substantiality of the main course, well – what can I tell you? – it is Christmas, after all. But, while I make no claims for the dietary restraint of this menu – *as if* – it is actually the case that the cheesecake has, in each more-ish mouthful, just the tang and the melting lightness that you want after the tagine. The maple syrup that cascades lightly on top and sometimes down the sides is sweet enough to hold its own after the swelling fruitiness of the dates, but not so sweet that it creates overload.

An easy, no-cook alternative for getting this balance of sweet first, tang after, is to provide, instead of pudding, a snowy log or two of tender goat's cheese, and perhaps some honey to drizzle over it.

And I'm sure you know my views by now on the enduring desirability of loading the table with seasonal fruits, so both you, and those you're feeding, can play it any way you or they want, to finish dinner.

LAMB AND DATE TAGINE

3–4 x 15ml tablespoons goose fat (or
   olive oil)

2 onions, peeled and chopped

1 teaspoon ground cinnamon

1 teaspoon ground turmeric

1 teaspoon ground ginger

1 teaspoon ground cumin

1 teaspoon ground allspice

1kg diced leg of lamb

250g soft dried pitted dates, or pitted
   Medjool dates

250ml pure pomegranate juice, from a bottle

250ml water

2 teaspoons Maldon salt or 1 teaspoon table
   salt, or to taste

If you're not using a funnel-lidded tagine, but a regular, preferably shallow, casserole, then you do
have the option of cooking this for 2 hours in a
150°C/gas mark 2 oven.

MAKE AHEAD TIP:
Make the tagine, then transfer to a non-metallic
bowl to cool. Cover, and store in the fridge for up to
3 days. When ready to serve, return the tagine to
the pan and add 75ml water. Bring slowly to the
boil, stirring occasionally, and let it bubble very
gently for 2–3 minutes. Reduce the heat to a bare
minimum and simmer the tagine, still stirring, for
15–20 minutes or until piping hot. Be prepared to
add a little more water to thin it out as it reheats.

FREEZE AHEAD TIP:
Make the tagine as directed and freeze in an
airtight container for up to 1 month. Thaw overnight
in the fridge and reheat as above.

I admit, I often call a stew a tagine because it sounds more appealing, but this can more authentically claim rights to the title: it is, after all, Moroccan in substance and inspiration and I have indeed cooked it in the tagine – that Moroccan funnel-lidded casserole – which gives the stew its name.

You don't need to have a tagine to cook it, so don't worry. What the traditionally shaped tagine – with its shallow base and conical lid – does is to allow a lot of steam to circulate so that a relatively small amount of liquid gives a lot of flavour and intensity to the dish. But, conversely, I find using a pan into which all the ingredients fit snugly, with a tight-fitting lid, does the trick just as well. As to size, what you need here is a tagine base, or wide, shallow, lidded pan or casserole, with a 3-litre capacity.

Strangely, my local supermarket sells diced leg of lamb for stewing in 340g packets; if I'm not getting the neat kilo of meat from my butcher, I buy three of these packets. I have chosen goose fat as a cooking medium here only because I always have some in the house over Christmas, but do use regular olive (not extra virgin) oil if you prefer.

The dates make this tagine rich and sweet, which is just how it should be; the fragrant, almost-sourness of the pomegranate helps to punctuate this. The spices permeate the atmosphere with warmth and festive spirit. If you wish to, you could serve some plain couscous alongside – prepare 500g as for the Festive Couscous on p.97, but leave out the sultanas and the post-soaking adornment.

❆ Warm the goose fat (or oil) in your cooking vessel of choice and scrape in the onions from the chopping board, letting them cook gently over a low heat for 10 minutes or until softened, stirring occasionally.

❆ Add the ground cinnamon, turmeric, ginger, cumin and allspice, and turn well in the onions.

❆ Turn up the heat and add the meat, turning it patiently in the pan so that it sears equally; this is why a wide, shallow pan is better than a narrow, deep one.

❆ Drop in the dates, pour in the pomegranate juice and water, then add the salt and bring to a bubble. Put the lid on, turn down the heat to an absolute minimum; it's important that this cooks ultra-gently for 2 hours. Or choose the oven option (see left) if appropriate.

❆ I prefer to cook this a day or two in advance and reheat; on serving, top with some of the Red Onion and Pomegranate Relish (see opposite), transferring the rest to a small bowl.

RED ONION AND POMEGRANATE RELISH

I don't normally like raw onion much, but the pomegranate and lime juices take any acrid sting away. I could eat this by itself, frankly. It gives a fruity, sharp edge to the gratifying richness of the tagine – and is worth bearing in mind whenever you need to add glorious seasonal adornment to a meal fast; it is as delicious with some cold turkey as heaped onto a hot, fluffy-fleshed baked potato.

❄ Peel and cut the onion in half, then slice into very thin half-moons.

❄ Put the onion slices into a bowl with the lime juice and pomegranate juice, and let them steep for half an hour.

❄ Drain the steeped onion into a little bowl, discarding the too-oniony juice, and add the pomegranate seeds.

❄ Toss with the chopped coriander and season with a little salt.

❄ Strew a little relish on top of the tagine and put the rest in a small bowl for people to add to their own portions.

1 red onion

60ml lime juice

**juice and 40g seeds from 1 large pomeg-
ranate, or 60ml pure pomegranate juice
from a bottle and 40g pomegranate
seeds from a tub/packet**

2 x 15ml tablespoons chopped coriander

salt to taste

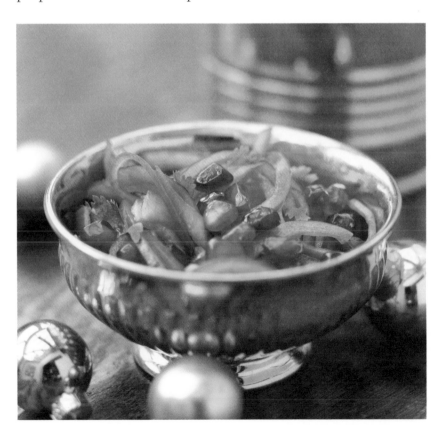

GLEAMING MAPLE CHEESECAKE

FOR THE BASE:

8 digestive biscuits

75g pecan halves

75g soft butter

FOR THE FILLING:

3 x 200g packets cream cheese, at room
temperature

50g sugar

2 teaspoons cornflour

125ml maple syrup, plus more for drizzling

4 eggs

1/2 teaspoon cider vinegar or lemon juice

I've broached the sweetness issue earlier, but know that this pudding makes converts of even those who claim never to want something sweet: it's a cheesecake (baked in a bain-marie, which is the smartest route to the lightest, most delicate set) sitting on a base made of digestives, crushed pecans and a dash of maple syrup, the cheese layer itself smokily sweetened with the syrup. This cheesecake is best made well in advance, so you can sit back at dinner and enjoy the feast.

The one thing I need to be strict about is that the cream cheese be taken out of the fridge a good 2 hours before you start. I know you'll obey me when I tell you to bake the cheesecake in a tin of water (don't worry, it's perfectly straightforward) but I suspect that the stipulation for room-temperature cream cheese may not be as dutifully observed. But it must be: you will never get the requisite voluptuously smooth texture if the cream cheese starts off cold.

❋Preheat the oven to 170°C/gas mark 3.

❋Blitz the biscuits in a food processor until they turn to crumbs, then add the pecan halves and blitz again to a crumb mixture. Add the butter and process everything together until it clumps up, and then press into the bottom of a 20cm springform tin to make a smooth base. Sit the tin in the fridge to chill while you get on with the topping.

❋Put the cream cheese into the cleaned processor bowl with the sugar, cornflour and maple syrup.

❋Turn the motor on and, with the engine running, break the eggs down the funnel, processing until you have a smooth mixture. Add the vinegar or lemon juice, and pulse to mix.

❋Take the springform tin out of the fridge, and line the outside with a layer of special ovenproof clingfilm, bringing it up around the top outer edge of the tin; this is to make a waterproof layer for when the cheesecake is cooked in a water bath. Do the same again, over the plastic wrap, with a double layer of foil, making sure that this, too, is brought right up to the top edge of the tin.

❋Sit the foil-wrapped springform in a roasting tin, then pour in the smooth filling. Fill the roasting tin with freshly boiled water, to come about halfway up the wrapped springform.

❋Bake the cheesecake in the oven for about 1¹/4 hours, though start checking it after an hour; it should be set on top but still have a hint of a wobble in the middle.

If you can't get ovenproof clingfilm, just use the double layer of foil.

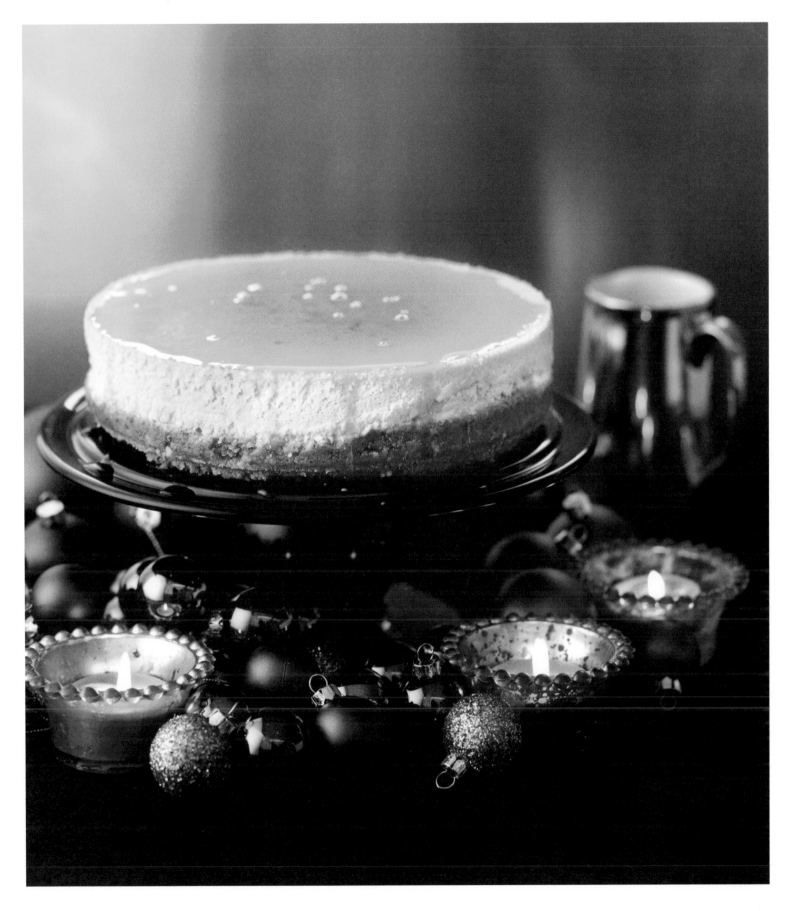

✳ Take the whole shebang-marie out of the oven and carefully lift the cheesecake out of its water bath. Peel away the foil layers and let it cool in its tin on a rack. Once cooled, refrigerate the cheesecake for at least 4 hours, or ideally overnight.

✳ The following day, or up to 2 days later, let it come to room temperature before springing it out of the tin.

✳ Sit it on a serving plate and pour some maple syrup over the top of the whole cake, drizzling a little more over each slice as you serve the cheesecake.

MAKE AHEAD TIP:
Make the cheesecake and leave to cool as directed. When cool, cover the tin with clingfilm, making sure the film doesn't touch the top of the cheesecake, or pop a plate on top. Keep in the fridge for up to 2 days. Add maple syrup only on serving.

FREEZE AHEAD TIP:
Only cheesecakes made with full-fat, softened cream cheese will freeze. Leave the cheesecake in the tin to cool, cover with clingfilm, as above, and freeze for up to 3 months. Thaw overnight in the fridge. Add maple syrup only on serving.

GROWN UP NURSERY SUPPER FOR 6

I have never much liked formal entertaining. I love cosiness: I want people to feel welcomed, not impressed and I want to feel happily surrounded by my friends rather than wind myself up into a frenzy of hissing, self-loathing panic because I've got people coming for dinner.

And this time of year, above all, should be about relaxed expansiveness, about succour as well as celebration. This menu says it all: the supper you want to eat to make you feel that all will be well.

The fish gratin is the lazy person's answer to a fish pie. I *love* fish pie, but mashing a sinkful of potatoes is no one's idea of a low-effort enterprise; of course, it's not hard, but it takes time when time itself is at a premium. Topping the fish with finely sliced, unpeeled baking potatoes is the easy answer. And as for the fish itself, rather than cook and flake it and then make a sauce, I simply make an extra-thick white sauce (my version is too basic, really, to be called a béchamel), turn it green with a garden of freshly chopped parsley and leave it for up to 3 days before snipping in some smoked and unsmoked fish, giving it a stir-up, topping with the sliced potatoes and whacking it in the oven. You don't have to make the sauce in advance, but I find it makes my life easier. If you're not making it in advance, slice the potatoes before you put the fish into the warm sauce so that the minute the raw fish is in the sauce you can top with the potatoes and put the gratin straight in the oven.

This is best eaten with a big bowl of buttery peas, fresh from the freezer. I love to add a few handfuls of mangetout to the pea-cooking water for the last minute of cooking time, before draining and dousing them in butter and a fresh grinding of white pepper.

The pudding must be made up in advance; though, again, this is a boon not a burden for me.

PARSLEYED FISH GRATIN

PROSECCO AND POMEGRANATE JELLY

PARSLEYED FISH GRATIN

❄ Make a white sauce by first melting the butter in a large saucepan and then adding the flour, stirring together for a minute or so. Then, off the heat, whisk in the vermouth (or wine), mace (or nutmeg), salt and mustard.

❄ Next, whisk in the milk, and put the pan back on the heat, continuing to whisk the sauce as it thickens. Once the sauce appears to be getting thicker, which will be a matter of 3 or so minutes, keep cooking it for a further 3 minutes until very thick.

❄ Take it off the heat and stir in the chives and parsley. Then decant into your gratin-type dish (mine is a round shallow casserole about 26cm x 5cm deep).

❄ Once cool, you can leave this dish covered, in the fridge overnight or for up to 3 days.

❄ When ready to cook, preheat your oven to 200°C/gas mark 6 and slide a baking sheet in as you do so. Take your gratin dish out of the fridge and uncover it.

❄ Slice the unpeeled potatoes as thinly as you possibly can.

❄ Scissor or cut both types of fish into large bite-sized pieces (approx. 6cm x 4cm), and mix into the parsley sauce.

❄ Layer the potatoes in concentric circles over the fish in parsley sauce, overlapping halfway across each potato slice as you go around the dish.

❄ Melt the garlic oil and butter in a small pan, then paint the circles of potato with this mixture, using a silicone pastry brush (or just dribble it over), to slick the top of the gratin.

❄ Grind some fresh white pepper over the top and place in the oven to cook for 50–60 minutes; the top should be golden and the underneath of the gratin bubbling.

FOR THE SAUCE:

50g butter

50g plain flour

1 x 15ml tablespoon dry white vermouth or dry white wine

1/4 teaspoon ground mace or nutmeg

1/2 teaspoon Maldon salt or 1/4 teaspoon table salt

1/4 teaspoon Dijon mustard

350ml full-fat milk

1 1/2 x 15ml tablespoons finely chopped chives (or 1 spring onion, finely chopped)

75g flat leaf parsley, finely chopped (to give about 50g chopped weight)

FOR THE FISH MIX AND POTATO TOPPING:

2 medium-sized (400g total) baking potatoes, unpeeled

300g pollack or other white fish fillet, skinless

750g smoked haddock or cod fillet, skinless

FOR THE GLAZE:

1 teaspoon garlic oil

25g butter

good grinding of white pepper

MAKE AHEAD TIP:
Make the parsley sauce up to 3 days ahead. Decant into gratin dish and cover directly with clingfilm or the lid to prevent a skin forming. Cool and keep in the fridge.

FREEZE AHEAD TIP:
For fresh, not previously frozen fish, make the parsley sauce, and leave to cool in its dish. When cool, stir in the fish, then cover and freeze for up to 1 month. Thaw overnight in the fridge, then, when ready to cook, finish with the potatoes and cook as directed.

PROSECCO AND POMEGRANATE JELLY

1 x 75cl bottle Prosecco or other white wine

250ml water

300g caster sugar

25g leaf gelatine

1/2 teaspoon vanilla

3 teaspoons Cointreau, Grand Marnier or
    Triple sec, plus more to serve

seeds from 1 pomegranate, or 75g
    pomegranate seeds from a tub/packet

flavourless oil for greasing

double cream to serve (optional)

I love wine and liqueur jellies, and I think I've had a version – sauternes and lemon balm, gin and tonic, slut red raspberries in chardonnay jelly, blackberries and Muscat – in pretty well all of my books. They are delicate, luscious and incredibly easy to make, providing, that is, you use leaf gelatine: I have never been able to make the powdered stuff work for me.

There's no absolute need to use Prosecco: any good white wine would do. What's important is simply to make this: the pale glint of the jelly against the red jewels of pomegranate makes it as beautiful to look at as to eat.

❄ Lightly grease a 1-litre jelly mould with flavourless oil and sit it on a small tray so it's easy to convey it to the fridge later.

❄ Pour the Prosecco and water into a saucepan, add the sugar and stir to help it dissolve (but do not stir once the pan is on the heat). At the same time, put the gelatine into a dish and cover with cold water, letting them soak for 5 minutes.

❄ Put the pan on the heat, bring to the boil and let it boil for a minute.

❄ Add the vanilla and keep the pan bubbling gently for another minute, before taking it off the heat.

❄ Carefully ladle about 250ml of the wine–sugar mixture into a measuring jug.

❄ When the gelatine leaves have had a good 5 minutes' soaking, lift them out, squeezing and squelching them to remove excess water (this is curiously pleasurable) and whisk them into the jug of hot wine–sugar mixture to dissolve.

❄ Pour the jugful of liquid back into the pan (which must be still off the heat), whisk again, and tip it all back into the jug, before pouring it into the prepared jelly mould. (This may sound a kerfuffle, but it ensures the gelatine is thoroughly dispersed.)

❄ Put the filled-to-the-brim mould, still on its tray, into the fridge and leave to set overnight. It has a gentle set, which is what makes it so delectable.

❄ Just before you are ready to serve, fill a sink or plastic washing up bowl with warm water to come about halfway up the mould, and sit the as-yet-unturned mould in the warm water for half a minute.

The amount of gelatine leaves is deliberately low; packets will instruct you to use more, but a voluptuously soft set is desirable. This does mean, however, that the jelly needs an overnight set in the fridge and cannot be unmoulded in advance.

MAKE AHEAD TIP:
Make the jelly up to 3 days ahead. If it's possible to cover the mould with a tight seal of clingfilm without it touching the jelly, then do so. Otherwise, leave uncovered and put in the fridge, but make sure you have nothing heavily flavoured with garlic in the fridge at the same time!

❊ Take the mould out of the sink, wipe the water off the outside and place your serving plate on top. Then, with one hand on the plate and the other on the mould, tip them both over and lift off the mould to reveal the jelly. It will look smaller than it did in the mould; that's expected.

❊ Dribble the Cointreau (or your choice of alcohol) over the jelly (putting the bottle on the table so people can anoint with more as they eat) and scatter with pomegranate seeds, a few on top, but most around the side. It spoils the jewel-like clarity of the jelly, but this is out of this world with a little double cream poured over each portion. Put a small jugful on the table as encouragement.

If you want to dispense with the worry of unmoulding, simply divide the warm jelly mixture between six stemmed glasses of under 200ml capacity each and set in the fridge.

MEANWHILE, BACK AT THE RANCH...

BOURBON-GLAZED RIBS
SPOONBREAD
SPINACH AND BACON SALAD
GIRDLEBUSTER PIE

...A FINGER-LICKIN' SUPPER FOR 8–10

This is the perfect relaxed holiday supper, though there's no reason it couldn't be a button-bursting lunch when you're not at work, either. It's big and friendly and gives an atmosphere of homestead warmth. You may feel mightily full when you get up from the table, but you will feel happy.

BOURBON-GLAZED RIBS

24 pork spare ribs

100g dark muscovado sugar

175ml bourbon

2 x 15ml tablespoons soy sauce

2 x 15ml tablespoons American mustard

2 x 15ml tablespoons tomato ketchup

I can't think of any way of cooking ribs I dislike, but this bourbon and muscovado marinade-cum-glaze does double-duty, tenderizing the meat before it cooks and slicking it with a conker-shiny, delicious-beyond-words glaze after, and is frankly more inviting – the rich scent in the air as it cooks, the sweet stickiness as you eat – than is decent. I salivate both in memory and in hope.

This glaze is stickily perfect for **sausages**, too, in which case roast 24 pork sausages for 40 or so minutes at 220°C/gas mark 7. Mix together the marinade ingredients but forget the marinating and simply boil up and reduce the glaze as below, pouring over the cooked sausages as you serve them.

❊ Put the ribs into a freezer bag and add the other ingredients to form a marinade. Place in the fridge, putting the bag into a bowl to avoid drips or spillages, and leave overnight.

❊ The next day, remove the ribs from the fridge, and preheat the oven to 220°C/gas mark 7.

❊ Pick the ribs out of the marinade and put them into a shallow roasting tin, then pour the marinade into a saucepan.

❊ Cook the ribs for 1 hour, turning them over halfway through cooking.

❊ When the ribs are cooked, bring the marinade to a boil and cook for about 7 minutes or until it is thick and glossy. Plate up the ribs, then pour the bourbon sauce over them.

MAKE AHEAD TIP:
Chill the ribs in the marinade for up to 3 days.

FREEZE AHEAD TIP:
Freeze the ribs in the marinade for up to 1 month.
Thaw overnight in the fridge, and cook as directed.

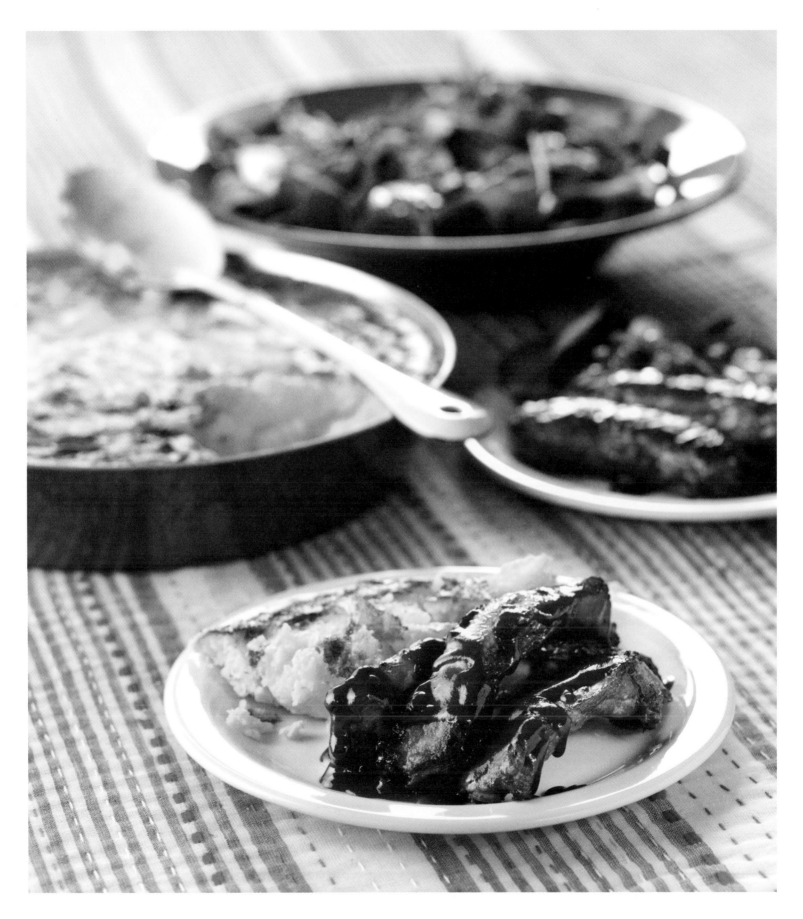

SPOONBREAD

75g soft butter, plus more for greasing

450g sweetcorn kernels, drained

4 spring onions, roughly chopped

150g mature cheddar, roughly chopped

4 eggs

350g yellow cornmeal

2 teaspoons baking powder

1 litre full-fat milk

This is something of a cross between cornbread and creamed sweetcorn – a kind of Southwestern polenta. It is perfect with ribs or sausages as here, but I love it, too, with some sizzled bacon (in which case no need to add bacon to the salad) or to jazz up a fridgeful of cold cuts.

I mostly use the kernels drained from their cans, but do use frozen sweetcorn if you prefer; if you haven't got time to let it thaw, put it in a sieve and pour boiling water over it for a quick defrost.

I like to bake this in a round, shallowish copper roasting tin (28cm x 5cm deep with a capacity of 2.25 litres), so be prepared to adjust cooking times if your ovenproof dish has different dimensions.

❊ Preheat the oven to 220°C/gas mark 7. Grease your ovenproof tin or dish, melt the 75g butter in a saucepan over a low heat and leave to cool.

❊ Put the sweetcorn, spring onions and cheddar into a food processor with the eggs.

❊ Process to chop the vegetables and cheese, then add the cornmeal and baking powder.

❊ Process again until the mixture becomes paste-like, then, with the motor running, add the milk and melted butter.

❊ Pour into the greased tin or dish and bake for 1 hour until just set.

❊ Remove the spoonbread from the oven and let it stand for 10 minutes – it will continue cooking as it stands – before taking to the table.

SPINACH AND BACON SALAD

I love those Eighties salads, tossed with bacon-cubes and a warm dressing that makes the leaves begin to wilt. "Begin" is the operative word: though spinach, even young, relatively tender-leaved spinach, stands up to the warm drizzle well, as does the chicory. I like to go for the rusty-red blades, but if all you can find is the regular pale jade chicory, it won't make any difference: they taste the same; my preference, here, is aesthetic.

And even though this is a spinach salad, some other bag (or two) of salad leaves would do just as well. Similarly, if you haven't got any pancetta, just snip up some streaky bacon.

200g baby spinach, or similar salad

4 small heads red chicory

1 teaspoon garlic oil

75g pancetta cubes

75g pecan pieces

2^1/$_2$ x 15ml tablespoons cider vinegar or white wine vinegar

2 x 15ml tablespoons maple syrup

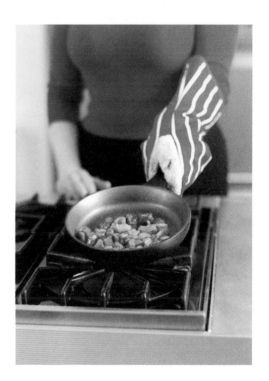

❀ Arrange the spinach in a large salad bowl. Add the chicory, separated into leaves and then torn into bite-sized pieces, and toss together.

❀ Warm the garlic oil in a frying pan over a medium heat, and drop in the pancetta cubes, cooking until they are crisp and bronzed.

❀ Add the pecans, and mix well with the pancetta in the fatty pan.

❀ Take off the heat, and stir in the vinegar – be prepared for a lot of sizzle.

❀ Now stir in the maple syrup, quickly pour over the salad and toss swiftly, serving immediately.

GIRDLEBUSTER PIE

I confess: it was the title that lured me. Tell me you don't feel the same. I came across this in a recipe by Elinor Klivans, whom I often turn to for chocolatey solace, in her *The Essential Chocolate Chip Cookbook*, which includes the wonderful phrase "let the chocolate chips fall where they will".

Although her recipes always work to the letter, my recipe is not hers. I am inspired by the digestive and chocolate base and coffee ice cream filling (though if you're feeding children, I'd suggest vanilla) but I like a butterscotchy topping, which sets the minute it hits the ice cream. Sometimes bits of ice cream bubble up to the surface, making the top gloriously Florentined.

And the joy of the girdlebuster (as it is known for short at home) is that, should there be any left, you can put it back into its dish and just stash in the freezer again for midnight feasts. Admittedly, this is not huge, but a small slice is all that's needed. Do not let it "ripen" out of the freezer before slicing because it all gets too sticky and drippy and messy.

❄ Process the biscuits with the butter and chocolate pieces or chips until it forms a damp but still crumb-like clump.

❄ Press into a 23cm pie plate or flan dish. Form a lip of biscuit a little higher than the plate or dish if you can. This process takes patience as you need ideally to form a smooth even layer. Sorry.

❄ Freeze this biscuit-lined layer for about an hour so it gets really hard. In the meantime, let your ice cream soften, just enough to be scooped, in the fridge.

❄ Spread the ice cream into the hard-biscuit-lined dish to form a layer. Then cover in clingfilm and replace in the freezer.

❄ Put the syrup, sugar, salt (if using) and butter into a saucepan and let it melt over a low to medium heat, before turning it up and boiling for 5 minutes, then turn off the heat and add the bourbon, letting it hiss in the pan.

❄ Add the cream and stir to mix into a sauce, then leave to cool. And once the sauce is cool, but not set cold, pour it over the pie to cover the ice cream layer and then put it back in the freezer. Once frozen, cover with clingfilm again.

❄ When ready to serve, remove from the freezer, take the whole pie out of its dish and cut into slices. Should you have any pie left over, slip it quickly back into the dish and return, covered with clingfilm, to the freezer.

FOR THE BASE:

375g digestive biscuits

75g soft butter

50g dark chocolate pieces or chips

50g milk chocolate pieces or chips

FOR THE ICE CREAM FILLING:

1 litre coffee ice cream

FOR THE TOPPING:

300g golden syrup

100g packed light muscovado sugar

75g butter

1/4 teaspoon Maldon salt or pinch of table salt (optional)

2 x 15ml tablespoons bourbon

125ml double cream

FREEZE AHEAD TIP:
Make and freeze the pie in its dish, as directed, but cover with clingfilm *and* a double layer of foil. Freeze for up to 6 months.

EASY ELEGANT DINNER FOR 8

EFFORTLESS HOME-CURED PORK
APPLE AND ONION GRAVY
TIRAMISU LAYER CAKE

I actually did this dinner for my brother Dominic's birthday last year, but I think of it as a Christmastime menu simply because his birthday is 17th December and so he helps usher in the family festivities. My seasonal celebrations, anyway, are regulated by the family diary: my daughter's birthday is the 15th and so no tree, no mention of Christmas, no festive distractions of any kind are allowed to intrude until after that date. To tell the truth, it is a very convenient curtailment.

When I say that the curing of the pork is effortless, I am not making any false promises. I suppose it is not quite accurate to call it "curing", since that implies preserving: what I am really doing is "brining" (as with my Spiced and Superjuicy Turkey on p.115). But I avoid that word because it hardly tempts, whereas the effect it produces, which is rather to tenderize and imbue with flavour, is more of an obvious inducement. All it involves is putting the pork in a pan or bowl, covering it with water, apple juice, spices and a few other bits and pieces and your work is done, save for bunging it in the oven later.

With this, I make an apple and onion gravy, which is really halfway between a gravy and a sauce; it's thick but just pourable. All this, the light-toned pork and the equally pale apply, oniony gravy that anoints it, is not supercharged aesthetically and I would go for a vegetable to add depth of colour as well as taste. My choice is the Red Cabbage on p.60, though I love it with the bacony, creamy peas (*Piselli con Panna e Pancetta*) on p.63 as well. But it's an either or; don't do both. And you can either bake fluffy potatoes in their jackets alongside, and put some chive-flecked sour cream on the table to dollop in them, or steam some small, sweet and tight-fleshed waxy potatoes.

I created the Tiramisu Layer Cake especially for my brother, since there is nothing he likes more than coffee, chocolate and creaminess all in one over-indulgent package, but I also recommend here the Christmas-Spiced Chocolate Cake on p.183, a seasonal favourite I came up with to celebrate another seasonal birthday – on the 21st December – for the·voice coach and pocket venus, Joan Washington.

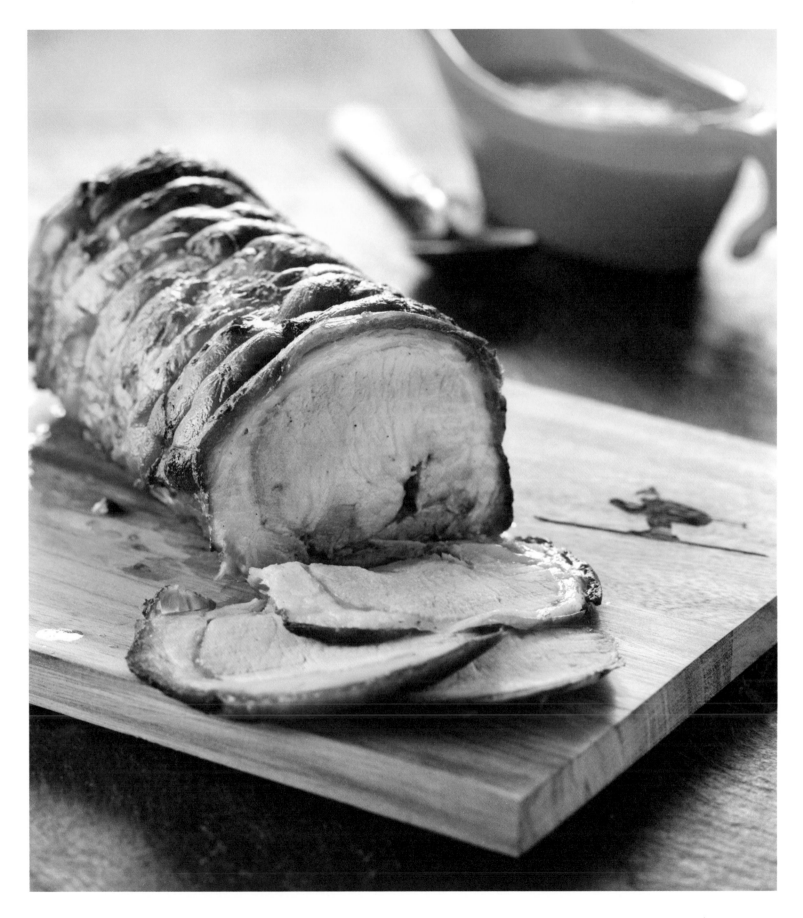

EFFORTLESS HOME-CURED PORK

1.6kg boneless pork loin roast

1 litre apple juice, preferably pressed

1 litre water

100g Maldon salt or 50g table salt

250ml cider vinegar

4 small onions, peeled and quartered (or 2
   large onions, cut into eighths)

stalks from large bunch of parsley (optional)

cloves from 1 head garlic, bruised but not
   peeled

80ml maple syrup

1 teaspoon cardamom seeds

1 teaspoon caraway seeds

4 teaspoons garlic oil

These days pork is reared to be so lean that it is barely digestible when you just plain roast it. Of course, you can stuff and roll it, as I do when going all-out in my Rolled Stuffed Loin of Pork on p.158, but that is work – work that rewards, but work just the same. This is altogether easier. Indeed, it is impossible to think of any kind of preparation that would involve less effort; not only does it make the pork juicily delicious, but it also makes it easier to carve thinly, which means it goes a lot further, too.

Because of the magic-soaking treatment, a supermarket pork loin joint is just fine, though go for organic or proper farm-sourced for choice. And it comes all ready for you – fat removed, boned, rolled and tied. This size joint certainly looks small, but once carved ultra-thinly – as the cure helps you do – there's plenty to go round.

❈ Put the skinned, boned and rolled pork joint in a pan or stockpot (with lid).

❈ Add the remaining ingredients except the garlic oil, put a lid on the pan or stockpot and place in the fridge or in a cold place for at least a night and a day and up to 2 days.

❈ Half an hour before the pork needs to go into the oven, preheat the oven to 200°C/gas mark 6, then take the pork out of its brine and sit it on a rack in the sink to let the liquid drain off and the meat get less cold.

❈ Transfer the pork to a roasting tin, pour the garlic oil over it and roast for $1^1/_2$ hours, before removing to a carving dish. A meat thermometer, inserted, should read 75°C when the pork is cooked through.

❈ Carve the pork thinly – the joy of the quasi-cure is that it makes it easy even for a bad carver like me to do this, and you can be sure of feeding 8 people. Serve with the apple and onion gravy, opposite.

MAKE AHEAD TIP:
Keep the pork in its "curing" mixture for up to
2 days. Leave it in a cold place or in the fridge if
you have room.

APPLE AND ONION GRAVY

Although I'd pretty well go along with the Wildean aphorism that one should try anything once except incest and morris dancing, I am in certain matters, most of them culinary, rather a novelty-eschewing traditionalist. If I'm having pork, I want to have apple sauce with it. My grandmother always mixed her apple sauce with horseradish, a radical departure I, too, am happy to make. I can also accommodate the corresponding tart fruitiness of cranberry sauce, but not with this apple-brined pork roast; it wouldn't be right.

And while I wouldn't want to upset anyone who just wants plain old regular apple sauce alongside, I happen to feel better myself when I make this apple and onion gravy. Not that it's quite a gravy in the traditional sense, but it's runnier than the customary sauce: you pour it from a jug, maybe with a little cutlery-coaxing; it's a grauce.

Somewhat untraditionally, I use eating apples here: Gala would be my first choice, although Braeburn or Granny Smith should be fine, too. And because I think bacon fat is such a wonderful cooking medium, I always pour off the fat from the pan when I've been cooking bacon, to keep in a little cup in the fridge for exactly these occasions, and advise you to do likewise (fish fried in bacon fat is fantastic), but otherwise use butter. The onions, which are mushed up with the apples then fried, give depth and savouriness, and the maple syrup – yes, maple syrup again, and I don't have shares in any Vermont orchard I promise – brings its resiny sweetness to play along with the peppy heat, just a hint though, of the ginger.

❋ Put the onions and apples into a food processor and process to mush.

❋ Put the bacon fat (or butter) and the garlic oil into a pan and cook the processed onions and apples over a very gentle heat for about 30 minutes, stirring every now and again.

❋ Add the maple syrup and cook for another 15 minutes.

❋ Stir in the cornflour and ground ginger, then turn up the heat as you, still stirring, pour in the stock.

❋ Continue stirring as you bring the gravy to a boil and season with the soy sauce. Cook until the gravy has thickened slightly, almost into a sauce, and there is no floury taste; this is probably no longer than 3 minutes.

2 onions, peeled and quartered
2 eating apples, peeled, cored and quartered
2 x 15ml tablespoons bacon fat (or butter)
1 teaspoon garlic oil
1 x 15ml tablespoon maple syrup
2 teaspoons cornflour
¼ teaspoon ground ginger
500ml chicken stock
4 teaspoons soy sauce

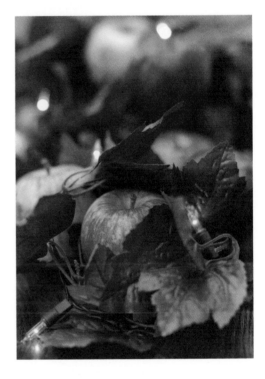

MAKE AHEAD TIP:
Make the gravy, then transfer to a non-metallic bowl, cover with clingfilm and keep in the fridge for up to 2 days. You may need to add some more stock or water on reheating.

FREEZE AHEAD TIP:
Make the gravy, pour into an airtight container and freeze for up to 1 week. Thaw overnight in the fridge, then pour into a pan and gently reheat, with a little extra liquid if needed, until piping hot.

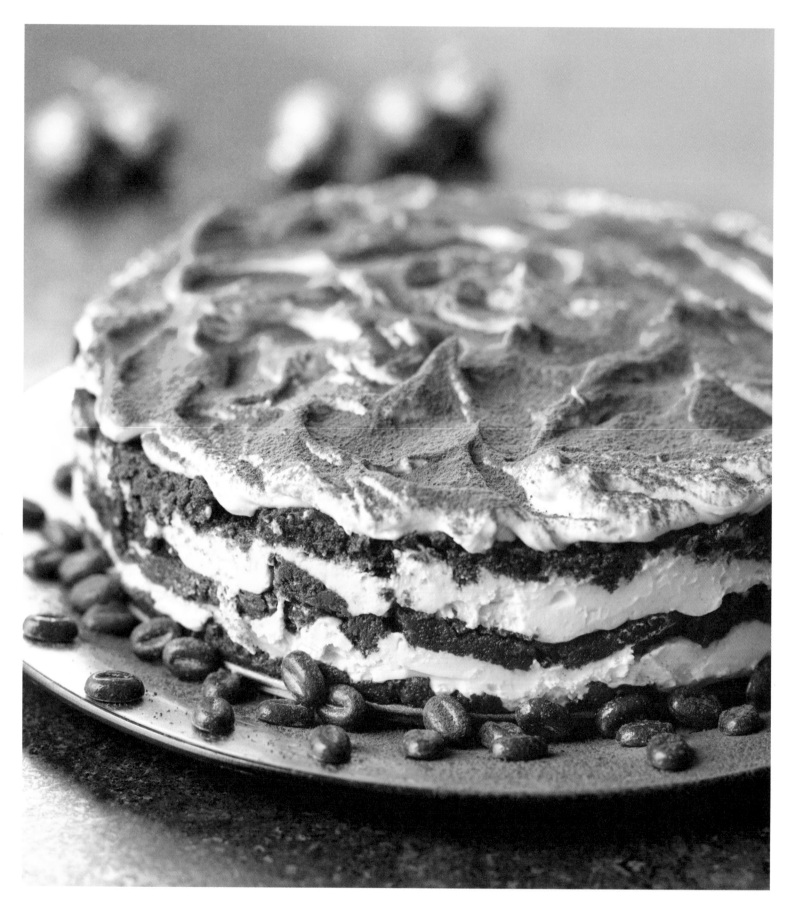

TIRAMISU LAYER CAKE

There is no shortage of tiramisu recipes in the world, many of them emanating from me. I started off with a certain hauteur, stemming from the certainty that tiramisu was the Black Forest gâteau of the Nineties; you can see how long ago the prejudice and the countering compulsion started. But now I know that when things work, they work, and that I'm happier adding to, rather than chipping away, at the canon.

This recipe reads harder than it cooks. Or rather, doesn't cook. It's an assembly job more than anything, and it doesn't take very long or require much in the way of skill or patience: it's just that the number of layers make the recipe on the page seem more complicated than it is.

I don't deny its vulgarity: the original, hardly the apotheosis of chic, relies on *savoiardi* (ladyfingers), or boudoir biscuits, dunked in coffee and liqueur, before being built up with eggy, marsala-laced mascarpone and topped with a dusting of cocoa; I cut to the chase, by using chocolate sponge (shop-bought loaf cakes seem to soak in more than homemade or deli-sourced chocolate cake, so you might not need as much liqueur if you're not getting the wherewithal from the supermarket) and dipping it only in coffee liqueur, before layering up into a big fat cake which cuts easily into greedy wedges.

I wish I were the sort of person who could make enough but no more, but that's never going to be the case: when I made this for my brother's birthday, he came back round for a couple of slices the next day. And that's the way I like it.

❋ Wrap the outside of a 23cm springform cake tin with some clingfilm or foil to avoid leaks from the base.

❋ Slice the chocolate cakes thinly, and pour the 300ml (or more if needed) of Tia Maria into a shallow dish, ready for soaking the cake slices as you need them.

❋ Before you start to layer the cakes, whisk the eggs and sugar, and then beat in the mascarpone and double cream; I use an electric whisk for this, but there is no need to if you're feeling muscley. Then add, gradually, the 125ml Tia Maria to make a creamy spreadable layer for the cake.

❋ Using approx. 1 cake per layer, dunk the slices in Tia Maria before lining the tin with them. Squidge them down, pressing confidently as you go; each layer should not be too thick, but juicily compact and solid.

❋ Spread a third of the cream mixture over the soaked cake slices.

3 x 350g chocolate loaf cakes (shop-bought variety is fine)

300–400ml Tia Maria

1–2 teaspoons cocoa for dusting

chocolate-covered coffee beans (optional)

FOR THE FILLING:

2 eggs

75g caster sugar

500g mascarpone

250ml double cream

125ml Tia Maria

MAKE AHEAD TIP:
Make the tiramisu, cover with clingfilm, and store in the fridge for up to 4 days. Unmould and finish as directed.

FREEZE AHEAD TIP:
Unmould the tiramisu, finish with the remaining cream then open freeze. When solid, cover securely with a double layer of clingfilm and return to the freezer for up to 3 months. To use, unwrap the tiramisu, place on a serving dish and thaw overnight in the fridge. Dust with cocoa and serve.

❊ Repeat with another layer of soaked chocolate cake slices, and then cream again.

❊ Finish with a layer of chocolate cake slices – not as soaked as the first 2 layers – reserving the last third of the cream mixture for later in a covered bowl.

❊ Press the cake layer down to make it as smooth as possible, then cover it with clingfilm and put the cake in the fridge overnight, or for up to 4 days.

❊ When you are ready to serve, take the cake out of the fridge, unmould, sit it on a plate or cake stand, then spread with the final third of cream mixture, before dusting with cocoa and serving. The cake is too deliciously damp to lift it off the tin's base, but I shouldn't let that worry you; if you want, though, you can scatter some chocolate-covered coffee beans around the cake, once it's sitting on its serving plate, to deflect critical gaze away from the visible edge of tin.

SEDUCTIVELY SIMPLE SUPPER FOR 6

PARTY POUSSINS
SPICED ROAST SQUASH
FESTIVE COUSCOUS
CHESTNUT CHOCOLATE POTS

The shorthand for this, chez moi, is pouss-pouss with couscous, and there is a reason for that: this is one of the most reliable fallback suppers that can be stuck in the oven and left to cook itself, with only a bit of stoveside fiddling, in order to provide a party-mood, feel-good festive supper even when you're chock-a-block with after-school activities, office parties, or sackfuls of wrapping; this is my seasonal get-together without tears.

I love the silky richness of the Chestnut Chocolate Pots afterwards, but if you don't have the sort of timetable that accommodates advance preparation, simply pile up some **Quickly Scaled Mont Blancs** in glasses at the last minute. These were my mother's seasonal speciality, and need no further full-on explanation from me, since I have banged on about them before (in *Nigella Express*, for instance) but, just in case, here's what you need to do: get out 6 smallish glasses, with a capacity of about 125ml each, and in them drop a layer of chopped dark chocolate (you'll need a 100g bar altogether); on top of the rubbly shards of chocolate, dollop some sweetened chestnut purée from a can (a 500g can is more than generous); then whip 500ml double cream until thick but still soft, fold in one crumbled meringue nest (about 10cm in diameter) from a packet and spoon this on top of the chocolate and chestnut layers; then crumble another meringue in a snowy layer on top. Couldn't be easier – but then nor could the silky Chestnut Chocolate Pots on p.98. The choice is undemandingly yours.

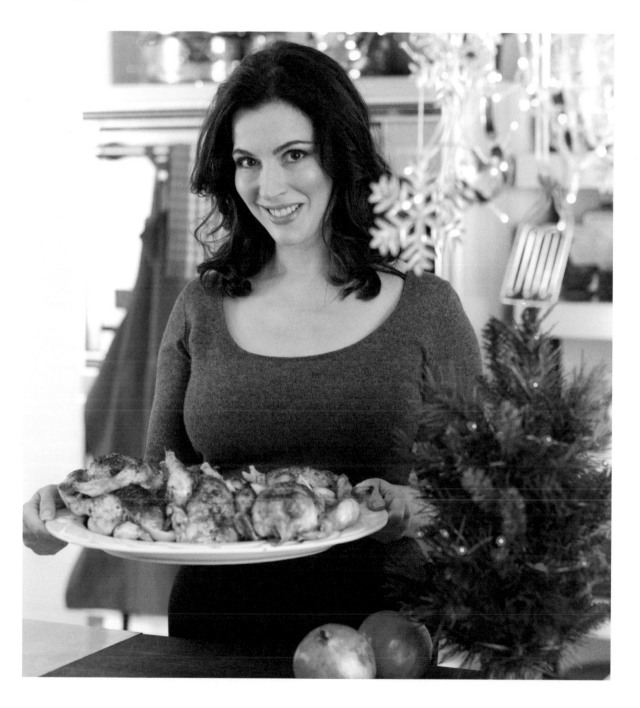

PARTY POUSSINS

6 poussins

4 x 15ml tablespoons chilli oil or olive oil

1 x 15ml tablespoon Maldon salt or
   1¹/₂ teaspoons table salt

pinch of sugar

¹/₄ teaspoon ground cinnamon

¹/₂ teaspoon paprika

1 lemon, preferably unwaxed

1 head garlic

These small birds make a big feast, and with ease. For me, one reason why this produces such a relaxing supper is that there's no work once you're at the table, either. It's not only that I am a bad carver (though I am), but elaborate serving-up makes me feel flustered. This must obviously be avoided – but without sacrificing the sense of occasion.

The pouss-pouss need no more than the couscous to eat alongside, but I often like to make (since I have room in the oven and the flavours are so right) a tray of **Spiced Roast Squash** at the same time. In fact, this is a regular festive fall-back of mine, as it provides a luscious accompaniment, without much work. You need a whole butternut squash – about 1kg in weight – and don't bother to peel but deseed it and cut into, roughly, 3–4cm cubes. Arrange these on a low-lipped baking tray (I use a swiss roll tin) and pour a couple of tablespoons of regular olive oil over, sprinkle with 1 teaspoon each of ground mace and paprika and smoosh everything around to mix, before baking on the rack below the poussins for about the same amount of time. If you're cooking the squash on its own, you may find 50 minutes at 220°C/gas mark 7 is enough. Either way, I love the squash served with a generous sprinkling of Maldon salt and a judicious spritz of lime juice; both bring out the earthy sweetness of the squash.

And incidentally, if you have any butternut or couscous left over, add the one to the other to make a very more-ish salad. A final note: the poussin carcasses, after, make a great stock or soup.

❉ Preheat the oven to 220°C/gas mark 7. Sit the poussins snugly in a roasting tin, and pour the oil slowly over, making sure you get good, equal coverage.

❉ Mix together the salt, sugar, cinnamon and paprika in a small bowl, and sprinkle this spice mixture over the poussins.

❉ Cut the lemon into quarters, then cut each quarter into 4 so you have 16 small pieces, and tuck these pieces along with the garlic separated into cloves (unpeeled), around and in between the baby birds.

❉ Cook the poussins for 1–1¹/₄ hours, then let them rest for about 10 minutes in their tin out of the oven before serving.

MAKE AHEAD TIP:
Put the poussins in the roasting tin with the oil, salt, sugar and spices. Cover with a roof of clingfilm and leave in the fridge overnight. The next day, add the lemons and roast as directed.

FESTIVE COUSCOUS

The correct way of cooking couscous is to cover it with cold water for about 20 minutes, and then place the dampened couscous in the top part of a couscoussier or a steamer to steam it. The best way to tell when it's ready is to put a thin slab of butter on top: when the butter starts melting, the couscous is done.

However, even though the following method is, strictly speaking, incorrect, it is the way I most often do it, and feel it is only fair to encourage you down this shameful, lazy path, too. If you want, do replace the golden sultanas with dried cherries or dried cranberries or even, should you live near a Middle-Eastern store, some dried barberries.

***

❊ Just before the poussins come out of the oven, put the couscous into a heatproof bowl or a pan (which has a tight-fitting lid), add the sultanas, spices and salt, and give everything a stir.

❊ Pour the freshly boiled water over and cover with clingfilm or the lid; let it sit for 10–15 minutes, by which time it should have absorbed the water.

❊ Fluff the couscous through with a fork to separate the grains, then carefully pour in some of the juices that have collected in the roasting tin of poussins.

❊ Fork through again and check the seasoning before transferring to a serving dish.

❊ Drop half the pomegranate seeds over the mounded couscous, mixing them in gently with a fork.

❊ Scatter the remaining pomegranate seeds over, sprinkle with some chopped coriander and serve.

❊ Serve each person not only a poussin and some couscous but some oven-charred lemon pieces and garlic cloves as well – and some sweet spiced squash if you've chosen to add it (see opposite).

500g couscous

75g golden sultanas (see Stockists p.267)

1/4 teaspoon ground cinnamon

1/2 teaspoon paprika

1/2 teaspoon ground cumin

1/2 teaspoon ground coriander

2 teaspoons Maldon salt or 1 teaspoon table salt

800ml freshly boiled water, from a kettle

seeds from 1 pomegranate, or 75g seeds from a tub/packet

small bunch of fresh coriander, chopped

CHESTNUT CHOCOLATE POTS

175g best-quality dark chocolate

125ml double cream, plus more to serve if wished

125ml full-fat milk

1 egg

1 x 250g can sweetened chestnut purée

2 x 15ml tablespoons dark rum

I'm almost embarrassed by how easy these are. It's true that you do need a processor, though you could just chop well and whisk using a lot of elbow grease. Or you could make the machinery-eschewing Quickly Scaled Mont Blancs (see p.94) if that suits better.

As an experiment, I also tried the chestnut chocolate pots as chestnut chocolate mousses: the mousses were more work and not as good; this – lazy – way provides a much more meltingly luscious texture. Good to know . . .

The remainder of the chestnut purée can either be brought out to make these for another day, or can be profitably put to use to make the Hot Chocolate-Chestnut Sauce, unspeakably good swathed over ice cream, and see p.169.

❋ Crush the chocolate to smithereens in the food processor.

❋ In a saucepan, heat the cream and milk until just about boiling and, with the motor off, pour into the processor through the funnel over the chocolate.

❋ Let it stand for 30 seconds. Process for 30 seconds, then crack the egg down the funnel and process for 45 seconds more.

❋ Add the chestnut purée and rum through the funnel, and process until everything is incorporated.

❋ Remove the blade and, using a rubber spatula and a spoon, fill 6 x 125ml glasses or pots. Put them in the fridge to set for at least four hours.

❋ If wished, put a jug of unwhipped double cream on the table and let people pour it over their pots as they eat.

MAKE AHEAD TIP:
Make the pots up to 2 days before, cover with cling-film and store in the fridge.

FREEZE AHEAD TIP:
Spoon the mixture into freezable, ceramic serving dishes, cover and freeze for up to 1 week. Thaw overnight in the fridge.

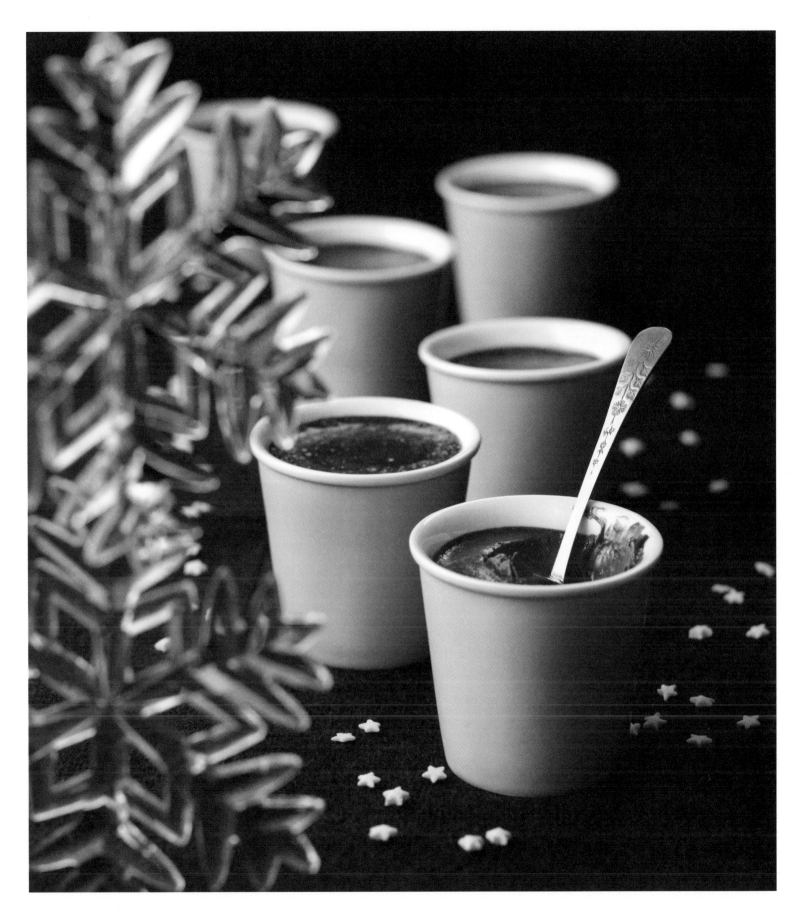

MY CHRISTMAS EVE SUPPER FOR 10–12

GINGER-GLAZED HAM
MACARONI CHEESE
SPRUCED-UP VANILLA CAKE (P.198)
RHUBARB AND STRAWBERRY COMPOTE

The tradition in Continental Europe is to have fish on Christmas Eve. That's never felt right for me. I rather plan ahead and make the supper before Christmas Day something I can call into service afterwards. My mother routinely baked a ham to go with the turkey on Christmas Day but, given all the vegetables and bits and pieces that need to be seen to, I think that is making life hard on yourself. This, then, is my way of ensuring there is cold ham to eat alongside cold turkey for the rest of the week.

It also provides the perfect cross-generational supper. When my children were younger, I didn't do dinner on Christmas Eve, preferring instead to have a big late lunch – sausages and mash and a rhubarb crumble – and to pack the children off early to bed where, excitedly, they didn't sleep. Now, I invite friends and their families over for an early supper, knowing that ham and macaroni cheese will keep everyone happy.

The Spruced-Up Vanilla Cake, with its snowy fir-tree peaks, is a must for my Christmas Eve table, though you'll find the recipe for this impressively festive yet simply made cake in the baking chapter (see p.198) where it, strictly speaking, belongs. But, with the Rhubarb and Strawberry Compote that follows here, it makes the perfect pudding to give everyone a feeling that Christmas has come. Furthermore, should you not want to bother with the Christmas Morning Muffins the next day (see p.214), know that this cake, toasted, makes for the most fabulous breakfast, with or without the rhubarb and strawberry compote drizzled over. With a scoop of vanilla ice cream, the toasted cake doubles as an exquisite pudding; think unfried French toast, a creation of extreme vanilla-and-eggy scrumptiousness.

GINGER-GLAZED HAM

I make no excuses for the fact that this is far too big a joint for the planned supper. Even were I to invite a crowd, I know I could count on leftovers. But that, after all, is the point. Anyway, you can adapt it freely, depending on the number of people you want to feed at the first sitting (I did this for 11 adults and 6 children last year) and how many days you want to eke it out for afterwards. But what *is* important, given that this is probably the most labour-intensive time of year in the kitchen, is that this dispenses with any fiddly steps. The gammon is simply simmered in ginger ale and, although you need to strip off the rind to glaze it, the glaze is straightforward. My patience is pretty well exhausted by Christmas Eve and knowing that I've still got the stockings to fill and the next day to get through, I don't go in for clove-by-clove studding on the ham: instead I let the golden cubes within the ginger preserve (or jam) give a criss-cross effect as they rise to the surface. It works glowingly well.

It won't give that same crowning effect, but if you cannot get hold of ginger preserve, you could use ordinary orange marmalade and add a teaspoon of ground dried ginger or, indeed, grated fresh, as you heat it up.

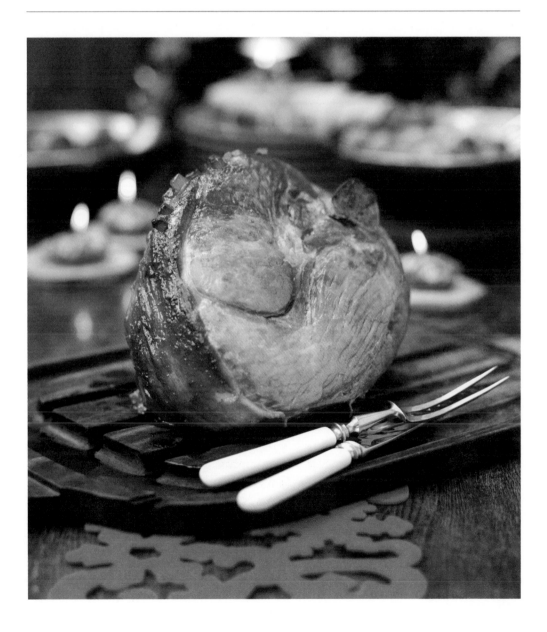

1 x 5.5kg joint (mild cure boneless) gammon

3 x 2-litre bottles dry ginger ale

350g chunky ginger preserve (or orange
    marmalade)

2 x 15ml tablespoons hot English mustard

100g soft dark brown sugar

1/2 teaspoon ground cloves

MAKE AHEAD TIP:

About 6 hours before serving, cook the ham for 3
hours only, take the pan off the heat, remove the
rind and return the ham to the hot liquid. Set aside
in a cool place for about 3 hours. One hour before
serving, preheat the oven to 220°C/gas mark 7.
Put the ham in a shallow, foil-lined roasting tin,
cover with a tent of foil and place in the oven for
20 minutes. Then glaze and return to the oven for
20–30 minutes or until golden and burnished.

FREEZE AHEAD TIP:

Any leftover ham can be thinly sliced, wrapped in a
double layer of foil, or put into a sealable bag, and
kept in the freezer for up to 1 month.

✳ Place the joint in a large pan over the hob and pour the dry ginger ale over it, topping up with water so the ham is just about covered with liquid.

✳ Bring to the boil, then lower the heat to keep the joint bubbling gently for 3 1/2 hours.

✳ Towards the end of cooking, preheat the oven to 220°C/gas mark 7 and start on the glaze.

✳ Put the chunky ginger preserve (or marmalade) into a small bowl, and spoon in the hot English mustard. Add the soft, dark brown sugar, sprinkle in the ground cloves and stir to mix.

✳ After the ham has had its 3 1/2 hours (and check that it's ready by inserting a meat thermometer – it should read 71°C), gently lift it out of the pan – no mean feat – and place in a foil-lined roasting tin. Carefully cut away the skin, leaving a thin layer of fat. There is no need to score the surface, simply slap on the glaze and place in the hot oven for 20 minutes.

✳ Transfer to a carving board where it can be admired before being carved as thinly as possible; I try to get someone else to do this.

MACARONI CHEESE DE LUXE

175g soft butter, plus more for greasing

150g plain flour

2 teaspoons Dijon mustard

3 x 170g cans evaporated milk, 500ml total

1.5 litres semi-skimmed milk

2 x 500g packets macaroni

275g Emmental, chopped or grated

300g red Leicester or Cheddar, chopped or
    grated

75g Parmesan, chopped or grated

salt

I'll come clean, I am making a vatful here, but I can't stop myself. At any time of the year, I take the view that welcome is conveyed by plenty and am, frankly, never knowingly undercatered. However, at Christmas, there isn't a pan that isn't overflowing, a dish that isn't full to the brim, a table that isn't groaning. I'm not apologizing, and nor do I suggest you minimize quantities (though you could probably halve the amounts here if you have a different temperament). I admit I had more than enough for the children and 11 adults, packing up half the left-overs for my sister to take home, and half to heat up for tea when I couldn't be bothered to cook later on in the week.

If the notion of evaporated milk appals you, use single cream in its stead (or replace both the evaporated and semi-skimmed milk with 2 litres of full-fat milk), but it's the former that gives that very necessary almost-packaged taste which makes the macaroni cheese so sweetly comforting and gorgeous against the pink saltiness of the ham.

You could add a simply dressed crisp green salad to the supper table, but nothing more is worth considering.

❋ Preheat the oven to 220°C/gas mark 7, lightly grease a roasting dish or tin (approx. 36cm x 26cm x 6cm deep) with butter, and start heating a large panful of water on the hob to cook the pasta.

❋ Put another pan (with lid), though not quite as big, to heat on the hob for the cheese sauce; melt the butter over a medium to low heat, add the flour, stirring until you have formed a paste – roux – in the pan. Cook, still stirring, for 5 minutes over a low heat.

❋ Add the Dijon mustard to the pan, stir well, then take off the heat.

❋ Pour the evaporated and the fresh milk into a jug and slowly whisk this into the roux. Be patient or you will get lumps.

❋ When you have whisked in all the liquid, put the pan back on the heat and cook, stirring with a wooden spoon, for about 10–15 minutes, or until all the flouriness has gone.

❋ When the sauce is ready, add the chopped or grated cheeses (reserving a small handful). Stir until the cheese has melted, season to taste and take off the heat, with a lid on so no skin forms.

❋ Meanwhile, when the water in the first pan has come to the boil, salt it extravagantly and cook the macaroni for a couple of minutes less than directed on the packet, and drain.

❋ Tip the drained pasta into your prepared dish or tin, and scrape the cheese sauce on top. With a couple of spatulas or your already dirty wooden spoon and a spatula (why add to the washing up?), mix the two together until the pasta is coated with the sauce.

❋ Sprinkle over the reserved cheeses and transfer to the oven and cook for 15–20 minutes or until the top has scorched slightly and the underneath is bubbling. This is best left to stand for another 20 minutes or so out of the oven before serving.

MAKE AHEAD TIP:
Make up the macaroni cheese, pour into the prepared oven dish, cool, cover with clingfilm and keep in the fridge for up to 3 days. When ready to use, preheat the oven to 200°C/gas mark 6. Remove the macaroni from the fridge while the oven is heating and cover with foil. Place the dish in the oven for 20 minutes, then uncover, sprinkle over the reserved cheese and reheat for a further 20–30 minutes until piping hot and golden (the time will depend on the depth and thickness of your dish). To check, push a metal skewer or table knife into the centre of the dish; if the macaroni is hot enough, the tip of the skewer or table knife will be piping hot.

FREEZE AHEAD TIP:
Make the macaroni, cool, cover and freeze for up to 3 months. Thaw overnight in the fridge and reheat as above.

SPRUCED-UP VANILLA CAKE WITH RHUBARB AND STRAWBERRY COMPOTE

(see p.198 for cake recipe)

1kg rhubarb (weighed with leaves) or 2 x 400g packets trimmed rhubarb
1 x 340g jar best-quality strawberry jam

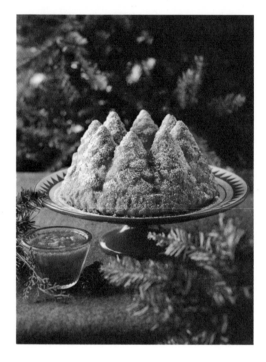

One of my oldest friends – school, university and now children the same age – Tracey had a grandmother who, over-rouged and frizzy-haired, was known cruelly by us when we were young as Elizabeth I. She was, though, a fantastic old-fashioned cook and at the end of the summer used to make a pie with rhubarb and strawberries or raspberries from her garden. This is my deep mid-winter version, made with gorgeously forced pink rhubarb and a pot of good strawberry jam (Wilkin & Sons Little Scarlet is the favourite, but any good strawberry or raspberry jam will do). It could scarcely be easier and can cook, and cool, while the cake bakes and cools. I love it, too, with Greek yogurt, or you can fold it into whipped double cream to make a heavenly fool.

Strictly speaking, that early, tender, puce-pink forced rhubarb is not meant to appear in the shops until January, but for the past two years, I've found it from the second week of December. I'm hoping, obviously, my luck holds. If not, then you can either add the same weight of some frozen berries to the jam, and simmer that up into a pulpy compote or serve the Spruced-Up Vanilla Cake, in all its glory, with the Antioxidant Fruit Salad on p.254 or with an accompanying bowl of crème fraîche sprinkled with pomegranate seeds.

✷Trim the rhubarb and cut into 2.5cm slices.

✷Put into a saucepan (with lid) with the jam and stir together.

✷Put the lid on the pan, and over a low to medium heat cook for 10 minutes, removing the lid only briefly now and then to give a stir.

✷Then, take the lid off altogether, and turn up the heat so that the pan bubbles away for about 4 minutes.

✷Tip into a wide-mouthed measuring jug and allow to cool, before transferring to a prettier jug or two for the table, to be poured at will over the yellow, eggy, thick slices of Spruced-Up Vanilla Cake (see p.198).

MAKE AHEAD TIP:
Make the compote, spoon into a heatproof bowl and leave to cool. Then cover and chill for up to 3 days. To reheat, place over a pan of gently simmering water (you may need to add a splash of water or a squeeze of orange juice) until liquid again. Pour into a jug and allow to cool before serving.

FREEZE AHEAD TIP:
Make the compote and freeze for up to 1 week. Thaw overnight in the fridge and reheat as above.

THE MAIN EVENT

THIS IS IT. The title of the chapter says it all, and if this unsparing statement of fact adds to the pressure, I have to admit, there is no point denying it. This is not just lunch: it is the focus of our expectations. It is also a huge undertaking. So, to feel a twinge of anxiety is not a sign of weakness or impending failure. It's reasonable. No one, absolutely no one, can just breeze through Christmas Day. I love the whole thing, so I'm not complaining, but I think it is best to accept that it's going to be a stretch.

The work itself, however – all the preparation and organization needed to pull everything together – is actually not so terrible. Like most things in life, when you actually do what you dread, you find that the fear is dispelled. But then, most things are better to do than to think about. Having to make the best lunch of the year feels daunting: peeling potatoes and trimming brussels sprouts, writing out a list of what must be done, and ticking it off as you go, is hugely satisfying. You don't have to operate quite like this, but I find it helps, and so have included here a tight timetable that demands, but delivers. This doesn't need to be followed to the letter, but I suggest that if you want to go off piste, you chart your own proposed trajectory. You need some means of containing and controlling your workload. I have concentrated on two days, Christmas Eve and Christmas Day, simply because that's my favoured M.O. You may find it easier to start the preparations a few days earlier, and sometimes – if you're at work on Christmas Eve, for example – you will have no choice. But if you look at the Make Ahead suggestions printed alongside each recipe, you can check how many days you can work ahead and finesse the timings to suit your schedule. Should you be someone who finds long-term, advance preparation and freezer-filling the best way to diminish panic and prep-proliferation, then look at the Freeze Ahead tips beside each recipe, and plan a strategy that works for you.

That – the nuts and bolts of the lunch as a purely practical undertaking – is the easiest part. But the stress-factor, incipient panic, the general hysteria that can colour this day – this is where the danger lies. I think we all have to make a conscious effort to keep this under control; and by under control, I don't mean keep it to yourself, but rather ensure you don't risk getting worked up into a state of explosive, put-upon martyrdom. No lunch is worth that. What is the use of fabulous food and blip-free efficiency if everyone is cowed into misery by the stress you give off? My mother's hysteria is an enduring lesson to me. By Christmas Eve, every year, she'd be in tears, and her tension leaked throughout the house. Now, I want to enjoy Christmas.

To some extent, this means working out a way of making this feast your own. Friends of mine who get the nerviest are those who have mothers (or mothers-in-law) coming over and, haunted by the perfect Christmas these dames have apparently delivered effortlessly, they live in fear of the harsh judgement their own shameful simulacrum will surely elicit. You have a choice here: you either take charge of your Christmas and enjoy (as I do) the slightly less structured event you decide to let unfold; or you recognize that disapproval of your slap-dash efforts bestows such a sense of superiority in those finding fault that you are in fact doing them a favour. Think how threatened they'd feel if you'd upstaged them.

But that brings us to a difficult area. What makes Christmas lunch so important is also what makes it so fraught; reader, I have one word to say to you, and it is Family. I love to have as many of mine around me as I can, but I have learnt they need to be leavened. Why not invite some friends, and not necessarily old friends, though it's lovely to have them round the table, too? What you need is the stabilizing effect of the stranger factor: someone with whom your family doesn't feel quite at home enough to behave badly. And I include myself here, too. We can all regress quite alarmingly with family, and we need to be inhibited out of this behaviour.

As I said, I want the lunch to have a certain relaxed informality, and if that seems at odds with the brisk, clipboard-and-pen style of my detailed preparations, well, it's because only the military precision of the planning enables me to relax for the lunch.

And, for the meal itself, I want – as will become clear – the food to be plentiful but I want, too, the feel of a feast not a banquet. I have, in recent years, let my lunch become more of a help-yourself than a silver service affair. That's to say (not least because I make so much food there's too much of it to go on our table and still leave room for us) I put all the food on another table, and let everyone pile up their own plates as they go. Sometimes, I hover, adding spoonfuls or helping people if I feel the need, but, generally, I'm happy to carve or get someone else to, and make sure they all know exactly what everything is. Then we can all take ourselves to the main table to eat, returning for a refill at will. It's not an elegant solution, but it feels cosy.

My other, more recent, accommodation was suggested by my sister. I was worried that I wouldn't fit everyone around one table, and I didn't want a sprawled out affair but something warm and compact. So, at my sister's bidding, I put an oilcloth out on the floor underneath the Christmas tree and let the children have a Spruceside picnic lunch. They couldn't have loved it more, munching under the baubles and the lights, and everyone was happy. So much energy can be wasted trying to make sure small children stay seated, that not having this to worry about aided the mellowness of proceedings.

Informality doesn't preclude attention to detail. I want the table to look right, which, for me, means special cloths or napkins and bits and bobs of decoration, brought out once a year, with ceremony. It has to feel festive. I bring them out soon after the 15th December, and they are packed away again on Twelfth Night. I don't insist on a tablecloth – I like the warm gleam of plain wood – but I must have tealights or candles, and proper napkins, and I'm not beyond the odd bauble or pine cone. My favourite china, seasonally stashed away, is the somewhat obsessively collected, mainly 1950s Crown Devon Stockholm (and see my proud display, left), but I can go a number of pleasurable ways.

So aside from this basic, number one Christmas Table, I love, too, the elemental Christmas Red – you can see from the pictures, on pp.48 and 131, how glorious it looks when tablecloth, napkins, crockery are all aglow with holly-berry brightness. But, although the season allows for vibrant display, it doesn't depend on it. There is a part of me that longs, throughout Christmas, to evoke the wood cladding and rustic cosy calm of some alpine hut and this is the part that brought the table setting on pp.110 and 166 into being. It's hard to choose between my two other favourite tables, different as they are. One I think of as "I'm dreaming of a white Christmas" mode (p.109); the other, my designer and art director, Caz Hildebrand, nicknames Barbie Goes to Bollywood (right and p.viii). There is a brightness, airy calm and serenity about the white-on-white approach; and yet the other, with its preposterous pinkness and odd clashing touch of brazen orange, manages a spirit-lifting glamour despite its (or my) best efforts. But these are just my ways of playing with the Christmas table, and you, no doubt, will have yours. Of course, no one wants a new set of china each year, but it's surprising how different you can make a setting look just by playing about with a cloth, some napkins and a tealight or two.

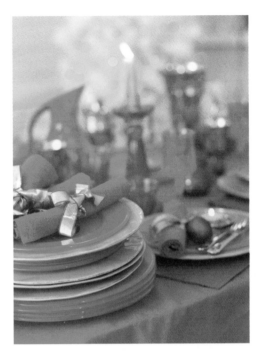

I try to be as permissive about the content of the lunch itself, and I am, I am, but I make no secret of the fact that *my* Christmas lunch is the one that opens this chapter: the lunch presided over by the turkey with all the traditional trim-mings; the lunch I ate as a child, and the one I eat so much more joyfully now, and which, with occasional variations, I've written about before. But I am, I'd hope, a zealot rather than a bully and happy to include ideas for those of you who want something different for a change, or who cannot embrace or even meekly go along with my exuberant championing of the Christmas turkey. A Christmas goose is the most obvious alternative, and a fabulous one (especially with pear and cranberry stuffing), but once I've ventured beyond the traditional, I am ready to take a broadly inclusive approach. So that means a vast and gor-geous rib of beef with a seasonal port and Stilton gravy; or a slightly Italianate, rolled, stuffed loin of pork, both of which bring their own splendour and special-ness to the occasion. A glazed ham (p.32), if you wanted to bring this into the equation, and were not already following my Christmas Eve supper plans (see p.100), would also do the trick. Within all these suggestions are provisions for vegetarians, but I'm happy, too, to include a full-on, meatless Christmas Feast, in the form of a beautiful, whole, stuffed pumpkin. Some of you may have teenage children and their tyrannical fads to accommodate, others may simply prefer, if in mixed carnivore and veggie company, to have just one meal for all, and this is one that everyone can relish.

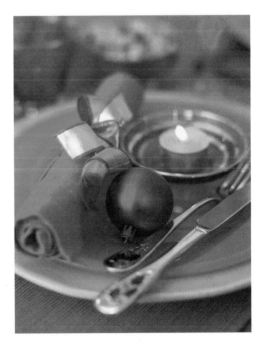

And, although each of the menus makes any Christmas lunch feel like the Main Event it is, these are meals that can also lend themselves to any big-deal dinner throughout the season.

MY TRADITIONAL CHRISTMAS LUNCH

CHRISTMAS LUNCH MENU FOR 10–16

SPICED AND SUPERJUICY TURKEY WITH ALLSPICE GRAVY

REDDER THAN RED CRANBERRY SAUCE

MY MOTHER'S BREAD SAUCE

GINGERBREAD STUFFING, PANETTONE AND ITALIAN SAUSAGE STUFFING OR CHESTNUT STUFFING

BACON-WRAPPED CHIPOLATAS

PERFECT ROAST POTATOES

MAPLE-ROAST PARSNIPS

BRUSSELS SPROUTS WITH CHESTNUTS

BUTTERNUT ORZOTTO

RED CABBAGE WITH POMEGRANATE JUICE (p.60)

ULTIMATE CHRISTMAS PUDDING WITH EGGNOG CREAM

CHOCOLATE PUDDING FOR CHRISTMAS PUDDING HATERS WITH CHOCOLATE SAUCE

SATSUMAS OR CLEMENTINES

LYCHEES

FRESH MIXED NUTS IN THEIR SHELLS

When I read the menu that follows, I feel exhausted, hungry, flabbergasted and proud. How could I have cooked so much? How could we all have eaten so much? But how I want to eat it now. I am warmed by recollection and anticipation.

For this is what I made last year, which is – give or take – what I make every year and will be making every year that – *d.v.* – follows. It used to be worse, I used to make two stuffings; now, I concede that one suffices. But then, in my two-stuffing days, I went without bacon-wrapped chipolatas, so a balance has been maintained.

In fairness, I should say that the menu is inflated, as two of the people (out of a total of nine adults and five children) round my table were vegetarians and I wanted to make sure they could feast as richly as the rest of us. In previous years I had only intermittently added the red cabbage and never the butternut orzotto, but both made sense and neither was any trouble since I prepared them in relative quiet the day before and simply reheated them as I cooked the rest. I had to do something for non-meat eaters as I knew I couldn't forgo the goose fat on my roast potatoes (although I had decided to take pancetta out of the sprouts). I did *think* about the goose fat, and consulted my sister who was, after all, bringing the vegetarians. I gave her three options: cook the potatoes in vegetable oil; cook them in goose fat and don't tell the vegetarians; cook them in goose fat, tell them and deprive them. She felt strongly that we'd already given up the pancetta, so enough was enough – they would have the orzotto, plus we hadn't forced them to become vegetarians. At this time of year, one can get frenzied and beyond reason – so I was grateful for her coolly brutal logic.

I have printed a timetable for guidance, my own Christmas Lunch Countdown, but obviously there are variables. I hope, at least, it helps you to structure your own timetable. That much is crucial: if you don't run the cooking like a military campaign, you won't get lunch on the table in time. Having said that, I should admit one thing: I invited everyone for 2pm, with a thought that we would eat at 2.30pm, and got started in the kitchen at 10am, having not been released from rapacious present-opening by my children before then. By the time everyone arrived, I was unmade-up, shiny-faced with the exertions and still in my dressing gown. So I'm not pretending that any of this can be done with a mere snap of the fingers or wiggle of the nose. But the pleasures that are to be had from the slow build-up as you prepare a feast, as well as from quickly eating it, are not to be underestimated. For me, this lunch is the lynchpin of the year.

The menu opposite, in the quantities I cook, is what I'd do for 10, and it would certainly stretch to 16. This may sound odd, but caterers routinely downsize portions the greater the number of guests. The one thing you needn't worry about is not having enough: there are so many elements to a proper Christmas feast, you'd be surprised just how little people take of each. And simply, the fewer the guests, the more leftovers you'll have. That, too, is part of the rich, full point of the exercise.

There is no reason why you couldn't do some of what follows in advance, but this is how I tackle it.

CHRISTMAS EVE (at the latest)

- First thing, take the turkey out of the fridge. (Take the giblets out as soon as you get the bird home and stash them separately in the fridge, throwing away the liver, I'm afraid to say.) Put all the giblets into a saucepan (with lid) along with the other ingredients to make the stock for your Allspice Gravy (see p.118), then put it all on the heat and get on with preparing the turkey while the stock comes to a boil.
- Get out a very large pan (with lid) – one that will fit the turkey roomily – or a clean bucket or plastic bin and add all the ingredients you need for brining the Spiced and Superjuicy Turkey (p.114). Stir well and lower the turkey into the brine, adding more water if needed. Cover with the lid and put it somewhere cold. This now just sits, infusing, until Christmas morning.
- Meanwhile, once the giblet-water has started boiling, cover with a lid, turn down the heat to very low and leave for 2 hours.
- You could use this time to get on with everything else, so in whatever order you like – or you can man several pans at once, which is more efficient so long as it doesn't stress you out:
  – Redder Than Red Cranberry Sauce (p.119); or make this further ahead.
  – your chosen stuffing (pp.122–26), but don't add the eggs yet.
- The above are non-negotiable, I feel. You may want to add (or not) the following, and if so, start on these today:
  – Bacon-Wrapped Chipolatas (p.127): wrap them ready for cooking.
  – Red Cabbage (p.60); or this can be made further ahead.
  – Butternut Orzotto (p.134), but only up to the point before the mascarpone is added.
- When the above are either done or under control:
  – Take the giblet-water, after its simmering time, off the heat, remove the lid and leave to get cold.
  – Check you've got all the plates, cutlery and napkins you need for tomorrow and that there's champagne, white wine, fizzy water (or any combination you want to serve) in the fridge, or in a small clean plastic bin stuffed with ice, to save fridge space.
  – Count the Christmas crackers and, if this applies, put them beyond any child's reach.
  – Slice a good-quality white loaf, cut crusts off and leave on a rack to stale for the Bread Sauce tomorrow (p.121).

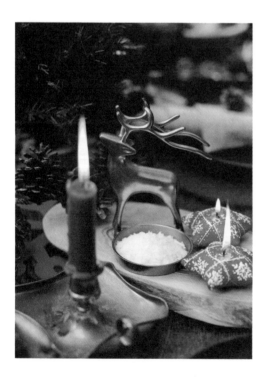

CHRISTMAS DAY

This is a brutal schedule, but better to go into battle properly prepared than enter the fray buoyed up with optimistic ignorance. You can draw up your own timetable, and it's often wise to, as the act of scribbling things down on paper helps you to get a good measure of what's involved, more than just reading can. I still scrawl down my own schedule. Plus, of course, you may have a different weight turkey, want to eat later or introduce any number of your own traditions and elements or have to fiddle and edit to accommodate your particular kitchen set-up.

The following, unsparing, schedule is based on a 2.30pm lunch, cooked with the benefit of a double oven. I know not all of you will have two ovens, and this is all perfectly possible, if harder, with one oven. In many ways it's more of a conjuring trick than a culinary exercise. Once cooked, the turkey can sit for an hour, or longer, out of the oven so long as it is not in a draught; and as it comes out, the oven can be turned up for the potatoes. A hot oven for the spuds is the only crucial factor – or that and the gravy. As I've said before, so long as the turkey is cooked, the potatoes are crisp and the gravy piping hot, everything else can be warmish, whatever the health and safety officers say.

No doubt, you would give yourself a less frenetic timetable were you to schedule lunch for later, say 4pm, but old habits die hard, so that's too late for me. I hear my mother's voice in my ear talking disdainfully about "Spanish hours". Besides, if you have a later lunch, you run into the difficulties of having hungry people hanging around the kitchen wanting to be fed beforehand. But the choice is yours. Good luck!

10.00am • Peel and cut potatoes, then leave in cold water, as directed (p.128).
• Take bacon-wrapped chipolatas out of fridge.

10.30am • Take turkey out of brine, sit it on a rack in the sink (or over a tin) and leave to drip, drain and come to room temperature.
• Preheat 1st oven to 200°C/gas mark 6.
• Trim brussels sprouts and leave in a colander.
• Take prepared stuffing out of fridge.

10.40am • Put chipolatas in oven.
• Infuse milk for Bread Sauce (p.121).
• Measure out ingredients for Chocolate Pudding (p.140) and set aside.

11.00am • Put prepared potatoes (p.128) in pan on heat to parboil.

11.10am • Take chipolatas out of oven and leave wrapped in foil.

11.20am • Melt basting liquid for turkey (p.114).

11.30am
- Baste turkey with half the liquid, and put in 1st oven.
- Potatoes should be at parboiling stage, or will be within the next 10 minutes, so keep an eye on them, then drain, dredge (p.128) and leave in pan.

12 noon
- Baste turkey with remaining liquid.
- Put large pan of water with steamer attachment (for puddings) on to heat.
- Now sit down calmly with a glass of wine, or cup of tea, and look over everything else that needs to be done so you are not panicked by the quick-fire work later.
- Lay the table.

12.45pm
- Put Christmas Pudding (made a few weeks earlier, p.137) in bottom part of pan-with-steamer attachment to steam (for 3 hours).

12.50pm
- Prepare Maple-Roast Parsnips (p.130), and leave in a tin, preferably a foil throwaway one.
- Put sprout water on and let it to come to the boil. You can leave it with its lid on, with the heat switched off once it boils.

1.00pm
- Preheat 2nd oven (if available) to 250°C/gas mark 9, putting in a roasting tin with goose fat to heat up at the same time (this will be for the potatoes).

1.30pm
- Put potatoes in hot fat in 2nd oven.

1.45pm
- Add prepared bread to infused milk and finish off Bread Sauce (p.121).
- Put parsnips in oven on rack below potatoes.
- Check sprout water, bring back up to boil, then cook and drain sprouts.
- Finish off stuffing, by adding eggs etc. (pp.122–26), put in dish and pop in oven below turkey.
- Baste turkey at the same time.

2.00pm
- Turn potatoes over.
- Check turkey; it should be done. Take out of oven and leave tented with foil.
- Pop foil parcel of chipolatas in oven to reheat.
- Process ingredients for Chocolate Pudding (p.140), put in basin, and put basin in steamer above Christmas pud to steam.

2.10pm
- Put Red Cabbage (p.60) on to reheat.
- Put Butternut Orzotto (p.134) on to reheat.
- Warm chestnuts in butter, add drained sprouts and toss in pan (p.132), leaving with lid on and heat off till lunch.
- Fork through Cranberry Sauce (p.119).

2.20pm
- Finish Allspice Gravy (p.118).
- Take parsnips out and plate up.
- Check seasoning and heat of bread sauce.
- Take stuffing out of oven.

2.30pm
- Bring everything to the table, leaving potatoes and hot gravy till last.
- LUNCH

3.30pm
- Have a quick nip out to the kitchen, whip up Eggnog Cream (p.140) and melt ingredients for Chocolate Sauce (p.140).

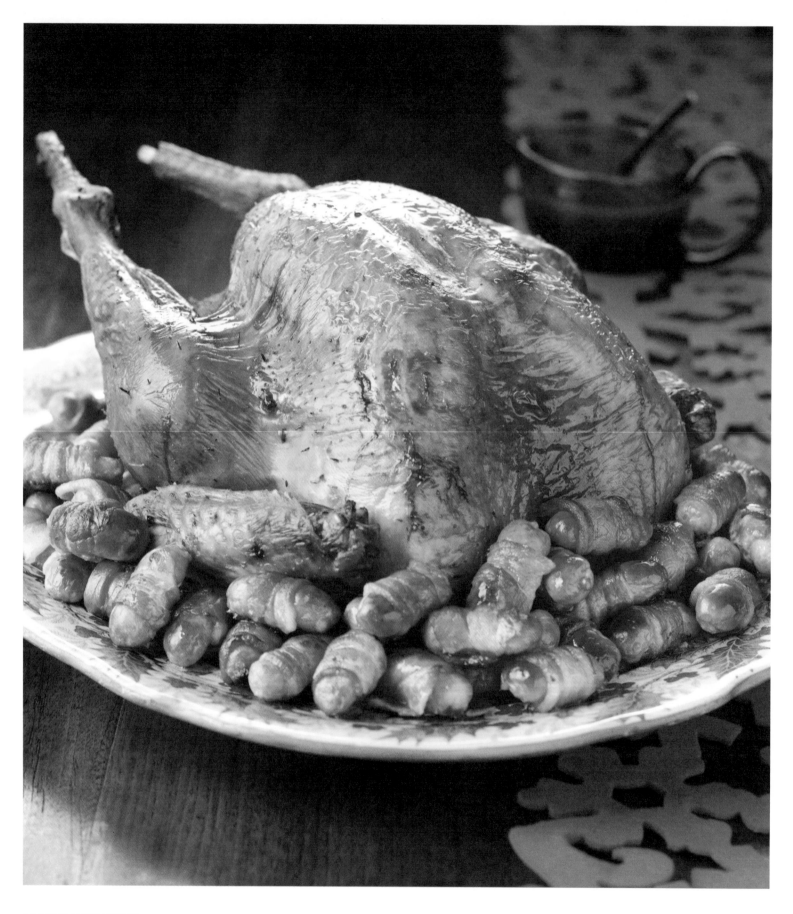

SPICED AND SUPERJUICY ROAST TURKEY WITH ALLSPICE GRAVY

I know I have done an awful lot of jumping up and down and shouting about my way of making sure your turkey is going to be surefire-succulent, but I don't think I can rest until I have converted every last person. This is feasible: you have only to try this method to be utterly convinced. It's not egomania that motivates me here: indeed, I take no credit for an age-old tenderizing technique; brining is a discovery not an invention. My evangelical zeal is more a combination of altruism, control-freakery (if I'm honest) and enthusiastic faith. But then, these factors are probably behind all kinds of evangelism – and cookery books.

But I don't wish to be lacking in compassion for those who don't choose this path. I can offer another way of making sure a turkey doesn't end up stringy and dry, namely my **Sausagemeat-Bosomed Turkey** (see photo p.110). It is simple, consisting of a minor, but amply satisfying, procedure. You take your turkey and, using your fingers, wiggle some space between the skin and breast of the bird, being careful not to tear the skin. (Mind you, turkey skin is so tough, you'd probably need talons to rupture it.) Into this space you've made, squeeze good sausagemeat, or the contents of your favourite butcher's sausages (900g of either should be enough for a 5.5kg/12lb turkey), pushing, pressing and coaxing so that it covers the whole breast. Then from on top of the skin, mould it a little with your hand so that the breast is voluptuously but smoothly bulging. Secure the flaps of skin over the cavity with a metal skewer so that the sausagemeat doesn't escape during cooking. The skin really crisps up as this turkey roasts, and the sausagemeat, which drips down into the breast as it cooks, keeps the meat from drying out. To ensure the turkey doesn't brown too rapidly, cover it loosely with a sheet of buttered foil until halfway through the cooking time. You could then dispense with the chipolatas (or stuffing if you can live without it), so this is a good way of cutting down on dishes to prepare, without making huge sacrifices.

But still, my Christmas turkey is the brined one. For not only does it tenderize and add subtle spiciness, but it makes carving the turkey incredibly much easier.

And I mean to say: how hard is it to fill a pan or large plastic bin or bucket with water and spices and lower a turkey into it? At this time of year, it's fine just to leave it in a cold place. I sit mine by an open window in the kitchen. It means everyone freezes, but who am I going to put first – my turkey or my family? Out in the garden if you're lucky enough to have one would also be fine, though the pan must be securely covered: if I've got a bucket or bin out in the open, I cover it twice with foil and then put my son's skateboard on top to prevent foxy foraging.

As I've said before, though you might find it hard to believe sight unseen, a raw turkey covered in brine – with its oranges, cinnamon sticks, and scattering of spices – looks so beautiful as it steeps that I can never help lifting the lid for quick, blissfully reassuring peeks.

Serves 10–16 as part of the Christmas feast, or 8–10 if not

approx. 6 litres water

1 large orange or 2 smaller, quartered

1 x 250g packet Maldon salt or 125g table salt

3 x 15ml tablespoons black peppercorns

1 bouquet garni

1 cinnamon stick

1 x 15ml tablespoon caraway seeds

4 cloves

2 x 15ml tablespoons allspice berries

4 star anise

2 x 15ml tablespoons white mustard seeds

200g caster sugar

2 onions (unpeeled), quartered

1 x 6cm piece ginger (unpeeled), cut into 6 slices

4 x 15ml tablespoons maple syrup

4 x 15ml tablespoons runny honey

stalks from medium bunch of parsley (optional, if you have some parsley hanging around)

1 x 5.5kg/12lb turkey

FOR THE BASTING GLAZE:

75g goose fat or butter

3 x 15ml tablespoons maple syrup

MAKE AHEAD TIP:
Leave the turkey submerged in the brine, securely covered, in a very cold place for up to 2 days.

I give a turkey this size, without stuffing, 2¹/₂ hours' cooking. You have read correctly: as long as it goes into the oven at room temperature, that is enough time, along with 20–40 minutes' standing time, tented in foil, once it's out of the oven. See the chart opposite for a slightly more structured guide. But remember that ovens vary enormously, so check by piercing the flesh between leg and body with a small sharp knife: when the juices run clear, the turkey's cooked. Or, if you want to be really scientific, put a meat thermometer in, and when it reads 65–71°C, you know it's cooked. Don't worry: the note opposite will explain everything fully.

❋ Put the water into your largest cooking pot or a bucket or plastic bin. Squeeze the juice from the orange quarters into the water before you chuck the husks in, then add all the other ingredients, stirring to combine the salt, sugar, syrup and honey.

❋ Remove any string or trussing from the turkey, shake it free, remove the giblets, if not already done, and put them in the fridge (or straightaway set about making the stock for the gravy), then add the bird to the liquid, topping up with more water if it is not completely submerged. Keep covered in a cold place, even outside overnight or for up to a day or two before you cook it, remembering to take it out of its liquid (and wipe it dry with kitchen paper) a good hour before it has to go into the oven. Preheat said oven to 200°C/gas mark 6.

❋ Melt the goose fat (or butter) and maple syrup together slowly over a low heat. Paint the turkey with the glaze before roasting in the oven, and baste periodically throughout the cooking time. Roast for 2¹/₂ hours.

❋ When you think it's ready, pierce the turkey with the point of a sharp knife where the body meets the leg, and if the juices run clear, it's cooked; if still pink, cook it for longer until they run clear, or use a meat thermometer. Then take the turkey out of the oven, and let it sit, tented with foil, for 20–40 minutes or even longer if you like, as I do.

HOW LONG TO COOK YOUR TURKEY FOR

The cooking times here always seem shockingly short to other people, but the truth is we've all been overcooking turkeys for years, and then complaining about how dull and sawdusty they are. If your turkey starts at room temperature, and is untrussed and without stuffing, and your oven thermostat is working correctly, these cooking times hold.

I've given instructions on how to check your turkey is cooked through, opposite, but so long as you use my brining method, if you want to ignore me and give your poor old bird longer, you can rest assured that a turkey so prepared is not going to taste dry, even if it is untrustingly overcooked. I beg you, though, for the sake of succulence, to have the courage of my convictions.

A turkey is generally held to be cooked through when a meat thermometer, inserted into its thickest part, reaches 71°C, though some cooks recommend 75°C. However, Paul Kelly of KellyBronze Turkeys says his birds are cooked through at 65°C and this is what his turkey thermometer indicates. Any such free range turkey also cooks faster than a very lean, more mass-produced bird, since the free range turkeys have more marbling and this conducts the heat faster. The timings here are for free range birds, put in the oven at room temperature rather than fridge-cold. If you have stuffed the bird, add the weight of the stuffing to the weight of the bird to calculate the total weight and cooking time; if you choose to stuff the cavity, do so loosely and add a further 1/2 hour.

TURKEY COOKING TIMES

Weight of bird	Cooking time
2.25kg/5lb	1$\frac{1}{2}$ hours
3.5kg/8lb	1$\frac{3}{4}$ hours
4.5kg/10lb	2 hours
5.5kg/12lb	2$\frac{1}{2}$ hours
6.75kg/15lb	2$\frac{3}{4}$ hours
7.5kg/17lb	3 hours
9kg/20lb	3$\frac{1}{2}$ hours
11.5kg/25lb	4$\frac{1}{2}$ hours

ALLSPICE GRAVY

giblets from turkey (not including liver)

1 litre water

1 x 15ml tablespoon allspice berries

1/2 teaspoon black peppercorns

3 bay leaves

1 x 4cm stick cinnamon

1 stick celery, halved

2 carrots, peeled and halved

1 onion (unpeeled), halved

1 x 15ml tablespoon Maldon salt or
   1/2 tablespoon table salt

juice of 1 clementine/satsuma (approx.
   60ml), plus pulp from fruit

2 x 15ml tablespoons plain flour

2 x 15ml tablespoons honey

Generally speaking, the best gravies are made by deglazing a joint's cooking juices in the roasting tin, but, with a brined bird, the liquid it gives off is just too salty; you can't use more than 2–3 tablespoonfuls. You could, of course, simply drain off the excess, but given the stress of Christmas Day, making the gravy in a saucepan is a better route: you avoid the smoking you can get from a roasting tin on the hob; and you can make it all ahead – the stovetop will be quite busy enough as it is.

❊ Put all the ingredients, except the flour and honey, into a saucepan and bring to a boil. Cover with a lid and simmer gently for 2 hours.

❊ Strain the gravy stock through a sieve (or just pour, holding back the bits) into a large measuring jug: this should give you approx. 1 litre. All this can be done well ahead (and see tips).

❊ On the Day itself, whisk the flour in a saucepan with 2 tablespoons of the salty juices from the turkey roasting tin, then put the saucepan on the heat and slowly whisk in the rest of the stock and the honey.

❊ Let the gravy bubble away, stirring every now and again with a wooden spoon, until it thickens a little and the floury taste disappears.

❊ If you are preparing the gravy stock ahead, make sure when you add the flour and juices and reheat that it gets piping hot; preferably fill the gravy jug with hot water for 10 minutes before draining, drying and filling it with hot, invitingly aromatic allspice gravy.

You can use the unused juice and pulp of one of the clementines/satsumas from the Gingerbread Stuffing on p.124, if making.

MAKE AHEAD TIP:
Simmer the gravy stock for 2 hours and stir in the honey. Cool, cover and keep in the fridge for up to 2 days. Finish the gravy with flour and turkey juices as directed.

FREEZE AHEAD TIP:
Make the stock as directed, cool and freeze for up to 1 week. Thaw overnight in the fridge, and finish as above.

REDDER THAN RED CRANBERRY SAUCE

When I was a child, I don't think fresh cranberries were ever seen in England. For me, cranberry sauce came out of a jar – and my mother was the sort of person who made her own mayonnaise. Actually, I have nothing against shop-bought cranberry sauce (and recommend it in various recipes), but I personally don't quite see the point: it is ridiculously easy to make, and tastes so much better homemade that it feels like the wrong thing to cut out of your cooking schedule.

Having a kitsch weakness for déclassé liqueurs, I love the cherry brandy element (not the sophisticated see-through kirsch, but the rich, red, sweet and viscous maiden-aunt's tipple), though Cointreau, Grand Marnier, Triple sec or ruby port would be just dandy, too. But you can simply substitute some freshly squeezed orange juice (blood orange juice out of a carton would keep you tonally correct) and be prepared to up the sugar slightly – probably by an extra 100g, but don't add it all at once – as the sweet liqueurs counter the fierce sharpness of the cranberries. If you're squeezing an orange for juice, go that extra inch and zest it first over the cranberries in the pan.

❉ Put everything into a pan and let it bubble away until the berries start to pop, stirring every now and again with a wooden spoon. This will take about 10 minutes.

❉ The one thing you should bear in mind, though, is that the pectin-rich nature of the fruit means it solidifies enormously on cooling, so although it will be cooked when the berries have burst, it will still look runnier than you think cranberry sauce should.

❉ At this stage, give the sauce a final, vicious, whipping stir to help crush the berries into the liquid, and taste – making sure not to burn your mouth – to check whether it needs more sugar; if you find it too sweet, which is unlikely, just spritz in some lemon juice. Transfer to a bowl to cool.

❉ If you cook this sauce way in advance, it will jellify a lot so thrash it through with a fork before serving.

Serves 10–16 as part of the Christmas feast, or 8–10 if not

1 x 340g pack fresh cranberries
200g caster sugar
45ml cherry brandy
75ml water

MAKE AHEAD TIP:
Make the sauce up to 1 week ahead. Cover and keep in the fridge. Stir well before serving.

FREEZE AHEAD TIP:
Make and freeze for up to 1 month. Thaw overnight at room temperature. Stir well before serving.

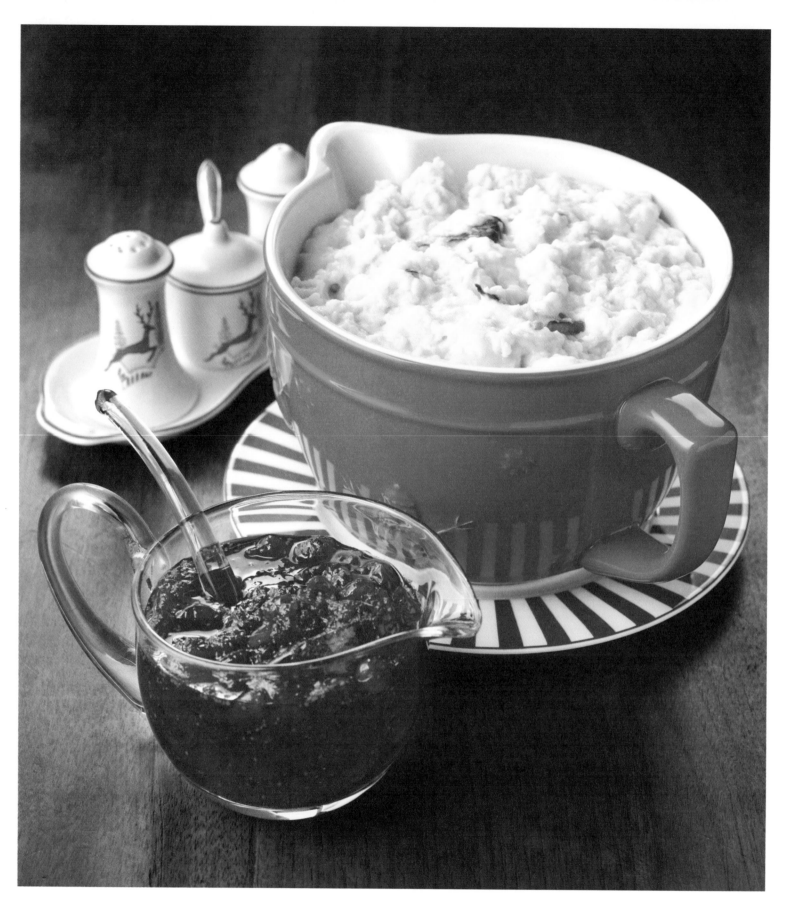

MY MOTHER'S BREAD SAUCE

Proper recipes tell you to use breadcrumbs and it isn't simply laziness that makes me cut out that step, though I suspect it played some part in my mother's decision. I don't mean that rudely: she was a wonderful cook, and much of that came from her impatience; stripping away unnecessary processes is an important part of real cooking, and no one should feel guilty about that.

The real truth is that bread sauce made with torn-up cubes and strips of bread has a much better texture than the almost gruel-like, uniformly smooth sauce made with semolina-sized crumbs.

I couldn't have Christmas lunch without bread sauce: just the smell of the milk, infusing on the hob, giving off that familiar scent of onion, mace, bay and clove, lets me know it is Christmas. The idea of a bread sauce remains intensely baffling, possibly even disgusting, to any person who hasn't been brought up with British traditions, but I have, so far, been able to convert Italians, Austrians and even (admittedly with some condescension on their part) a French contingent. I regard bread sauce as not only my legacy from my mother, but every Briton's sacred and stodgy inheritance. I shouldn't have to say it but, given the kind of bread our nation willingly consumes (and my children lead the way here, eschewing all proper loaves), let me warn you now: do not even consider making this with the plastic, sliced stuff.

❄ The day before you make this, slice the bread thickly, cut off the crusts (not with too much dedication, as a few bits of brown crust won't matter) and lay the slices on a rack to stale. And as you don't need the 2 end-crusts for the sauce, I'd eat these while they're nice and fresh. I'm afraid I often end up eating the strips of discarded crusts from the slices, too (with a thick layer of butter and a thin one of Marmite).

❄ If you've forgotten to stale the bread, or don't have time, you can speed the process by putting the slices in a very low oven until they feel dry to the touch (though not toasted) – but just don't forget they're there.

❄ On Christmas Day (see p.111), though you could make this before, prepare the sauce, which is scarcely hard work. Put the milk into a pan. Peel and quarter the onion, stud each quarter with a clove, and drop them, as you do so, into the pan of milk. Add the bay leaves, peppercorns and the blades of mace (or sprinkle the ground mace over) along with the salt and bring to an almost boil, but *do not let it boil*.

❄ Remove from the heat, cover the pan and let it foggily infuse.

Serves 10–16 as part of the Christmas feast, or 8–10 if not

1 x 800g good-quality white loaf, sliced thickly and left to stale overnight (see step 1 below)

1 litre full-fat milk

1 onion

4 cloves

2 bay leaves

1 teaspoon white peppercorns

2 teaspoons Maldon salt or 1 teaspoon table salt

2 blades mace (or heaped $1/4$ teaspoon ground mace)

30g butter

2 x 15ml tablespoons double cream (optional)

fresh nutmeg

MAKE AHEAD TIP:
Make the sauce up to 2 days ahead. Remove the clove-studded onion pieces. Melt the butter and spoon over the sauce to prevent a skin forming. Cover with clingfilm and keep in the fridge. To reheat, return the sauce and butter layer to the saucepan, and stir over a gentle heat for 3–4 minutes until everything has blended together. Adjust the seasoning to taste.

FREEZE AHEAD TIP:
Make the bread sauce (without adding the butter) up to 1 month ahead. Cool and freeze. To reheat, thaw overnight in the fridge and return to the saucepan. Stir over a gentle heat for 2–3 minutes then beat in the butter, and season as above.

OPPOSITE:
My Mother's Bread Sauce (top);
Redder Than Red Cranberry Sauce (bottom)

❊ Tear the slices of bread into rough cubes over a bowl, so you catch all the crumbs, too.

❊ When you're not far off serving up, put the pan back on a very low heat, add the bread cubes and cook for about 15 minutes, by which time the sauce should be thick and warm and evocatively fragrant. I have to say I don't bother with removing any of the bits – the onions, the peppercorns and so on – but you can strain the milk before adding the bread if you want to.

❊ Just before serving, stir in the butter and, if you happen to have a carton open, the cream (otherwise, splosh in a little more milk) and some more salt if you think it needs it. Grate over quite a bit of nutmeg, adding more once you've decanted it into a warmed bowl or gravy boat.

CHESTNUT STUFFING

This is my modest reworking of the stuffing, as made by Lidgate's of Holland Park, which the constant reader will recognize. I've fiddled a little, but not in a major way – it didn't need it – and this makes enough to fill a turkey or dish of approx. 26cm x 21cm x 5cm deep, though I often use a similar-sized foil container. Neither of these needs any more than 30 minutes' baking time, maybe 40 if the oven is very loaded. I can't make any aesthetic claims for this stuffing, but it is unreasonable to expect wodged-up chestnuts and chestnut purée to cast off their claggy brown looks and, besides, the taste dispels any worries about its appearance.

This is not a huge amount of stuffing, but I find a large spoonful per person is all that's needed, though if you want to make more – say the size of the Gingerbread Stuffing on p.124 – just double everything.

It is the perfect amount for fitting inside the turkey's cavity, which is all well and good, but I have found that stuffing and trussing a bird on Christmas morning, while very satisfying Obs & Gyne work on its own account, is the one step that can tip me over the edge. And my brining method means that moisturising from within is no longer necessary.

As for breadcrumbs, I highly recommend you use stale real bread that you've crumbed yourself in a processor. If you need to, buy a loaf, slice it and leave it to stale overnight as for the bread sauce, above; it doesn't have to be as dry as dust, just not still squidgy. I often make breadcrumbs as I go, throughout the year – I can never throw anything away, least of all stale bread – and stash sealable bags of them in the deep freeze.

❄ Peel and roughly chop the onion and stick the pieces in the processor with the bacon and parsley. Or chop finely by hand.

❄ Melt the 75g butter in a large-ish, heavy-based pan and, keeping the heat fairly low, cook the processed mixture until it softens, about 10 minutes.

❄ Remove to a bowl and, using your hands, crumble in the chestnuts so that they are broken up slightly, then mix in the breadcrumbs and chestnut purée. This isn't very hard to do by hand (a wooden spoon and brutal manner will help), but an electric freestanding mixer with the paddle attachment is the agreeably lazy option.

❄ If you are making this in advance, then let it get cold now, otherwise, beat in the eggs, season with only a little salt (remember the bacon will contain some) and a good grating of fresh nutmeg and fresh pepper.

❄ If you want to stuff the turkey with this on Christmas morning, be my guest; otherwise butter your dish or foil container, add the stuffing, spread the 15g butter on top, and bake, uncovered, in the oven underneath the turkey for 30–40 minutes, depending how full your oven is.

Serves 10–16 as part of the Christmas feast, or 8–10 if not

1 large or 2 small onions
100g streaky bacon
large bunch of parsley, from which you can get a good 2 handfuls of leaves
75g butter, plus more for greasing dish and extra 15g for buttering top (if not stuffing turkey)
250g vacuum-packed whole chestnuts
250g breadcrumbs
1 x 435g can unsweetened chestnut purée
2 eggs, beaten
good grating of fresh nutmeg
salt and pepper

MAKE AHEAD TIP:
Make the stuffing, leave to cool completely then beat in the eggs. Cover and keep in the fridge for up to 2 days.

FREEZE AHEAD TIP:
Make the stuffing, with the eggs, and freeze for up to 2 weeks. Thaw overnight in the fridge.

GINGERBREAD STUFFING

Serves 10–16 as part of the Christmas feast, or 8–10 if not

500g (3 medium-sized) onions
2 eating apples, peeled and cored
45g butter
1 x 15ml tablespoon vegetable oil
750g streaky bacon
zest of 2 clementines/satsumas
2 x 400g gingerbread loaves (such as McVitie's Jamaica ginger cake), loosely crumbled
2 eggs, beaten
approx. ½ teaspoon freshly ground pepper

MAKE AHEAD TIP:
Make the stuffing, leave to cool completely then beat in the eggs and pepper. Cover and keep in the fridge for up to 2 days.

FREEZE AHEAD TIP:
Make the stuffing, with the eggs and pepper, and freeze for up to 2 weeks. Thaw overnight in the fridge.

Sometimes, it makes sense to use one's obsessions to advantage. I know that most people don't have trivial light-bulb moments when the notion pops into an already food-filled head to make a stuffing in which crumbled gingerbread cake replaces breadcrumbs, but that's, unfathomably, how my mind works.

You can use dark brown, dense gingerbread, or the lighter, sandier loaves. I buy spiced bread rather than make it (though those who want to could turn to p.201) and you will often find it sold, even still in loaf-shape, as ginger cake. It all works. Indeed any sweet, spiced bread would, and the Italianate version opposite is a case in point.

❋ Using a food processor or by hand, finely chop the onions and apples.

❋ Put the butter and oil in a large, wide saucepan over a medium heat and fry the chopped onions and apples until soft, about 10–15 minutes.

❋ Finely chop the bacon in the processor, or by hand, and add this to the softened onion and apple mixture. Cook everything, stirring frequently, for about 5 minutes more.

❋ Add the zest of the clementines/satsumas, reserving the bald fruit (you can use some of their juice in the Allspice Gravy on p.118).

❋ Take the pan off the heat and let it cool a little before mixing in the gingerbread crumbs. You can let this get properly cold now if you want.

❋ Just before you want to cook the stuffing, add the beaten eggs and pepper, and use it to stuff the cavity of your turkey, or cook all of it (or what's left after stuffing your bird) in a buttered baking dish. I don't stuff the bird but put all of my stuffing in a very generously buttered old Le Creuset terrine, with internal dimensions of approx. 25cm x 9cm x 7cm deep.

❋ Bake it in a hot oven (200°C/gas mark 6) with your turkey for about the last 45 minutes. If the stuffing's going into a full oven – which it no doubt is – there should be no need to cover the dish. If the oven is less full, and therefore hotter and less steamy, you could cover with foil for the first 30 minutes.

❋ Let the cooked stuffing sit in its terrine for a good 10 minutes out of the oven before turning it out and slicing it. Or just spoon from the dish if that's less stressful. (I love a slice of this, cold, in a Christmas night or Boxing Day turkey sandwich.)

PANETTONE AND ITALIAN SAUSAGE STUFFING

This is nothing more, really, than an Italian-inspired take on the gingerbread stuffing, opposite. The finished product is very different, however. Whereas the Olde Englishe stuffing is rich, dark and dense, this one is light, spicy and spoonable.

I go for hot Italian sausages here, since it's the contrast between the sweet, fruited bread and the fieriness of the sausage that I love; but it would work with the milder variety, too. You can't, however, substitute normal breakfast sausages: the rusk in them would add too much breadiness; that element is elegantly provided already.

If you don't like the dried fruit in panettone, then go for a tall, round loaf of pandoro instead. In either case, be sure to brush off all the bits of visible sugar from the top. I just slice off the sugar-covered bits.

For stock, I simply use good shop-bought concentrate whisked into cold water. If you're starting off with hot stock, make it up first and leave it to cool a little before mixing in with the eggs.

Serves 10–16 as part of the Christmas feast, or 8–10 if not

2 onions, peeled
3 sticks celery
4 x 15ml tablespoons olive oil
1kg Italian sausages
4 eggs
500ml chicken stock
500g panettone, cut into 2–3cm cubes
salt to taste
large handful of chopped parsley, plus more to serve

❋ Preheat the oven to 200°C/gas mark 6. Lay out the panettone cubes on a large baking sheet, and toast them in the oven for 10 minutes, till they are crisp and golden at the edges. Allow to cool. Obviously, this step can be done well in advance, just be sure to keep the toasted cubes in an airtight container.

❋ Chop the onions and celery finely, but don't go so far that you end up with a mush.

❋ Put 2 tablespoons of the oil into a pan and, when warm, add the celery and onion and cook gently, stirring every now and again, for 10–15 minutes until softened.

❋ Add the remaining oil to the pan, then squeeze the sausages out of their casings into the pan and squish and turn with a wooden spoon to break the pieces up as much as possible and mix with the celery and onion. Cook the sausage-meat for about 10 minutes, or until the pinkness has left it, stirring regularly with your wooden spoon. You can do everything up till this stage in advance if you like.

❋ Preheat the oven to 200°C/gas mark 6 (if it isn't on already) and grease an ovenproof dish (approx. 33cm x 19cm), pretty enough to serve from, put in the toasted panettone cubes and add the sausage, celery and onion: I use my hands to blend everything together well.

❋ In the bowl that had the sausages, celery and onion (to save on washing up)

MAKE AHEAD TIP:
Make the sausagemeat and celery mixture. Cool, cover and keep in the fridge for up to 2 days. Toast the panettone cubes and store in an airtight bag or container for up to 1 week. Finish with the eggs and stock, as directed overleaf when ready to use.

whisk the eggs with the stock (adding salt if it isn't already salty, so taste the stock first) and pour this over the stuffing, leaving it to soak in for 5 minutes or so before baking, uncovered, in the oven for 45 minutes. It will be dark golden and crisp on top, eggily soft – but utterly firm – underneath.

❋ Sprinkle with chopped parsley and use a large spoon to serve.

BACON-WRAPPED CHIPOLATAS

It's embarrassing – or should be, though happily I don't believe in feeling ashamed of anything I eat – but I used to be a little sneery about bacon-wrapped chipolatas. How foolish one can be. They are now a must-have.

I make life easy for myself by cooking them early – about an hour or two in advance – and then covering with foil (in the main to stop marauders, and I include myself here as they are dangerously pickable) and reheating at the last minute in a very hot oven, such as the one the potatoes will be roasting in later.

If the bacon's not very thin, it makes sense to roll it out: you can do this most efficiently by putting lots of rashers on some clingfilm on the kitchen surface, covering with another layer of cling, and rolling with your rolling pin. Half a rasher is plenty for one little sausage; pancetta slices, if you opt for these, are best used one per chipolata.

Cooking 50 of them may seem over the top, but these get snaffled up (especially by children) faster and more greedily than you could believe.

❋ Preheat the oven to 200°C/gas mark 6; though if I'm doing this much earlier and don't need the oven at this temperature anyway, I cook them for 40–45 minutes at 180°C/gas mark 4.

❋ Make sure your bacon (or pancetta) is thin enough to be unbulkily pliable (pancetta comes thinner sliced, but it generally costs a lot more) and if not, roll out to make thinner, then cut each rasher of bacon in half vertically. Wrap each fine half-slice of bacon round each cocktail sausage; there's no need to firm with a cocktail stick, as I've never had any unravelling. The bacon, when thin, seems to get sticky and adheres dutifully to its sausage.

❋ Spoon the oil into a roasting tin and arrange the sausages, each with the end bit of bacon down (though they may roll), and roast for 30 minutes or so, until the bacon is crisp and the sausages cooked. The only way to be sure is to make the ultimate sacrifice and taste one.

❋ Take out of the oven and wrap the tin in foil. If you've let the sausages burn a little, however, it may be better to remove them to a large piece of foil and wrap them in it, forming a loose but tightly sealed package; otherwise the sausages will continue to fry a little in the tin.

❋ When you are almost ready to eat, reheat the sausages by posting the foil-wrapped tin, or parcel, in a hot oven for about 10 minutes. Or cook them from scratch about 45 minutes before you need them.

Serves 10–16 as part of the Christmas feast, or 8–10 if not

25 thin rashers streaky bacon, or 50 very thin slices pancetta

50 cocktail sausages or small chipolatas

approx. 3 x 15ml tablespoons vegetable oil

See these beauties nestling around the turkey on p.114.

MAKE AHEAD TIP:
Roll the chipolatas in bacon, as directed, cover and keep in the fridge for up to 2 days ahead. Cook in the oven as directed.

FREEZE AHEAD TIP:
Freeze the bacon-wrapped chipolatas in sealable bags for up to 3 months. Thaw overnight in the fridge. Cook in the oven as directed.

PERFECT ROAST POTATOES

Serves 10–16 as part of the Christmas feast, or 8–10 if not

2 x 320g jars goose fat
2.5kg potatoes, such as King Edward's
2 x 15ml tablespoons semolina

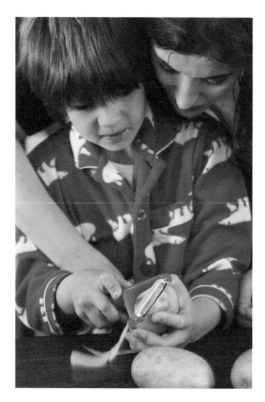

MAKE AHEAD TIP:
Peel the potatoes the day before. Keep submerged, whole, in cold water in a cold place. Drain, cut and cover with fresh, salted water to parboil and then roast as directed.

Needs must and all that, so I have always been an open anti-perfectionist, but in truth (and I'm sorry to repeat what I've said before) it is impossible to cook roast potatoes without needing them to be perfect, which to me means sweet and soft inside and a golden-brown carapace of crunch without. And, strangely, no matter how many tricksy things you may succeed at in cooking, no matter what techniques you may master, nothing gives quite the contented glow of achievement that cooking a good tray of roast potatoes does.

Unfortunately there is concomitant decline when you feel you've failed. The brutal truth is that you either get it right or you don't, and anything less than perfect is a disappointment.

There are three crucial things that I think make the difference: the first is the heat of the fat – if it's not searingly hot, you don't stand a chance, and since goose fat has a very high smoking point and tastes good, it is my annual choice here; the second is the size of your potatoes – you want them relatively small, so that the ratio of crunchy outside to fluffy interior is optimized; and, finally, I think dredging the potatoes – and this is a family practice, inherited through the maternal line – in semolina rather than flour after parboiling, then really rattling the pan around to make the potatoes a bit mashed on the surface so they catch more in the hot fat, is a major aid.

❋ Preheat the oven to 250°C/gas mark 9. If you don't have a double oven, you will have to do this as soon as the turkey is out of your single oven, which, for me, is very much later than the parboiling stage.

❋ Put the fat into a large roasting tin and then into the oven to heat up, and get frighteningly hot. 20–30 minutes should do it.

❋ Peel the potatoes, and cut each one into 3 by cutting off each end at a slant so that you are left with a wedge or triangle in the middle.

❋ Put the potatoes into salted, cold water in a saucepan, and bring to a boil, letting them cook for 4 minutes.

❋ Drain the potatoes in a colander, then tip them back into the empty, dry saucepan, and sprinkle the semolina over.

❋ Shake the potatoes around to coat them well and, with the lid clamped on, give the pan a good rotate and the potatoes a proper bashing so that their edges fuzz and blur a little: this facilitates the crunch effect later. I leave them to rest at this stage. If you don't, you'll need to have preheated the oven earlier!

❄ When the fat is as hot as it can be, tip the semolina-coated potatoes carefully into it (they splutter terrifically as you put them in) and roast in the oven for an hour or until they are darkly golden and crispy, turning them over halfway through cooking.

❄ If the oven's hot enough, they may well not need more than about 25 minutes a side; but it's better to let them sit in the oven (you can always pour off most of the fat) till the very last minute.

❄ When everything else is served up, transfer the potatoes to a large (warmed if possible) serving dish and bring to the table with pride in your heart.

MAPLE-ROAST PARSNIPS

Serves 10–16 as part of the Christmas feast, or 8–10 if not

1kg parsnips
125ml vegetable oil
80ml maple syrup

These used to be, until about three years ago, honey-roast parsnips, but I prefer the less intense sweetness, the smokier richness, of the maple syrup. Added to which, being runnier, the syrup makes a better, and lighter, coating for the nips. I have got a bit lazier, too: when cooking them in the very hot potato oven, I used to parboil the parsnips first and then cook them in the higher heat for 15 minutes. Now, I don't parboil, and I don't even peel. I find they are fine, and won't burn in the potato oven, so long as they are given about 10 minutes less time, plus are lower down in the oven and cut as uniformly as you can. I make sure the thick parts of the parsnip are thinly sliced and leave the thin part long and straggly. Nevertheless, do keep an eye on things and don't leave them in the oven for longer than they need.

❄ It seems foolish to say "preheat the oven", when it's frankly going to be on anyway, but if you were cooking these to go alongside, say, some cold, leftover turkey, then you need a hottish oven, say 200°C/gas mark 6, and would need to cook them for around 35 minutes. If you're using the potato oven, 20–25 minutes should be fine.

❋Halve the parsnips crossways, then halve or quarter each piece lengthways, so that you have a bundle of spindly, shard-like lengths. Cut any thick part into a thinner – rather than square – chunk.

❋Put these fawn twigs of parsnip straight into a roasting tin, pour the oil over, smoosh them about and then dribble the maple syrup over them and roast until tender and stickily brown.

❋Be careful as you taste to test: the sugar content of the parsnips, more even than the syrup, make these blisteringly hot.

MAKE AHEAD TIP:
Cut the parsnips into lengths the day before and keep in the fridge in a sealable bag.

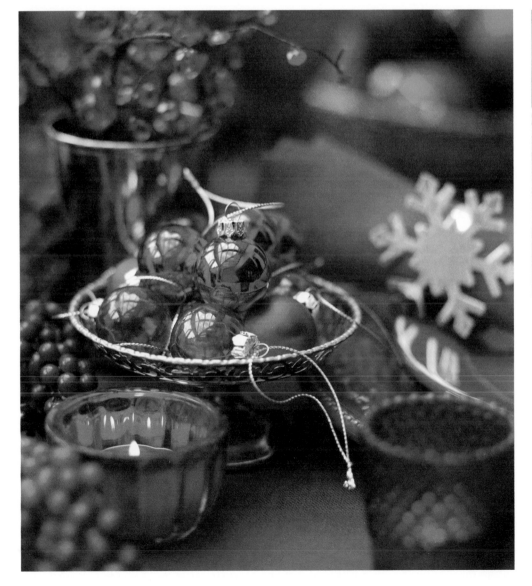

CHRISTMAS SPROUTS

Serves 10–16 as part of the Christmas feast, or 8–10 if not

1.5kg Brussels sprouts

250g vacuum-packed chestnuts

100g butter

fresh nutmeg

Maldon or table salt and freshly ground
   pepper to taste

This is the absolute basic, non-negotiable version of my Christmas sprouts. They need to be buttery, and they need crumbled, sweet chestnuts. I get my chestnuts in vacuum-sealed packs. My mother, against all her instincts, always roasted and peeled her own chestnuts, but then again, my mother always cried on Christmas Eve.

But if this is my basic version, there are many variants on the same theme. For my **Pancetta Sprouts** I start off (before the chestnuts) with 250g pancetta cubes, fried in 2 teaspoons of vegetable oil, so that the chestnuts are softened in bacon fat (to which I add 2 tablespoons of butter) and then splosh in 60ml marsala and let it bubble away to become a thick syrup before returning the drained sprouts to the pan along with 2 handfuls of chopped Italian parsley. For my **Pecan Sprouts**, I slice 4 fat or 6 thin spring onions and soften them in 2 teaspoons of garlic oil before adding the butter and chestnuts, then the drained, cooked sprouts, plus 100g toasted chopped pecans for the final tossing together, keeping some to sprinkle over. And for my **Bean Sprouts**, as it were, I throw 250g trimmed green beans, in short lengths, into the big pan once the sprouts have had a minute's bubbling and then carry on as for my basic Christmas Sprouts, but add the zest and juice of a lemon when the sprouts and beans are united with the buttery chestnuts; once the lemon juice has bubbled and reduced by about half, I decant and turn the mix, in the serving dish, in a drizzled tablespoon of best-quality olive oil. So, I like to play sometimes, but it's for pleasure not necessity: the sprouts here simply say Christmas.

❉ Bring a pan of water to the boil for the sprouts, adding salt once it boils.

❉ Cut the stalk-end off the sprouts, just a thin slice, and let the outer blowsier leaves fall away. If you have any large sprouts, cut an "X" in the bottom, so that they cook at the same time as the smaller ones do.

❉ Roughly chop or break the chestnuts so that some are cut in 2, some in 3; you don't need them whole but nor do you want mealy rubble. Plus, they'll break up further as they get turned in the butter.

❉ Cook the sprouts lightly, in the salted boiling water, for 5 minutes or so, then drain them. You don't want these mushy: you need them tight and nutty.

❉ Melt the butter – either in the pan the sprouts were cooked in, or in a casserole that you can serve them in – then toss in the chestnuts to warm through and add the cooked, drained sprouts.

❉ Add fresh nutmeg and salt and pepper to taste, then coat well with the butter in the pan before turning out into a warmed dish, or serving in your casserole.

MAKE AHEAD TIP:
Trim the sprouts the day before and keep in the fridge in a sealable bag.

OPPOSITE: Christmas Sprouts
ABOVE FRONT: Pancetta Sprouts; BACK LEFT:
Pecan Sprouts; BACK RIGHT: Bean Sprouts

BUTTERNUT ORZOTTO

Serves 10–16 as part of the Christmas feast, or 8–10 if not

1 butternut squash, approx. 1kg unprepared
    weight

4 x 15ml tablespoons olive oil or garlic oil

1 teaspoon ground mace

1 onion, peeled and finely chopped

500g barley

125ml dry vermouth, or white wine

1.2 litres hot vegetable stock, such as
    Marigold, plus more for reheating

1 x 250g tub mascarpone

75g pine nuts

1 teaspoon finely chopped fresh sage, plus a
    few small leaves

salt and pepper

MAKE AHEAD TIP:
Leave the cooked squash, mascarpone and barley
mixture, covered, in the fridge for up to 3 days.
Reheat as directed. Toast the pine nuts up to 3 days
ahead and keep in a sealable bag.

Let me first explain what I mean by "orzotto": *orzo* is the Italian word for barley; so an orzotto is a risotto that is cooked with *orzo* rather than *riso*.

Now, in the normal run of things, a risotto made with barley rather than rice would have disadvantages, chiefly that you wouldn't get that desirable, stickily binding starch emanating from the grains (due to their relative gluten content), so you wouldn't end up with a squishy risotto texture. But I use the barley for a reason: unlike proper risotto, orzotto can be made in advance and, indeed, seems to benefit from it. Stirring a risotto for visiting vegetarians at the same time as plating up Christmas lunch would be impossible: this one's easy. And it's very, very good: all you need to do is add a little mascarpone to the pan as it reheats, and tinker a little. Although I made this last Christmas for altruistic reasons, it became a truly self-serving exercise: I had three helpings.

✻ Preheat the oven to 220°C/gas mark 7 and slice the butternut, remove the seeds and cut into approx. 2.5cm cubes. I don't peel it, but you do need a big knife and a bit of brute force (and bravery).

✻ Tumble the butternut cubes out onto a shallow oven tray (I use a Swiss roll tin) with 2 tablespoons of the oil and half a teaspoon of the ground mace, and swoosh about to slick all the pieces before roasting for about 40–50 minutes, or until tender. Some of the butternut, chiefly the skin-sides, will be scorched and caramelized: this is a good thing.

✻ Meanwhile, gently cook the chopped onion for about 10 minutes in the remaining oil. I do this in my wide, shallow round casserole (about 30cm x 7cm deep) that I'm going to serve it in the next day.

✻ Turn up the heat to medium, add the barley to the onions, and stir for about 2 minutes, turning the barley in the mixture, then turn the heat up to high, add the vermouth or wine and let it bubble down a bit.

✻ Add the hot vegetable stock (unlike with a risotto, there is no need to add the liquid gradually and cautiously), put a lid on the pan and let the orzotto cook gently for about 30 minutes, or until done but still nubbly. In a narrower, slightly deeper pan, this could take 40 minutes and you might have to stir midway through.

✻ When the squash is tender, take it out of the oven and put half of it (judging by eye only) in a blender with half the mascarpone, and liquidize. Stir this into the cooked barley and season to taste. You can leave for a day or for up to 3 days at this stage.

✶ On reheating (or straight away if you're not doing any of this in advance), add the remaining mascarpone plus, if needed, some fairly weak vegetable stock (the longer the orzotto stands in advance, the thicker it will be so the more liquid you will need to add; I just boil some water and crumble in a few Marigold bouillon granules) along with the remaining squash cubes and mace. Stir gently but firmly and reheat; this should take about 15 minutes on a gentle heat, with the lid on.

✶ While the orzotto is reheating, or when it is hot (a few minutes on the hob but off the heat, with the lid clamped on, won't hurt it), toast the pine nuts by tossing them in a hot, dry frying pan until they turn deep gold.

✶ Stir half the pine nuts into the orzotto and scatter the remaining half, along with the chopped sage, on top. Garnish with a few sage leaves.

BEETROOT ORZOTTO

This is my favoured Christmas orzotto variant, which I wouldn't actually serve with the turkey first time around (though it's fantastic alongside cold turkey and generally breathes glamorous life into any meal of cold leftovers) but have done with goose (perfect, if you're willing to go without the red cabbage) and would love it with pork, too. I put it here simply because the ingredients, but not the method, vary (other than missing out the roasting stage, as cooked beetroot is used). It is a satellite recipe and needs to be near the Mother Ship.

✶ Cook the onions and barley as in steps 2 and 3 for the butternut orzotto, opposite; the only point of difference is that you add the teaspoon of dried thyme when the onion has softened.

✶ Liquidize half the beetroot cubes with half the sour cream, then stir into the cooked barley. When it is all mixed (and somewhere between puce and

Serves 10–16 as part of a feast, or 8–10 if not

1 onion, peeled and chopped

500g barley

2 x 15ml tablespoons olive oil or garlic oil

1 teaspoon dried thyme

125ml Noilly Prat or other dry vermouth, or white wine

1.2 litres vegetable stock, plus more for reheating

500g cooked beetroot (not in vinegar), diced into 1cm cubes

1 x 148ml pot sour cream, plus more for serving if wished

50g chopped pecans

3 x 15ml tablespoons chopped chives

ABOVE:

Beetroot Orzotto (back);

Butternut Orzotto (front)

MAKE AHEAD TIP:

Leave the cooked onion, barley and (half) beetroot mixture, covered, in the fridge for up to 3 days. Finish and reheat as directed.

magenta) you may put it aside for the time being if reheating later, or carry on.

✼ When reheating (or not), add the remaining beetroot cubes and sour cream, plus boiling water or weak stock to thin it down if necessary. As this beetroot variation yields less bulk than the butternut, you may find further liquid unnecessary.

✼ Toast the chopped pecans, as you do the pine nuts on p.135, and, before giving the orzotto one final stir, sprinkle with nuts and chives. If you wanted to, you could let everyone dollop a little sour cream on their serving of bright and sweet orzotto, too.

ULTIMATE CHRISTMAS PUDDING

I don't deny it: there is something unattractively boastful about calling one's own recipe "ultimate". But having soaked my dried fruit for this pudding in Pedro Ximénez – the sweet, dark, sticky sherry that has a hint of liquorice, fig and treacle about it – I know there is no turning back. It's not even as if it's an extravagance: the rum or brandy I've used up till now are more expensive and do the trick less well. This is sensational. I love the same fruits, too, steeped in the magic liqueur (see p.227), but this here is the Queen of Christmas puddings. It has to be tried, and clamours to be savoured.

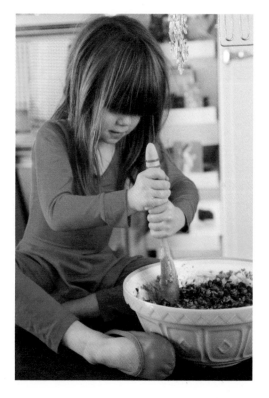

I know that many of you, tradition be damned, are resistant to Christmas pudding, and I do understand why. But you must try this. For until you do, you probably think all that dried fruit is, well, dry, and the pudding heavy. Yet this is far from the case: the fruit is moist and sticky, and the pudding mystifyingly, meltingly light.

A note on Christmas pudding generally, though I admit it's not my first foray into this; traditions, even if not followed to the letter, can't be wholly dispensed with just because they have lost their novelty – that is precisely their point. So, faithful readers, please forgive my ageing-lecturer style repetitiveness here. Traditionally, you should have all the family in the kitchen as you make your pudding, each one giving a stir in turn, the youngest first and going upwards in age. To honour the three kings, you are meant to stir from east to west, but I don't have a compass and am not good enough at geography to work that one out. Stir-up Sunday, when we are supposed to make our puddings, falls near the end of November, on the Sunday before Advent, and is – as I've told some of you before – a religious rather than a culinary injunction, as in "Stir up, we beseech thee, O Lord, the wills of thy faithful people". But personally I have never managed to make my puddings quite so efficiently in advance.

Some cooks like to use only 13 ingredients, symbolizing Jesus and his apostles, but a little bit of superstition enters in as well, since charms were traditionally included in the mix: a thimble, to suggest that whoever found it in their portion would stay a spinster, a coin to indicate riches, a ring to signify a wedding on the horizon, and so on. These days you'd be hard put to find such charms, though I own some pretty ancient ones. Clearly, we're just interested in money, as now it's coins that most of us bury in the pudding. (And some advice here: do clean them first; the best, if alarming way, is to soak them overnight in sugary cola. The Health & Safety recommendation is to wrap the coins in greaseproof paper even if they have been cleaned, but I unapologetically disobey. You must make up your own mind.)

There is still more than a whiff of the pagan about the pud: not only is each person meant to make a wish – superstition superseding faith – as they stir the mixture in advance; but the flaming of the pudding, as you serve it, is a nod to the pagan winter solstice celebration, in which fire and light and warmth are brought into our chill darkness.

Serves 10–16 as part of the Christmas feast, or 8–10 if not

150g currants

150g sultanas

150g prunes, scissored into pieces

175ml Pedro Ximénez sherry (see Stockists p.267)

100g plain flour

125g breadcrumbs

150g suet

150g dark muscovado sugar

1 teaspoon ground cinnamon

1/4 teaspoon ground cloves

1 teaspoon baking powder

grated zest of 1 lemon

3 eggs

1 medium cooking apple, peeled and grated

2 x 15ml tablespoons honey

sprig of holly to decorate

125ml vodka to flame

Eggnog Cream (see p.140) to serve

1 x 1.7 litre/3 pint heatproof plastic pudding basin with lid

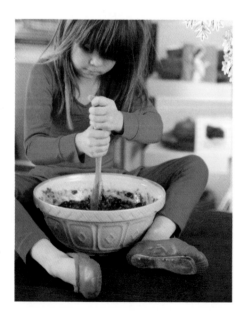

And to reiterate the little English history lesson I gave in *Feast*, actually, the Christmas pudding was once seen as a religious affront. Oliver Cromwell banned it as a "lewd custom", dismissing the rich pudding as "unfit for God-fearing people", and the Quakers magnificently condemned it as "the invention of the scarlet whore of Babylon". I used to fear that the Quakers made Christmas pudding sound more exciting than it is, so I've long done my bit to come up with a pudding that the scarlet whore of Babylon would be truly proud of. I don't recant any earlier recipes, but this one, definitively, is it.

❈ Although I stipulate a capacious 1.7 litre/3 pint basin, and cannot extol the utter gloriousness of this pud too much, I know that you're unlikely to get through most of it, even half of it, at one sitting. But I like the grand, pride-instilling size of this, plus it's wonderful on following days, microwaved in portions after or between meals, with leftover Eggnog Cream, or fried in butter and eaten with vanilla ice cream for completely off-the-chart, midnight-munchy feasts. But it wouldn't be out of the question – and it would certainly be in the spirit of the season – to make up the entire quantity of mixture, and share between smaller basins – a 2 pint one for you, a 1 pint one to give away. Three hours' steaming both first and second time around should do it; just keep the one pudding for yourself, and give the other to a friend, after it's had its first steaming, and is cool, with the steaming instructions for Christmas Day.

❈ Put the currants, sultanas and scissored prunes into a bowl with the Pedro Ximénez, swill the bowl a bit, then cover with clingfilm and leave to steep overnight or for up to 1 week.

❈ When the fruits have had their steeping time, put a large pan of water on to boil, or heat some water in a conventional steamer, and butter your heatproof plastic pudding basin (or basins), remembering to grease the lid, too.

❈ In a large mixing bowl, combine all the remaining pudding ingredients, either in the traditional manner or just any old how; your chosen method of stirring, and who does it, probably won't affect the outcome of your wishes or your Christmas.

❈ Add the steeped fruits, scraping in every last drop of liquor with a rubber spatula, and mix to combine thoroughly, then fold in cola-cleaned coins or heirloom charms. If you are at all frightened about choking-induced fatalities at the table, do leave out the hardware.

❊ Scrape and press the mixture into the prepared pudding basin, squish it down and put on the lid. Then wrap with a layer of foil (probably not necessary, but I do it as I once had a lid-popping and water-entering experience when steaming a pudding) so that the basin is watertight, then *either* put the basin in the pan of boiling water (to come halfway up the basin) *or* in the top of a lidded steamer (this size of basin happens to fit perfectly in the top of my all-purpose pot) and steam for 5 hours, checking every now and again that the water hasn't bubbled away.

❊ When it's had its 5 hours, remove gingerly (you don't want to burn yourself) and, when manageable, unwrap the foil, and put the pudding in its basin somewhere out of the way in the kitchen or, if you're lucky enough, a larder, until Christmas Day.

❊ On the big day, rewrap the pudding (still in its basin) in foil and steam again, this time for 3 hours. Eight hours' combined cooking time might seem a faff, but it's not as if you need to *do* anything to it in that time. And by the way, when I give it its Christmas Day steaming, I sit it in the bottom of my pot, in the water, and steam the Chocolate Pudding (see p.140) in the top part of my steamer.

❊ To serve, remove from the pan or steamer, take off the lid, put a plate on top, turn it upside down and give the plastic basin a little squeeze to help unmould the pudding. Then remove the basin – and *voilà*, the Massively Matriarchal Mono-Mammary is revealed. (Did I forget to mention the Freudian lure of the pudding beyond its pagan and Christian heritage?)

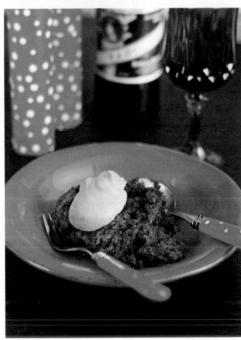

❊ Put the sprig of holly on top of the dark, mutely gleaming pudding, then heat the vodka in a small pan (I use my diddy copper butter-melting pan) and the minute it's hot, but before it boils – you don't want the alcohol to burn off before you attempt to flambé it – turn off the heat, strike a match, stand back and light the pan of vodka, then pour the flaming vodka over the pudding and take it as fast as you safely can to your guests. If it feels less dangerous to you (I am a liability and you might well be wiser not to follow my devil-may-care instructions), pour the hot vodka over the pudding and then light the pudding. In either case, don't worry if the holly catches alight; I have never known it to be anything but singed.

❊ Serve with the Eggnog Cream, overleaf, which you can easily make – it's the work of undemanding moments – while the pudding's steaming.

MAKE AHEAD TIP:
Make the Christmas pudding up to 6 weeks ahead. Keep in a cool, dark place, then proceed as recipe on Christmas Day.

FREEZE AHEAD TIP:
Make and freeze the Christmas pudding for up to 1 year ahead. Thaw overnight at room temperature and proceed as recipe on Christmas Day.

EGGNOG CREAM

350ml double cream

125ml advocaat liqueur

The traditional sauce for Christmas pudding is a "hard sauce", that's to say, brandy butter (and do make either the brandy butter, rum butter or, even better here, the bourbon butter, on p.190) but I can't help feeling that this corner-cutting Eggnog Cream, devised for my *Express* festivities last year, is best of all.

Actually, Dom, my long-suffering TV director, does a version of this with brandy, which also hits the spot (I think the cool cream factor is key), though you will need to whip in a tablespoonful or two of icing sugar – no more – as you go. And, you know, you might well consider the Cointreau Cream on p.183 to dollop alongside the pudding as a variation, too.

❊ Put the cream into a bowl and, using an electric whisk, start whipping to aerate and thicken. While it's still floppy, whisk in the advocaat, and once the yolk-yellow, eggnog-flavoured liqueur is combined and the cream thick but still soft, stop and spatula into a generous bowl and serve with the pudding.

CHOCOLATE PUDDING FOR CHRISTMAS PUDDING HATERS WITH HOT CHOCOLATE SAUCE

Christmas pudding isn't for everyone and, even though I have faith in my pudding's ability to convert, there's no point nagging or, indeed, fighting against real, die-hard antipathies. Besides, I have never met a child who likes Christmas pudding, and it seems unfair not to give a treat to everyone. The joy of this is that you can mix it all up in a processor while the Christmas pudding's in mid-steam (I dash into the kitchen in the middle of lunch to do just that, with ingredients measured out and ready, and basin prepared) then put it into the top part of the steamer, while the Christmas pud steams in the bottom part. Obviously, you can steam it in a separate pan if you want.

Whatever, don't be put off by having to steam another pudding. It's easier than trying to juggle to find oven space, and, actually, what makes the chocolate pudding Christmassy is that it looks like the traditional pud (I've never gone in for those round, cannonball moulds). Steaming 2 puddings is really no harder than steaming one. But if you feel you can't be doing with making 2 puddings, keep children happy by providing good shop-bought vanilla ice cream and red-white-and-green seasonal sprinkles to be scattered over at gleefully garish will.

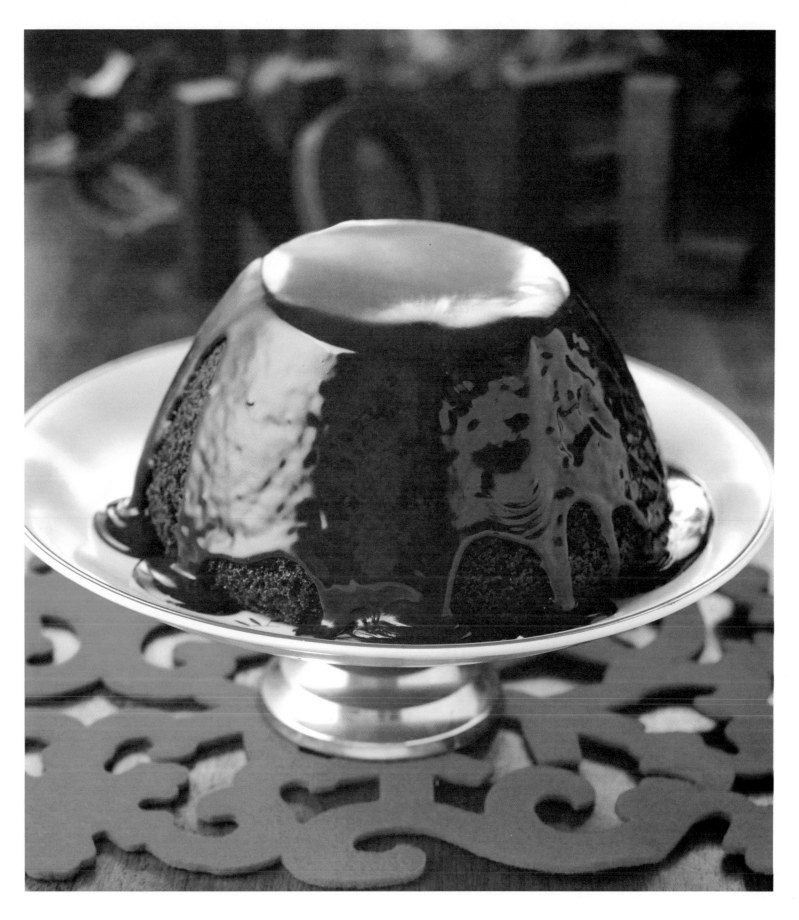

Serves 10–16 as part of the Christmas feast, or 8–10 if not

FOR THE PUDDING:

175g plain flour

1 teaspoon vanilla extract

40g cocoa powder

175g caster sugar

175g soft butter

60ml plain yogurt

3 eggs

2 teaspoons baking powder

1/2 teaspoon bicarbonate soda

1.7 litre/3 pint heatproof plastic pudding basin with lid

FOR THE SAUCE:

125g milk chocolate, chopped

125g dark chocolate, chopped

250ml double cream

75g golden syrup

4 teaspoons vanilla extract

❋ Butter your heatproof plastic pudding basin, remembering to grease the lid, too. Make sure you have adequate boiling water in a pan (or a conventional steamer) on the hob to steam the chocolate pud.

❋ Put the flour and cocoa powder into a processor and blitz to get rid of any lumps.

❋ Add all the remaining pudding ingredients to the processor and blitz, for longer this time, to mix. Take the lid off, scrape it down, then put the lid back on for 3 more long pulses, scrape the chocolate batter into the prepared basin, smooth it down (the batter will come only halfway up the basin) and put on the lid. Wrap the basin tightly in foil, so no water could possibly get in, and steam in the boiling water in the pan or steamer for $1^1/2$ hours (by which time the pudding will have risen to about 4cm below the lid). To cook it for longer will do no harm.

❋ To make the sauce, which can easily be done before you eat, and reheated just before you serve the pudding, put all the sauce ingredients into a saucepan and place over a gentle heat to melt, stirring every now and again and then whisking, off the heat, at the very end, to combine smoothly.

❋ When the pudding is ready, remove it carefully from the pan or steamer without burning yourself, then unwrap from its foil casing, unclick and remove the lid. Put a plate, or a stand, with a slight lip, on top, flip both upside down, so plate and pudding are the right way up, and wiggle off the basin.

❋ Pour some hot sauce over the pudding, so that it just covers the top and falls in glossy, licking drips down the side, and pour the rest of the sauce into a jug or bowl to be served with a spoon.

MAKE AHEAD TIP:
Weigh all the pudding ingredients the day before, ready to whizz together.
Make the chocolate sauce up to 1 week ahead, then cool and chill until needed, reheating gently on the hob or in the microwave.

FREEZE AHEAD TIP:
Make and freeze the chocolate sauce for up to 3 months, and reheat as above.

THOUGHTS FOR TURKEY LEFTOVERS

I have already greedily mentioned your options for leftover Christmas pudding; though the chocolate pudding is frankly good for nothing – unless you're truly desperate – once it's grown cold.

But with the turkey, and all those gorgeous bits that go alongside, the possibilities for fabulous leftover meals bring joy to my heart. My first suggestions are obvious, but I can't ignore them all the same. (And remember that your turkey – the carcass or the remaining meat stripped off it – must go in the fridge as soon as possible after Christmas lunch.) There are few things that can beat a leftover Christmas lunch sandwich: cold stuffing, cold turkey, cranberry and bread sauces, with some English mustard, and perhaps mayonnaise for those who can't contemplate a sandwich without it, or mango chutney for me, pressed between 2 slices of proper, white bread.

In fact, I relish any meal that's made up of cold cuts: I'll take turkey with ham (hence my insistence on the ham for Christmas Eve supper) and an array of chutneys, a jar of cornichons, some strong cheese, fresh bread and any of the salads from Seasonal Support (see pp.56–59) or simply some astringently dressed green leaves and a bowl of tomatoes, for people to pluck and slice as they go; and maybe bake some potatoes to go with them, should alcohol consumption seem to demand more carbohydrates. Of course, you can provide one of the soups from pp.50–55 of the same chapter to start with, to ring the changes or to make the meal feel more like a dinner; or produce a sprightly lunch by doing a turkey version of the Tortilla Soup on p.55 (using chicken stock just the same, or making turkey stock if you prefer), complete with its easily assembled accompaniments.

However, there are some recipes – the first new, the others older standbys which have appeared before but can't be missed out here – that I feel I have to suggest less sketchily. Please don't feel bound by the measurements or, indeed, the additional ingredients, in any way: leftover-sourced meals are by their nature provisional.

TURKEY PILAFF WITH POMEGRANATE AND DILL

WILD RICE, TURKEY, CRANBERRY AND PECAN SALAD

TURKEY AND GLASS NOODLE SALAD

ED'S VICTORIOUS TURKEY HASH

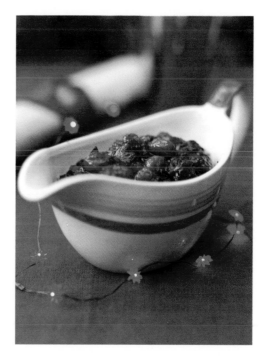

TURKEY PILAFF WITH POMEGRANATE AND DILL

Serves 4–6

275g brown basmati rice

200g shredded cooked turkey

125ml strong chicken stock (not needed if
   eating cold as a salad)

4 x 15ml tablespoons chopped dill

seeds from 1 pomegranate, or 75g pomegranate seeds from a tub/packet

2 teaspoons lemon juice

2 teaspoons extra virgin olive, or Mellow
   Yellow rapeseed oil (see Stockists p.267)

50g salted and herbed seed mix (I use The
   Food Doctor original seed mix, see
   Stockists p.267)

salt and pepper

❊ Cook the rice either in a rice cooker or in a saucepan according to the packet instructions.

❊ Put the shredded turkey in a generous-sized pan with the chicken stock. Bring to the boil and bubble gently for 1–2 minutes until piping hot.

❊ Drain the rice and transfer to a large bowl or dish, add the contents of the turkey pan and fork through to mix.

❊ Add the chopped dill and most of the pomegranate seeds, reserving some to sprinkle over the finished dish, and fork through again.

❊ Dress with the lemon juice, and a little oil, then scatter with the seeds, fork through again, and check for seasoning.

❊ Sprinkle with the remaining pomegranate seeds to decorate.

❊ If you happen to have leftover rice, this makes a great salad, but obviously you won't need the stock component: just mix all the other ingredients, cold, in the same ratio (when cooked, brown basmati increases its volume by $2^{1}/_{4}$, if that helps with the rough maths), and serve. Incidentally, this is a perennial possibility if made with leftover chicken; there's not a week I don't roast at least one.

WILD RICE, TURKEY, CRANBERRY AND PECAN SALAD

Serves 6–8

500g wild rice

75g dried cranberries

500g cold cooked turkey, diced or shredded

2 x 15ml tablespoons cranberry sauce or
   jelly

2 x 15ml tablespoons lime juice

60ml olive oil

75g halved pecans or pecan pieces

handful of parsley, chopped

❊ Cook the rice according to the packet instructions, and let it go cold. Always cool rice quickly; the best way is to turn it out into a large shallow dish.

❊ Add the dried cranberries and diced turkey to the cold, cooked rice.

❊ Make a dressing by whisking together the cranberry sauce (or jelly), lime juice and oil.

❊ Toss the dressing through the rice, cranberries and turkey. Add the halved pecans (or the pecan pieces) to the salad with most of the parsley, turn out onto a plate or into a serving dish, fork again to mix, then sprinkle with the remaining parsley.

TURKEY AND GLASS NOODLE SALAD

❆ First make the marinade/dressing by mixing all the dressing ingredients together. (This is very useful as a dipping sauce, or just as a dressing even if you're not going in for the glass noodles and so forth.)

❆ To make the salad, marinate the turkey strips in 125ml of the dressing; while this is going on soak the noodles in freshly boiled water (from a kettle) and, once re-hydrated (see packet instructions), refresh the noodles in cold water, then drain.

❆ Put the sugar snaps and beansprouts into a colander and pour some more freshly boiled water over them.

❆ Rinse them with cold water and drain – by shaking the colander – so they're not dripping wet.

❆ In a large bowl, mix the marinated turkey strips, and the dressing they're in, with the drained noodles, spring onions, sugar snaps and beansprouts.

❆ Dress with the oils and taste to see if you want to add more dressing.

❆ Sprinkle the chopped coriander over and toss everything together well before arranging on a large plate.

Serves 4–6

FOR THE DRESSING:

2 cloves garlic, minced or crushed

2 fresh long red chillies, deseeded and finely diced

2 x 15ml tablespoons finely minced ginger

4 x 15ml tablespoons fish sauce (nam pla)

juice of 1 lime

60ml water

2 x 15ml tablespoons caster sugar

FOR THE SALAD:

250g cold turkey, cut into fine strips

175g glass noodles (also called fine rice vermicelli)

125g sugar snap peas

125g beansprouts

3 spring onions, sliced into thin circles

2 teaspoons groundnut oil

1 teaspoon sesame oil

small bunch of coriander (approx. 20g), finely chopped

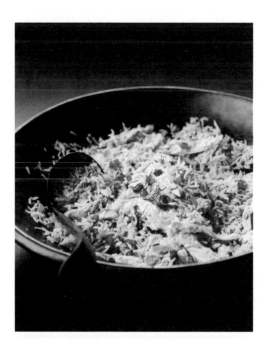

Turkey Pilaff with Pomegranate and Dill

Wild Rice, Turkey, Cranberry and Pecan Salad

MAKE AHEAD TIP:
The dressing can be made and kept in a tightly sealed jar in the fridge for up to 2 weeks.

ED'S VICTORIOUS TURKEY HASH

Serves 2 hungry people as a main course, or
4 with a baked potato and a green salad to
go alongside

50g flaked almonds
15g butter
2 x 15ml tablespoons olive oil
1 onion, peeled and chopped
2 red peppers, deseeded and chopped into
    approx. 1cm x 2cm pieces
1 clove garlic, peeled and minced
250g shredded cold turkey
75g pitted black olives
2 x 15ml tablespoons soured cream
2 x 15ml tablespoons leftover turkey stock
1 egg
few dashes of Tabasco sauce, or to taste
75g flaked Parmesan
1–2 x 15ml tablespoons chopped flat-leaf
    parsley to garnish (optional)

This turkey hash recipe, given to me by my friend and agent, Ed Victor, and in charmingly bossy letter form, has been a recurring feature in my books. Why drop it now of all times? Not least, of course, because it is a real winner.

    I've given it here as an actual recipe but, as with all these notions for leftovers, the quantities are meant to be a guide only. They are more of the "a handful of this, a handful of that" school of cookery, and that's how it should be.

    Anyway, this is my adaptation of the Victor Original: I've fiddled a bit, but remained essentially faithful, as, indeed, I will always be to him.

✷ Toss the flaked almonds in a hot, dry pan over a medium to high heat until toasted. Remove to a plate for a while.

✷ Add the butter and oil to the pan, then throw in the chopped onions and peppers and cook, stirring, over a medium to low heat for about 10 minutes.

✷ Stir in the garlic, then add the shredded turkey and cook until piping hot.

✷ Return the reserved toasted flaked almonds to the pan, add the olives and mix in.

✷ Whisk together the soured cream, turkey stock and egg, then pour into the pan, give a quick stir to combine and shake in the Tabasco sauce.

✷ Finally, add the flaked Parmesan and stir until it begins to melt into the hash.

✷ On serving, sprinkle with chopped parsley, if wished.

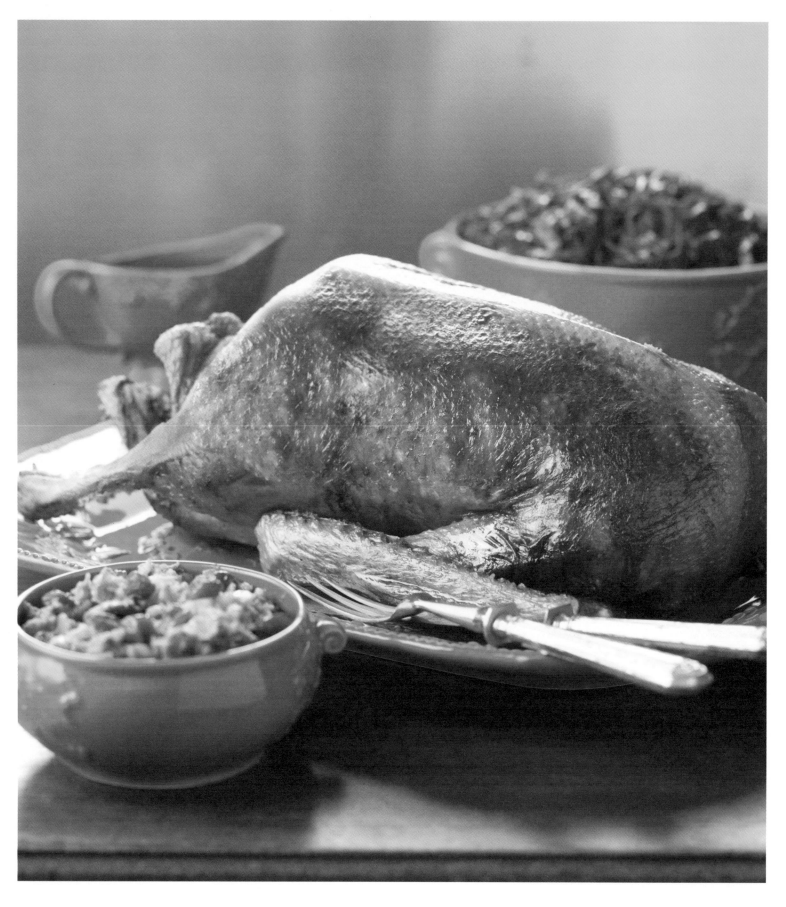

FOUR ALTERNATIVES TO CHRISTMAS TURKEY

THE GOOSE OPTION

ROAST GOOSE WITH PEAR AND CRANBERRY STUFFING
LIGHT GOOSE GRAVY
BACON-WRAPPED CHIPOLATAS (P.127)
PERFECT ROAST POTATOES (P.128)
CHRISTMAS SPROUTS (P.132)
RED CABBAGE WITH POMEGRANATE JUICE (P.60)
MY MOTHER'S BREAD SAUCE (P.121)
PRODIGIOUS PAVLOVA (P.45)

ROAST GOOSE WITH PEAR AND CRANBERRY STUFFING

It's true that goose has the older pedigree as the traditional Christmas roast, but if you are assembling in large numbers, it isn't actually feasible. This bird has such a large carcass which means that one only just fits in an oven and won't feed many more than 6, though with all the trimmings, it will probably stretch to 8–10. What the trimmings are, is up to you, of course, though I've suggested a similar line-up to the turkey's. I also suggest, unless there are 6 or fewer of you, that you don't reduce their portions; this way, if you wanted to be sure to feed 10 with a meat-mean goose, you probably could. It's just that I start panicking unless I make too much food for everyone, but I do know in my heart of hearts that 2 small slices of meat is plenty when the plate's piled high with stuffing, roast potatoes, sausages, bread sauce, sprouts and red cabbage.

Nevertheless, the disadvantage of the large carcass yields some positive returns, namely that you can fit in a lot of stuffing. And I do actually stuff the bird, as I no longer do my turkey, not least because a goose is so much easier to stuff than a turkey. And this sharp-sweet mix of grainy-fleshed dried pears and astringent cranberries – which becomes imbued with the flavour-deep juices of the goose as it cooks – is the perfect foil to the gorgeous richness of the dark meat.

If you have vegetarians coming, by all means make the Butternut Orzotto (p.134) to supplement, though I do love this with the Beetroot Orzotto (p.135);

Serves 6–8

FOR THE STUFFING:

500g dried pears (see Stockists p.267)

175g cranberries, fresh or, if frozen, thawed

100g dried breadcrumbs

¹/₂ teaspoon ground cinnamon

¹/₄ teaspoon ground cloves

1 teaspoon ground ginger

zest and pulpy juice of 1 clementine/satsuma

1 onion, peeled and chopped

2 x 15ml tablespoons maple syrup

125g pecans

1 x 15ml tablespoon Maldon salt or
   1¹/₂ teaspoons table salt

FOR THE GOOSE:

1 x 4.8kg fresh goose

MAKE AHEAD TIP:
Make the stuffing up to 2 days ahead and keep in the fridge. Then bring to room temperature and stuff the bird as directed.

FREEZE AHEAD TIP:
Make and freeze the stuffing for up to 2 weeks. Thaw overnight in the fridge and stuff the bird as directed.

but, as mooted earlier, if you want to serve the beetroot version, you must be prepared to lose the red cabbage. There's only so much Seventies maroon the eye can appreciate at one table.

❊ Either soak the dried pears overnight in cold water, or pour boiling water over them and leave to cool; this will take 2–3 hours.

❊ Drain the pears and put them into a bowl along with the cranberries and breadcrumbs.

❊ Add the cinnamon, cloves, ginger and clementine/satsuma zest and pulp.

❊ Stir in the chopped onion, maple syrup and pecans, and add the salt.

❊ Make sure everything is thoroughly mixed before you stuff the goose.

❊ Preheat your oven to 220°C/gas mark 7.

❊ Remove any excess fat from the goose cavity – this can go towards your roast potatoes – and remove the neck and giblets, reserving them for the gravy.

❊ Stuff the cavity of the goose with the pear and cranberry stuffing and, once stuffed, wrap the goose skin over, securing with a skewer.

❊ Sit the stuffed goose on a wire rack in a fairly deep roasting tin, as the goose will give off a lot of fat as it cooks and you don't want spillage.

❊ Cook the goose for 3 hours (after about an hour, drain off the excess fat in the tin, and again every half hour or so).

❊ Remove to a board and carve judiciously.

LIGHT GOOSE GRAVY

I'll be honest, my first impulse to make an unthickened gravy came out of my fear of trying to fiddle about with the goose-roasting tin: I didn't think I'd ever be able to skim off the fat and find some intense juice. But once I tasted the goose stock I'd made, I realized it didn't matter. Nothing could improve the taste, and a thicker or richer gravy would be too much for the strong meat. Now, I feel it's almost worth getting a goose just to make this delicate but, at the same time, deeply flavoured gravy. In fact, I may have to ask my butcher for as many goose giblets as he can spare, whenever he has them to hand. And don't throw away the liver, even though you don't need it here: unlike the turkey liver, this is well worth frying in butter and a few drops of garlic oil; add a glug of muscat wine (or sweet sherry if that's easier) once the liver's seared, then when it's cooked but still pink inside, wipe the pan out with some good brown toast, and squish the liver on top with a fork.

A final note: because you don't need the juices from the roast goose to make this lightest of gravies, you can make it ahead of the game, which I always find a boon.

Serves 8–10

neck and giblets of the goose (except the
   liver)
2 carrots, each snapped into 2 or 3
1 onion (unpeeled), quartered
5 cloves garlic (unpeeled)
1 stick celery, snapped into 4
generous bunch of parsley
1 1/2 teaspoons Maldon salt or 3/4 teaspoon
   table salt
1 x 15ml tablespoon peppercorns (white for
   choice, though black will do)
2 cardamom pods
1.2 litres water
1 x 15ml tablespoon maple syrup

❋ Put all the ingredients into a wide saucepan, and bring to the boil, then turn down and leave on a low simmer for 1 hour.

❋ Taste the stock or, now, gravy; it should be pronounced but delicate. If your saucepan is narrow, the water won't evaporate as quickly, so you may need to give it another 20 minutes. Let taste be your guide.

❋ Strain the gravy, discarding all the solids, then pour some over the carved goose and put the rest in a warmed gravy boat to take to the table.

MAKE AHEAD TIP:
As soon as you have bought your goose, remove the giblets and make the gravy. Cool, cover and keep in the fridge for up to 2 days.

THOUGHTS FOR GOOSE LEFTOVERS

The most important thing to say is that unless you let any leftover goose sit in any leftover gravy (you may not have the former, but I'd be surprised if you didn't have some of the latter), the goose isn't really worth discussing from this point on. I don't know why it should be so, since goose is so fatty, but it seems to dry incredibly if it's left to get cold untended. But pick off any bits of meat that you possibly can, and bathe them in the stock as it cools, and you have joy ahead.

I'm a fan of the thus-steeped cold goose (taken out of the fridge for a while first so it's no longer at fridge-temperature) with no more than a cold roast potato or two and a pile of pickled red cabbage from a jar. And although I warned against colour pile-up for the Main Event, I'm happy to add my Beetroot and Horseradish Sauce here (see p.68) even if it is tonally too much with the strands of red cabbage. Believe me, I am so grateful to find this gem (think ruby) of a no-cook, no-fuss but still sensational supper for one or two, that I am hardly going to start quibbling about the colour palette on my plate.

Otherwise, you can make the **Wild Rice, Cranberry and Pecan Salad** on p.144, with goose in place of the turkey leftovers, but so rich is this meat that you may want to use much less goose in proportion to the wild rice.

I have only one recipe proper for leftover goose: a cassoulet, though admittedly a corner-cutting, quick-time version, that no doubt would not find favour in the cassoulet and goose region of France, but that keeps me happy on a cold night after a long day at Christmastime.

QUICK CASSOULET

Serves 2–4 (depending on hunger of eaters and what else is being eaten alongside)

smear of goose fat

2 x 410g cans cannellini beans, or any good-quality canned beans, drained and rinsed

2 chorizo sausages, 110g total

250g leftover goose, chopped

200ml leftover light goose gravy

1 x 15ml tablespoon Armagnac, or brandy

75g breadcrumbs (or enough to cover dish)

2 x 15ml tablespoons goose fat

❊ Preheat your oven to 200°C/gas mark 6 and grease an oval gratin dish (approx. 25cm long) with a little goose fat.

❊ Put the drained and well-rinsed beans into a large bowl.

❊ Cut the chorizo sausages into fat coins, then cut each coin in half, and add to the bowl, along with the goose meat.

❊ Put this mixture into the prepared dish, pour the stock and Armagnac (or brandy) over, and sprinkle with the breadcrumbs to cover the top.

❊ Finally, pour the goose fat over and bake in the oven for 25 minutes – or until the crumbed top is golden and all is bubbling underneath.

✳ When cooked, the beans should have softened well in the liquid, though they won't have absorbed it: this cassoulet has a spoonable, generously gravied texture beneath the crisp crumb topping.

MAKE AHEAD TIP:
Assemble the cassoulet the day before, cover and keep in the fridge. Allow 30 minutes at room temperature before baking as recipe.

THE BEEF OPTION

ROAST RIB OF BEEF WITH PORT AND STILTON GRAVY
PERFECT ROAST POTATOES (P.128)
MAPLE-ROAST PARSNIPS (P.130)
CHRISTMAS SPROUTS (P.132)
BUTTERNUT ORZOTTO (P.134)
RED CABBAGE WITH POMEGRANATE JUICE (P.60)
BEETROOT AND HORSERADISH SAUCE (P.68)
PECAN-PLUS PIE (P.205) WITH CRÈME FRAÎCHE AND VANILLA ICE CREAM

ROAST RIB OF BEEF WITH PORT AND STILTON GRAVY

There is something about a big rib of beef sitting proudly on its carving board at the table that makes that table, and those around it, so immediately celebratory. The extravagance of it, the ridiculous vastness of it: this is a proper, stand-up-and-clap feast.

The Port and Stilton Gravy, grapily aromatic and tangy, is the perfect festive foil to the juicy meat. Although its inspiration – the gloriousness of blue cheese melting on top of a steak from an American grill – is not in itself seasonal, port and Stilton are the essence of an English Christmas. Just the words "port and Stilton" make me hear the crackling of logs in the fire, smell the chestnuts roasting there, see twinkling tree lights and hear descanted carols. Too much? Maybe, but isn't that the whole point of this time of the year.

Serves 8 (with leftovers), 14 without

3.8kg Scotch or black Welsh beef forerib (a 4-rib joint)
2 onions, peeled and cut into 1cm rounds
2 x 15ml tablespoons garlic oil
$1\frac{1}{2}$ teaspoons Maldon salt or $\frac{3}{4}$ teaspoon table salt
1 teaspoon dried thyme
$\frac{1}{2}$ teaspoon cayenne pepper

❉ Take your beef out of the fridge to bring to room temperature, which could take an hour or possibly more, and preheat the oven to 220°C/gas mark 7.

❉ Put the onion slices into a roasting tin and sit the rib of beef on top of them. Use the onion slices as props to help the rib sit up on its bones in an "L" shape.

❉ Smear the oil over the white fat of the rib, and sprinkle with the salt, thyme and cayenne pepper.

❉ Cook according to the beef's weight and your taste. I like my beef nice and underdone, so I give it 33 minutes per kg/15 minutes per lb, which means, for a joint this size, a cooking time of about 2 hours unless the beef's straight out of the fridge, in which case, add another 20 minutes or so. If you want medium beef, give the joint, from room temperature, 44 minutes per kg/20 minutes per lb, and if you like well-done meat, 66 minutes per kg/30 minutes per lb. As for feeding capacity, this size of joint will certainly look after a big tableful, from 8 with lots of leftovers to 14, without the definite promise of them.

❄ When the beef comes out of the oven, remove to a carving board and allow to rest in a warm part of the kitchen under a tent of foil for 30 minutes before carving; or just leave, tented in its tin, for the same time.

❄ Do not start clearing up the tin, even if you have taken out the beef, however, as you will need some of the pan juices and onions for the gravy, below.

PORT AND STILTON GRAVY

2 x 15ml tablespoons fatty juices, from the roast beef tin

1 x 15ml tablespoon plain flour

125ml ruby port, plus 1 x 15ml tablespoon

cooked onions from the roast beef tin (optional)

500ml organic beef stock, "fresh" from a shop-bought tub

125g blue cheese

1 teaspoon redcurrant jelly

salt and pepper to taste

extra juices from the roast beef tin and carving board

I love the mixture between rich, rounded ruby port and sharp, salty cheese. The onions, sweet and soft from the beef's roasting tin, add depth as well as texture if you liquidize them, in a blender (it doesn't work the same way in a processor) with the stock, which, in turn, is then combined with the port and Stilton.

But this Christmas gravy is good enough without, so if you don't feel like blending or your onions are too blackened from the tin, you can dispense with this step without cause for concern.

❄ Make a roux by adding the 2 tablespoons of fatty juices from the beef tin to a saucepan, whisk in the flour, and then the 125ml of port, and keep heating and whisking over a fairly gentle heat, until thick and bubbling.

❄ If you want to blend the onions and stock, do so now, by putting any but the blackened onions in the blender goblet with the beef stock, and liquidizing. Or leave the stock just as it is, straight out of the tub.

❄ Take the saucepan off the heat, and gradually whisk in the beef stock. When all the stock's added, put the pan back on the heat and cook, whisking to make sure any lumps are banished, over a medium heat for 2 minutes.

✤ Crumble in the Stilton, then drop in the redcurrant jelly and turn up the heat to let the gravy bubble for 5 minutes.

✤ Check the seasoning, adding salt and pepper as needed, and then the remaining tablespoon of port, along with any bloody juices – what we called red gravy when I was a child – from the carved beef. Pour into a warmed gravy boat.

THOUGHTS FOR BEEF LEFTOVERS

There is nothing, really, to be done to cold roast beef, and I say that in the best way possible. Cold, it's a dream with the Beetroot and Horseradish Sauce (see p.68), some bitter leaves – spiky witloof or a tangle of watercress – and a hot baked potato dolloped with sour cream and chives. In fact, there's not much that doesn't go with cold, sliced roast beef: echo the flavours it came with when it was hot by serving the beef cold alongside a green salad tossed in a dressing of blue cheese whisked with sour cream, a splosh of milk, a few drops of Worcestershire sauce and a spritz of lime; or perhaps add that tang another way by slicing the beef with some charred peppers (out of a jar is fine, if the quality's good) and drizzling the plate with some anchovies whisked to a viscous liquid with olive oil, a squeeze of lemon juice and very finely chopped parsley. Scatter more parsley on top of the divine but murky drizzle on the plate.

Or you can take this thought further East and drape a platter with slices of red roast beef, and make a dressing by whisking together some freshly grated ginger, brown rice vinegar, a little soft light brown sugar (to temper the vinegar), soy sauce, a scant amount of vegetable oil and a drop of sesame oil, then stir in some sliced spring onion, freshly chopped coriander and pour over the glistening rare beef.

My mother always made a salad, when any cold beef was coming to an end and what was left was too stubby to carve thinly, by shredding some crisp lettuce, chopping the beef, dicing some cornichons, throwing in a few capers and some small cooked, cooled and halved new potatoes, and making a thick, oily, Dijon-mustardy dressing. It's a hard one to beat.

THE PORK OPTION

ROLLED STUFFED LOIN OF PORK WITH RUBIED GRAVY

There is no denying that this is a complete showstopper. There is also no denying this is a fiddly undertaking, but it's worth it. Besides, if a meal isn't worth making a special effort for now, when is it?

The butcher can do a lot of the work for you; you certainly couldn't embark on this using a generic, untailored supermarket joint. So, ask the butcher for a fillet end of pork loin, with the rind and bones removed, but be sure you get to keep the rind and have it scored at the same time: this makes fantastic crackling when roasted separately in its own tin. You can also ask the butcher to open up the pork for you, so that you have a fairly level oblong of meat to stuff and roll up, but otherwise I've tried to show how you can do it yourself.

I like using smoked bacon to wrap round the stuffed joint, but whether the bacon's smoked or not is a matter of taste: what is essential is that it's streaky but fairly generously sliced; if the bacon rashers are too thin, they will burn before the pork's cooked.

Unlike the goose that is stuffed with fresh cranberries, the spicy filling that swirls its way through the pale pork meat here is studded with dried cranberries. Mixed with the sweet, tart berries, the garlic, cloves and cinnamon make this like a Christmas porchetta, with the bacon and its fat keeping everything juicy; so often, a pork loin is indigestibly lean, but not this one, for just as the stuffing keeps it tender from the inside out, putting the meat in a marinade while the stuffing cooks and cools starts the tenderizing from the off.

Inspired by the notion of a seasonal porchetta, I like to expand on that theme, by making sweet, soft diced Italian roast potatoes instead of the old-fashioned English roasties. But neither would be wrong here.

Serves 8–10

3.8kg fillet end loin of pork, rind and bones
    removed and reserved, to give approx.
    2.2kg loin
450g streaky rindless bacon, plus extra for
    stuffing (see below)

string to wrap round the rolled loin

FOR THE MARINADE:
250ml olive oil
125ml white wine or vermouth
30ml Worcestershire sauce
1 teaspoon Maldon salt or $\frac{1}{2}$ teaspoon
    table salt

FOR THE STUFFING:
125g streaky rindless bacon
2 onions, peeled and quartered
4 cloves garlic, peeled
1 teaspoon ground ginger
1 teaspoon ground cinnamon
$\frac{1}{2}$ teaspoon ground cloves
handful of fresh parsley
3 x 15ml tablespoons olive oil
200g dried cranberries

MAKE AHEAD TIP:
Stuff and tie the loin up to 6 hours ahead. Keep
covered in the fridge. Allow 20 minutes at room
temperature before putting in the oven.

❋ If the butcher hasn't already opened up the loin for you, lay it out in front of you vertically, and then slice partway through the centre of the meat laterally to open it out like a book, but without cutting through the "spine" as it were.

❋ Bash the meat (you may want to cover it with clingfilm first) so that it is as flat and as evenly thick as possible. It should now resemble a rectangle in shape.

❋ Put all the marinade ingredients into a large freezer bag, with the opened, flattened loin. Leave the bag overnight in the fridge (in a lasagne-type dish) or just while you are making the stuffing and waiting for it to cool.

❋ Put the 125g bacon into a processor with the onions and garlic cloves. Add all the spices and parsley, then process until it is pretty well mush.

❋ Heat the oil in a wide, shallow pan and fry the spiced mush gently for about 10 minutes, then add the dried cranberries and cook for a further 5 minutes before taking off the heat.

❋ Let the stuffing cool completely before you stuff and roll your loin.

❋ Twenty minutes before you want to stuff the pork for roasting, take it out of the fridge and preheat the oven to 200°C/gas mark 6.

❋ Take the pork out of its bag and marinade, shaking off any excess liquid, and lay it flesh-side up (de-rinded side down) on some baking parchment or greaseproof paper, with the long side facing you, and the short sides at right angles to you.

❋ Spread the stuffing over the pork but leave a good 2.5cm border all the way around the edge. Then roll up the loin from the long side to make a long, fat, stuffing-filled sausage. I know it looks, in the pictures, as though I'm rolling from the short side but, believe me, I'm not.

❋ Wrap the 450g bacon rashers around the loin to cover the white fat on top.

❋ Cut off lengths of string and, starting from the middle, slide the string under the meat, then tie up the sausage with a tight knot on the top.

❋ Tie the loin at intervals of about 4cm so that the meat is secured all the way along. Tuck in any rogue bits of meat or stuffing that may poke out at either end.

✤ Arrange the bones in a roasting tin so they form a rack to hold the stuffed loin, then sit the loin on top of the bones. Place in the oven for 2¹/₄–2¹/₂ hours.

✤ Once you've put the loin into the oven, place the scored rind in a separate shallow roasting tin and sprinkle with salt. Cook alongside the pork on a separate shelf – it will only need about an hour, so your best bet is to put it in the oven halfway through the pork's cooking time.

✤ Insert a meat thermometer, if you have one (and it's advisable), into the pork, to make sure the meat is absolutely cooked all the way through. When the thermometer reads 75°C, the pork's ready. If the bacon has browned too much but the pork needs more cooking time, just cover it with foil and put it back in the oven for 10–15 minutes before checking again.

✤ Once the pork is cooked, let it rest out of the oven, but leave the crackling in, while you make your Rubied Gravy, opposite.

✤ When the gravy is done and you are ready to carve the pork, cut off the string ties and pull them away from the meat. Then cut the pork into thick slices, about 2.5cm, that way each slice gets a good ribboning of stuffing without falling to pieces.

✤ Serve the pork dribbled with the rubied gravy, and break up the crackling to serve alongside.

✤ Should you have any pork left over, know that it is heavenly cold, just as is, or stuffed into a sandwich; mayonnaise and cranberry sauce are both gratifying additions here.

RUBIED GRAVY

The cranberry sauce from a jar gives an added fresh tang to the dried cranberries of the stuffing. If you want to go fresher still, make a downsized version of my Redder Than Red Cranberry Sauce on p.119, using ruby port in place of the cherry brandy. You could, indeed, make the regular-sized cranberry sauce and not bother with this gravy; but I'd rather proceed as follows, and unashamedly dollop some cranberry sauce out of a jar to make it.

And this gravy really is rubied: it glints gorgeously like a strange, savoury coulis as it's dribbled over the pinkish swirled rounds of pale meat.

1 x 195g jar cranberry sauce

1 teaspoon Dijon mustard

1/2 teaspoon Worcestershire sauce

250ml chicken stock

60ml ruby port

❅ Place all the ingredients into a saucepan and bring to a boil, stirring a little to dissolve everything.

❅ Let the gravy bubble away for 5 minutes. When it's ready – it should look glossy but still quite runny – pour into a jug, and serve with the pork, above.

MAKE AHEAD TIP:
Make the rubied gravy up to 3 days ahead. Keep covered in the fridge.

ITALIAN ROAST POTATOES WITH GARLIC AND THYME

❅ Preheat the oven to 220°C/gas mark 7. Cut the unpeeled potatoes into 2.5cm cubes and put them into a large roasting tin, or divide them between 2 tins.

❅ Add the unpeeled garlic cloves and sprinkle the thyme and olive oil over. Move the potatoes around so that they get slick with oil, evenly covered in thyme and dispersed with the garlic cloves.

❅ Roast the potatoes in the oven for 1–1$^{1}/_{2}$ hours, depending if they are in one tin or two, or until golden; if they are crowded in one roasting tin they will take longer to crisp up than if they are spread well apart.

❅ When the potatoes come out of the oven, turn them out onto a warmed platter to serve with the pork, sprinkling first with a little salt and a light scattering of fresh parsley.

Serves 8–10

1.5kg (about 8 medium) waxy potatoes

cloves from 1 head of garlic (unpeeled)

2$^{1}/_{2}$ teaspoons dried thyme

125ml olive oil

Maldon salt or table salt to taste

1–2 tablespoons chopped parsley

PANETTONE PUDDING

Serves 8–10

750g panettone

1 x 375ml bottle dessert wine, such as
    Beaumes de Venise or other reliable mus-
    cat

8 eggs

100g caster sugar

500ml full-fat milk

2 teaspoons vanilla extract

2 teaspoons icing sugar

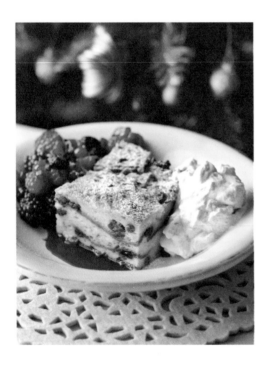

MAKE AHEAD TIP:
Assemble the panettone the day before. Cover and
keep chilled. Let the panettone stand out of the
fridge for 15 minutes before going in the oven as
directed.

I wanted to offer another suitable seasonal alternative to steamed Christmas pudding and since panettone is the sweet, fruited bread of Christmas in Italy, this pudding seemed perfect. It's not quite a panettone version of traditional bread and butter pudding. I wanted something with a little less of the nursery, and more elegantly, but not fussily, partified. This is it: the slices of fruit-studded, warm-spiced bread are baked in a custard made aromatic with muscat, without even a drop of cream to sully its winey clarity. Instead, you can serve some whipped cream (with or without a little Cointreau, Grand Marnier or Triple sec whisked in), or some vanilla ice cream if you prefer, on the side; and maybe a plate of frozen summer fruits, thawed – with all the vile mushy strawberries removed and a sprinkling of pomegranate seeds in their place – gently stirring in the zest of a clementine/satsuma, so that the orange-oil permeates this **Festive Fruit Salad**, and dusting with a little icing sugar or dousing with a small slug of Cointreau (or alternative) as you take it to the table with the pudding.

❉ Preheat the oven to 160°C/gas mark 2/3.

❉ Slice the panettone and lay the slices in a large baking dish (about 41cm x 25cm, or 26cm square, and just over 5cm deep) that you are happy to bring to the table.

❉ Put the dessert wine into a saucepan and bring to an almost boil, but *do not let it boil*. Take off the heat.

❉ Whisk together the eggs and sugar, then whisk in the warm wine, followed by the milk.

❉ Add the vanilla, and pour the liquid through a sieve over the panettone slices. Let the dish stand for 15 minutes before it goes into the oven.

❉ Bake for 50–60 minutes until the top is golden and the underneath soft but not wet.

❉ Let it cool down until warm, about 20 minutes, though longer would be fine, and then thickly dust the top of the pudding with the icing sugar pushed through a small sieve, before bringing to the table. The glorious puffiness of the pudding will subside once it's out of the oven, so don't worry about that. You can, indeed, make a virtue out of its fall from grace and even bake it in the oven before the pork goes in, so that by the time you serve it, the pudding will be set firm, and you can cut it into squares with neat ease.

YOU SHALL GO TO THE BALL:
THE VEGETARIAN OPTION TAKES CENTRE STAGE

CHILLI-CHEESE CROSTINI (P.17)
SEASONALLY SPICED NUTS (P.21)
ROAST STUFFED PUMPKIN WITH GINGERY TOMATO SAUCE
RED CABBAGE WITH POMEGRANATE JUICE (P.60)
CHRISTMAS SALAD (P.56)
AUSTRALIAN CHRISTMAS PUDDING WITH HOT CHOCOLATE-CHESTNUT SAUCE

ROAST STUFFED PUMPKIN WITH GINGERY TOMATO SAUCE

There is something so magnificent about a whole pumpkin stuffed with jewelled rice, that it doesn't really need too many side dishes to detract: its starchy interior means you can forgo potatoes or the orzotto; and the vibrant sauce precludes the need for a pile-up of condiments. Still, for once I think a couple of nibbly things on the table to start would balance this well, and you could add a sense of munificence and plenty – always important at this time of year – by having either the red cabbage with the pumpkin, or the pomegranate-scattered Christmas Salad (see p.56) after, or both. Indeed, why cut back? At Christmas there must be room, even before the richness of the Australian Christmas Pudding and its thick chocolate-chestnut sauce.

Obviously all pumpkins come in different sizes, and if yours is radically smaller (unlikely, I'd think, to be much bigger and still edible), here is an easy way to work out how much rice you need to stuff it: once you've sliced a "lid" off the top of your pumpkin and taken all the seeds out, put a freezer bag in the hollowed-out cavity. Now fill it with enough rice to come halfway up the cavity. Tip the rice into a measuring jug to see how much you've got, and simply use double the amount of stock to rice. If you're boosting rice quantities, augment the other ingredients accordingly.

You are slightly taking pot luck with pumpkin – it's very difficult to tell before you eat one whether the flesh is succulent and sweet or tasteless and grainy – but you should certainly avoid all Hallowe'en pumpkins, and try to buy from a trustworthy greengrocer who takes pride in his, or her, produce.

Serves 8–12

1 x 3–3.5kg preferably French pumpkin, unprepared weight

1 onion, finely chopped

1 x 15ml tablespoon vegetable oil or olive oil

3 cloves garlic, 2 minced plus 1 left whole

150g dried cranberries

1 teaspoon ground ginger

1 teaspoon ground allspice

good pinch of saffron strands

zest of 1 clementine/satsuma

approx. 400g basmati rice (but see intro left)

approx. 1 litre hot vegetable stock

salt and pepper to taste

❋ Preheat the oven to 200°C/gas mark 6. Slice a lid off the top of the pumpkin, and remove the seeds and fibrous flesh from the inside, keeping the top to put back on later.

❋ In a large saucepan (with lid), fry the onion gently in the oil until softened, then add the 2 minced garlic cloves, the cranberries, spices and clementine/satsuma zest. Stir in the rice, turning till it becomes glossy in the pan.

❋ Pour in the stock and let the pan come to the boil, then clamp on the lid and turn the heat down to the lowest it will possibly go. Cook for 15 minutes.

❋ Cut the remaining clove of garlic in half and rub the inside of the pumpkin with the cut side of each half, then, using your fingers, smear some salt over the flesh inside as well.

❋ The rice stuffing will be quite damp and not very fluffy at this stage, but check it for seasoning – adding more spice, salt or pepper if wanted – and then spoon it into the garlic- and salt-rubbed pumpkin cavity and tamp down well. Press the pumpkin lid back on top and squeeze it down as firmly as you can (it will sit up a bit proud of the top).

❋ Stand the pumpkin on a double layer of foil, wrapping the foil 4cm up around the sides and scrunching it there, to keep the pumpkin out of direct contact with the water later.

❋ Place the stuffed, partially wrapped pumpkin in a roasting tin and pour in freshly boiled water to a depth of 2cm. Cook the pumpkin for about 2 hours by which time it should be tender when pierced.

❋ Meanwhile, get on with the Gingery Tomato Sauce, overleaf.

❋ Take the pumpkin out of the roasting tin and let it sit for about 10 minutes before you slice it into segments like a cake.

GINGERY TOMATO SAUCE

1 onion, peeled and halved

2 cloves garlic, peeled

1 teaspoon dried ginger

3cm length fresh ginger, peeled

15g butter

1 x 15ml tablespoon olive oil

1 x 700g (700ml) bottle tomato passata

500ml water

1 teaspoon caster sugar

salt and pepper to taste

❊ Put the onion, garlic, dried ginger and fresh ginger into a processor and blitz to a pulp.

❊ Heat the butter and oil in a deep, wide pan, then add the onion–garlic mixture. Cook over a low heat for about 10 minutes, stirring occasionally so that it doesn't burn.

❊ Add the passata and water to the pan, and season with the sugar, salt and pepper.

❊ Cook for 15 minutes, at a gentle simmer, then taste for seasoning before decanting into a warmed jug or gravy boat and taking to the table, for people to pour over their slices of stuffed pumpkin.

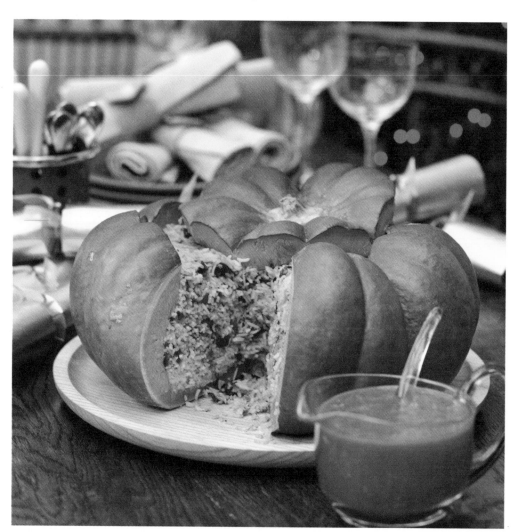

MAKE AHEAD TIP:
Make the sauce up to 3 days ahead and keep chilled in the fridge. Reheat gently before serving.

FREEZE AHEAD TIP:
Make and freeze the sauce for up to 1 month. Thaw overnight at room temperature and reheat as above.

AUSTRALIAN CHRISTMAS PUDDING WITH HOT CHOCOLATE-CHESTNUT SAUCE

My great aunt used to make something called Australian Christmas pudding, which was, in effect, all the ingredients from a Christmas pudding stirred into vanilla ice cream and set in a pudding basin. It was rather curious, but I have fiddled with it to turn it into something I love. First step: remove the candied peel; for me this is crucial. And I've reduced the bits and pieces, using only a mixed bag of dried fruit (without the peel), but otherwise go for currants, raisins and chopped glacé cherries. Importantly, for the look and taste, after soaking the fruit in rum, I fold it into chocolate ice cream rather than vanilla. Thus it looks like Christmas pudding – and it tastes divine, even before it's been swathed in the thick, rich, hot chocolate-chestnut sauce.

❄ Put the dried fruit and rum into a saucepan and bring to the boil. Turn down the heat and gently simmer for 5 minutes, then take off the heat and allow to cool. Or just pour cold rum over the fruit and leave to steep overnight.

❄ Add the slightly softened, but not runny, ice cream and mix to combine and spoon into your plastic pudding basin, cover with the lid and freeze.

❄ When it's almost time to eat, take it out of the freezer and let it stand for 20 minutes or so, to help unmoulding, then unmould and, if desired, put a sprig of holly on top or scatter flaked or chopped chocolate over on serving.

Serves up to 12

375g luxury mixed dried fruit

175ml dark rum

2 x 500g tubs chocolate ice cream

1.7 litre/3 pint plastic pudding basin with lid

FREEZE AHEAD TIP:
Make pudding and freeze for up to 1 month. Thaw and serve as recipe.

HOT CHOCOLATE-CHESTNUT SAUCE

This chocolate-chestnut sauce is so divinely rich, I think – unless it's Christmas Day – you don't need more than a tub of good vanilla ice cream to serve with it, which also makes this a fabulous seasonal standby.

❄ Spoon the chestnut purée into a heavy-based pan, tip in the chopped chocolate chips or buttons and pour in the cream and heat gently to melt together.

❄ Take off the heat, stir in the rum, then take to the table, and let people pour it generously over their pudding. You may have some left over. Don't complain.

250g sweetened chestnut purée

125g dark chocolate, chopped into chips (or use little cooking buttons)

250ml double cream

2 x 15ml tablespoons dark rum

MAKE AHEAD TIP:
Make the sauce up to 1 week ahead and keep, covered, in the fridge. Reheat gently to serve.

FREEZE AHEAD TIP:
Make and freeze the sauce for up to 3 months. Thaw overnight in the fridge and reheat as above.

JOY TO THE WORLD
CHRISTMAS BAKING AND SWEET TREATS

I AM NOT, I ASSURE YOU, any kind of self-proclaimed Domestic Goddess. True, I conjured her up, but when I did so, it was with gentle irony. It seems cruel to say that she doesn't really exist, and I don't wish to disown her; indeed, I still believe there are times when we need to feel like her. And Christmas, more than any other, is one of those times. In fact, the title of this chapter might easily be "The Return of the Domestic Goddess: This Time It's Personal".

But I stick to "Joy to the World", which is what the mythical Domestic Goddess wants to bring, and which we could all hope for at this time of year. Baking a Christmas cake or a batch of mince pies, mixing up muffins or a meltingly mouthwatering chocolate cake may not carry any moral weight, and it's not going to win you the Nobel Prize, but it makes you, and those around you, feel blissfully immersed in the sort of Christmas we'd like to believe in, all log fires, hushed snowfall and harmony.

Yet, if the picture-perfect Christmas is a dream, or an illusion, baking brings an irrefutable sense of satisfaction, and helps to bridge the wistful gap between fantasy and reality. The edible tree decorations you bake and ice and hang from the tree, the richly fruited pudding you stir up, or the dark, dense sticky gingerbread you give to friends who drop in for tea – these are all real components of that Christmas we want to feel exists beyond the mania which threatens to envelop us at this time of year. I don't promise you can cook yourself calm, but I believe it makes sense to snatch moments when you can quietly busy yourself in the kitchen – frankly doing nothing much more effortful than stirring – and give yourself up to the encompassing warmth that comes from a sense of purpose, the benediction of productivity.

If this book celebrates anything, it is the central, perhaps quintessential, feast of Christmas: it is the time when overindulgence is not just encouraged, it is pretty well ordained. But it also needs to be relished. So don't quibble over cake now: consider, deeply, pie crammed with nuts and gooey with eggy, amber caramel; all that is richly fruited, warmly spiced, luscious with chocolate beckons. Let the scent of Christmas baking fill the air and bring joy, if not to the whole world, then to your world. For Christmas, like charity, begins at home.

TRADITIONAL CHRISTMAS CAKE

Grateful though I am to Hazel Hook for giving me her foundation-stone recipe for a traditional Christmas cake, with its all-important table for weights, measures and tin sizes, so many Christmasses ago, I have departed somewhat from her strictures. To be honest, I don't always get it together to make a traditional Christmas cake (which needs a bit of time to stand and mellow to be as good as it can be) so I tend to rustle up either the Incredibly Easy Chocolate or Gorgeously Golden Fruit Cake (or both) at the last minute. But a traditionally iced and comfortingly decorative Christmas cake is a lovely thing, and if efficiency allows, should be embraced. This version builds on the Time-Honoured Christmas Cake of earlier books, but cuts down on varieties of dried fruits, augments alcohol (bourbon for preference, but brandy or sherry will also do), and adds ground almonds and chopped pecans. It bakes well, and can be iced beautifully, and is a satisfying way to get Christmas really going in the kitchen.

raisins	350g	700g	1kg
currants	150g	300g	500g
glacé cherries	50g	100g	150g
chopped pecans (or walnuts)	75g	150g	225g
bourbon (or brandy)	200ml	400ml	600ml
butter	150g	300g	450g
dark brown sugar	90g	180g	275g
lemon zest, grated	1 teaspoon	2 teaspoons	3 teaspoons
large eggs	2	4	6
black treacle or molasses	1 tablespoon	2 tablespoons	3 tablespoons
almond essence	$1/2$ teaspoon	1 teaspoon	$1^1/2$ teaspoons
plain flour	150g	300g	450g
ground almonds	75g	150g	225g
ground cloves	$1/4$ teaspoon	$1/2$ teaspoon	$3/4$ teaspoon
ground cinnamon	$1/2$ teaspoon	1 teaspoon	$1^1/2$ teaspoons
ground ginger	$1/4$ teaspoon	$1/2$ teaspoon	$3/4$ teaspoon
tin: round	18cm	23cm	25.5cm
or square	15cm	20cm	23cm
temperature	150°C/gas mark 2	150°C/gas mark 2	150°C/gas mark 2, reduce to 140°C/gas mark 1 after 1 hour
cooking time	$1^3/4$ – $2^1/4$ hours	$2^3/4$ – $3^1/4$ hours	$3^3/4$ – $4^1/4$ hours
yield	approx. 12 slices	approx. 16 slices	approx. 20 slices

✻ Place all the dried fruit in a saucepan, and add the bourbon or brandy. Bring to the boil, then take it off the heat, covering once cooled, and let it steep overnight, covered. And make sure you take your eggs and butter out of the fridge so that they will be at room temperature for the making of the cake tomorrow.

✻ The next day, preheat your oven to 150°C/gas mark 2, and prepare your tin, see right.

✻ Cream the butter and sugar together, then beat in the grated lemon zest.

✻ Add the eggs one at a time, beating well after each addition, then beat in the black treacle and almond extract.

✻ Sift the dry ingredients together, then mix the soaked fruit alternately with the dry ingredients into the creamed mixture, combining thoroughly. Fold in the chopped pecans.

✻ Put the cake mix into the prepared tin and bake in the oven, following the table opposite, or until a cake-tester or skewer inserted into the cake comes out cleanish.

✻ When the cake is cooked, brush with a couple of extra tablespoons of bourbon or brandy or other liqueur of your choice. Wrap immediately in its tin – using a double-thickness of tin foil – as this will trap the heat and form steam, which in turn will keep the cake soft on top.

✻ When it's completely cold, remove the cake from the tin and rewrap in foil, storing, preferably in an airtight tin or Tupperware, for at least 3 weeks to improve the flavour. And see the Make Ahead tip, too.

✻ To prepare your tin, line the sides and bottom of a deep, round, loose-bottomed cake tin with a double layer of greaseproof paper or baking parchment. The paper should come up a good 10cm higher than the sides of the tin; think of a lining that's about twice as deep as the tin. Cut out 2 circles of paper, and 2 very long rectangles that will fit along the sides of the tin and rise up above it like a top hat. Before you put the 2 rectangular pieces in the tin, fold one long side of each piece in towards the centre by about 2cm, as if turning up a hem, then take some scissors and snip into this hem, at approx. 2cm intervals, as if making a rough frill.

✻ Grease the tin, lay one paper circle on the bottom and get one of your long pieces and fit it down one side, with the frilly edge along the bottom, then press down that edge so it sits flat on the circle and holds it in place. Press the paper well into the sides, and repeat with the second rectangular piece. Now place the second circle on top of the 2 pressed-down frilly edges, to help hold the pieces around the edge in place.

✻ If you're making a big cake, it's worth wrapping the outside of the tin with a double layer of brown paper (also coming up about 10cm above the rim of the tin) but I don't bother if I'm making a normal-sized one (20cm–23cm).

MAKE AHEAD TIP:
Make the cake up to 6 weeks ahead and wrap in a double layer of greaseproof paper and then a double layer of foil. Store in an airtight container in a cool, dry place. (You could add a bit more bourbon or brandy over this storage time to feed the cake and keep moist.)

FREEZE AHEAD TIP:
Make the cake and wrap as above. Freeze for up to 1 year. To thaw, unwrap the cake and thaw overnight at room temperature. Rewrap and store as above until needed.

CHRISTMAS CAKE ICING AND TOPPINGS

There are a number of ways you can tackle the icing, and I will start with the more traditional; it seems fitting here. Some of the cakes below carry with them their own suggestions for decorating, but any of the methods here can be used for the first 3 cakes.

I love a plain white-iced cake: smooth icing, wrapping the cake almost like a hatbox. I am happy to have this decorated, but I'd just as soon the decorations were also white. I cut out bits of leftover rolled-out icing, using my snowflake or star cookie cutter, and perhaps throw a few silver baubles around, too. But play as you wish: red and green roll-out icing can be used to exuberantly Christmassy effect and wherever you buy the blocks of readymade, ready-to-roll icing or coloured sugar paste (see Stockists p.267) you should be able to get a holly leaf cutter, and it's not difficult to roll little bits into berries. If you are more dextrous than I am (not hard), you can be more adventurous. I long to bake a square cake and ice it like a present, but simple though I'm told this is, I know it's beyond me.

However, I have tried to get a bit artistic and have used white icing, cutting out a wibbly-wobbly hillscape and some trees and a star with my cookie cutters. The partially iced cake doesn't last as well as a fully covered one, but has a dramatic prettiness, if such is not a contradiction in terms.

If you want icing that gives the traditional snowy effect, I can also accommodate you. You still have to roll out the marzipan – and for what it's worth, I like yellow marzipan under the smooth icing, and white marzipan here – but the icing just needs to be whipped up, slapped on with a spatula and forked around to create the spikey effect that we all accept as snowy. This is the icing to go for if you have Christmas ornaments – a dinky sleigh, fir trees and reindeer, a red-breasted robin, or the whole, thronging nativity scene – stashed away in a cupboard or in the loft, ready to be brought out each year and put lovingly on top.

Finally, I am very fond of a topping more than an icing, and one that is not particularly British, but is the traditional way of decorating fruit cakes in Italy and America: and this is just a glaze-slicked mounding of nuts and candied fruits (and see p.177). Because the fruit is so sticky, it's not enormously less fiddly than the icing in the first two methods – and is more expensive – but it requires less dexterity and patience, and still looks beautiful. (It won't, however, keep the cake from drying out, as the layers of marzipan and sugar-icing do.) And a cake that has only a topping can look "finished" by having a ribbon tied or pinned around it. Understatement is not the order of the day at this time of the year, after all.

I don't think I ever make my Traditional Christmas cake bigger than 18cm in diameter, as a little goes a long way, and you really don't want it sitting on a table gathering dust in January. However, the amounts of ingredients for the icings below should be enough to stretch to a 23cm cake. If you're going big-time with a 25.5cm cake or more, then add half again to the ingredients.

MAKE AHEAD TIP:
The marzipan should have about 1 week to dry out before the icing goes on, otherwise the oils from the fruit cake gradually seep out and stain the icing. It's fine to marzipan and ice together if you're doing it one or two days before eating, but if you want to prepare the cake in the weeks running up to Christmas, the marzipan needs to be done first and dried out.

OPPOSITE:
Variations on Smooth Hatbox Icing (top left, top right and bottom right)
Snowscene Icing (bottom left)

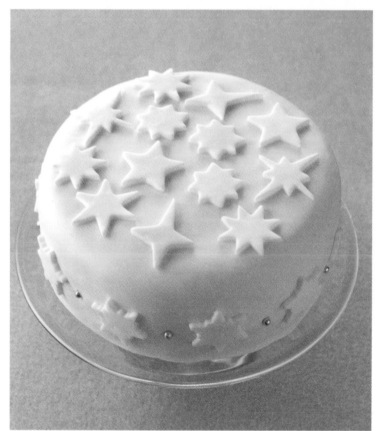

SNOWSCENE ICING

200g rindless marmalade or smooth apricot
   jam
500g marzipan
1 x 500g packet instant royal icing (see
   Stockists p.267)
icing sugar for dusting

❋ Follow the method for Smooth Hatbox Icing below only up to the point where the cake is covered with a neat layer of marzipan.

❋ Then make up the instant royal icing with cold water, as directed on the packet, and whisk until it is thick and gleamingly bulked up, so that it holds its shape if you try to make a peak with a teaspoon. Pile the icing over the cake with a spatula, to cover it completely, before forking to leave a rough snowy cover.

❋ Adorn with your treasured Christmas-cake decorations and leave to dry and set.

SMOOTH HATBOX ICING

200g rindless marmalade, or smooth apricot
   jam
500g marzipan
1kg ready-to-roll icing (more if you want
   different colourways)
icing sugar for dusting

❋ Warm the marmalade in a small saucepan over a low to medium heat. (If you are not using a rindless marmalade or smooth apricot jam, when it's hot and runny, strain into a bowl to remove rind or pips.)

❋ Place the cake on a cake board or cake stand and, with a pastry brush, paint the warm marmalade or jam all over the sides and the top of the cake to make a tacky surface.

❋ Dust a work surface with icing sugar, roll out the marzipan till it's about 2.5mm thick (don't be fanatical; you just want a supple and pliable layer) and drape over the cake. Then press the marzipan cloak against the cake so it covers it smoothly and cut off the excess with a sharp knife. If you find it easier to roll out two lots of 250g marzipan, that's fine, but be sure to smooth over any joins, so the icing will lie smoothly on top.

❋ Dust the work surface again with icing sugar and plonk down your block of icing. Beat it a few times with the rolling pin, then dust the top with icing sugar and roll out patiently until it's about 3mm thick.

❋ Cover the cake with it, cutting off the excess. If you need to stick bits together to patch up any breaks, sprinkle with cold water first; the water fuses breaks magically together.

❋ Cut out the shapes you want – stars, snowflakes, holly trees or ivy leaves – from leftover bits of icing and dibble or brush the undersides with cold water to stick them on to the cake.

GLOSSY FRUIT AND NUT TOPPING

I tend to order my glacé fruits online from France (see Stockists p.267) but around Christmastime, you tend to find them easily enough in the shops. The range is enormous, and it's up to you to decide how broad to make your choice.

8 teaspoons smooth apricot jam

175g assorted glacé fruits, about 3 whole fruits plus small handful glacé cherries

25g blanched almonds, whole

25g pecan halves

❄ Spoon the apricot jam into a little saucepan, add a tablespoon of water, heat gently, stirring to make a molten glaze, then take off the heat to cool it a little.

❄ Paint the top of the cake with the apricot glaze, and decorate with the fruits and nuts of your choice – I find it easier to cut the fruits into pieces and fit everything together like a jigsaw puzzle.

❄ When the top is completely covered in glacé fruits and nuts – although if you're going for a big cake, just pile the fruit and nuts in the centre, leaving a frame of plain cake all around – paint a second coat of apricot glaze over the top to give a glossy finish.

MAKE AHEAD TIP:
Decorate the cake with the fruit and nut topping up to 1 week ahead. Wrap a band of foil or ribbon around the cake to protect the sides. Store in an airtight container.

GORGEOUSLY GOLDEN FRUIT CAKE

Makes 10 fat slices

350g dried pears
250g dried apricots
250g golden sultanas (see Stockists p.267)
175g soft butter
200g sugar
125ml white rum
200g ginger jam or preserve (or use marmalade)
225g ground almonds
35g sesame seeds or mixture of sesame, sunflower and pumpkin seeds
seeds from 3 cardamom pods
1/4 teaspoon ground coriander
3 eggs

FOR THE TOPPING:
75g whole blanched almonds

GLUTEN-FREE CAKE

MAKE AHEAD TIP:
Make the cake up to 1 week ahead and wrap in a double layer of greaseproof paper and then a layer of foil. Store in an airtight container in a cool, dry place.

FREEZE AHEAD TIP:
Make the cake and wrap as above. Freeze for up to 1 month. To thaw, unwrap the cake and thaw overnight at room temperature. Rewrap and store as above until needed.

This is the fruity blonde sister to the brunette temptress overleaf. It delivers, as promised, a cake of apricot-pear-and-ginger goldenness and goodness, so squidgy and fresh-tasting, which comes perhaps not only from the amount of fruit in it, but also the lack of flour: this is a gluten-free treat for the greedy; fruit cake with the emphasis firmly on the first word.

The lack of flour makes for an exquisitely damp cake, but it does mean that unless you cut it into quite fat slices, it can break into fruity pieces rather than geometrically precise triangles. This is why it tastes so good of course. And, what's more, it makes a fantastic pudding at the end of a seasonal supper.

I do a Dundee cake-type studding of the top with blanched almonds before baking, so there is no need to ice it or adorn further.

❃ Roughly scissor the pears and apricots into small pieces and put them into a saucepan with the sultanas, butter, sugar, rum and ginger jam or preserve, or indeed marmalade.

❃ Simmer for 10 minutes and then leave to stand for about 30 minutes.

❃ Preheat the oven to 150°C/gas mark 2. Line the bottom and sides of a 20cm high-sided tin with a double layer of Bake-O-Glide or regular baking parchment; the lining should extend about 10cm above – and see the instructions for the Traditional Christmas Cake on p.172 if you want a more precise, step-by-step guide to the whole lining fandango.

❃ Stir the ground almonds, sesame seeds (or a mixture), cardamom seeds and coriander into the cooled saucepan. Beat in the eggs and spoon into the prepared cake tin, smoothing the top.

❃ Starting in the middle, work in concentric circles as you place the blanched almonds on top of the cake batter in decorative rings (rather like a Dundee cake).

❃ Bake for 1 hour 40 minutes, then leave to cool completely in the tin. Once cool, take out of the tin, wrap with baking parchment then foil, before stashing it away in its cake tin or other airtight container. Though, unlike a traditional fruit cake, it doesn't need to stand before being divinely edible.

INCREDIBLY EASY CHOCOLATE FRUIT CAKE

Makes at least 10 generous slices

350g prunes, scissored or chopped

250g raisins

175g currants

175g soft butter

175g dark muscovado sugar

225g (175ml) honey

125ml Tia Maria or other coffee liqueur

juice and finely grated zest of 2 oranges

1 teaspoon mixed spice

2 tablespoons cocoa powder

3 eggs, beaten

150g plain flour

75g ground almonds

1/2 teaspoon baking powder

1/2 teaspoon bicarbonate of soda

FOR DECORATION (see Stockists p.267):

25g dark chocolate-covered coffee beans

approx. 10 edible gold stars

edible gold mini balls

edible glitter, in Disco Hologram gold

MAKE AHEAD TIP:

Make the cake up to 2 weeks ahead and wrap in a double layer of greaseproof paper and then a layer of foil. Store in an airtight container in a cool, dry place. Decorate when needed.

FREEZE AHEAD TIP:

Make the cake and wrap as above. Freeze for up to 3 months. To thaw, unwrap the cake and thaw overnight at room temperature. Re-wrap and store as above until needed.

I think it's hard to improve on this cake: dark, damp, squidgy and luscious; you don't taste the chocolate full-on – the cocoa just leaves a hint of smokey richness. Nor, I should add, do you taste the prunes. When I was making this cake for my TV programme, the cameraman, Wee Nev (Neville Kidd, the eminent DOP, for all IMDb-addicts) said with force "Eugh, I HATE prunes!" But when he ate it, later, he proclaimed it to be the best Christmas cake he'd ever had. *And* he asked for the recipe so that he could ask his wife to make it for Christmas. I don't mean to crow; it sounds so undignified. But it's important that you know how universally seductive this cake is, for all that it starts off "350g prunes".

I don't know what it is in the prunes that gives the cake its damp bounciness; all I know is that it works. You don't need to make this in advance, although you can, and you don't have to do anything much to make it, either. You just melt everything together, give or take, in a saucepan, pour from saucepan to cake tin and bake. It needs no icing, though I have suggested – see p.267 if you need help with stockists – a little festive decoration, below.

And there's no reason why you couldn't vary this method to make a **Plain Dark Fruit Cake**: just replace the Tia Maria with rum (or brandy if you prefer), making up the sweetness by adding a heaped tablespoon of marmalade; take out the cocoa, adding 2 tablespoons of flour to the 150g; and decorate with a sprig of holly or any of the suggestions below.

❊ Preheat the oven to 150°C/gas mark 2 and prepare a 20cm x 9cm deep, round, loose-bottomed cake tin by lining the bottom and sides with a double layer of baking parchment, as for the Traditional Christmas Cake on p.172 (though I find that if you use one layer of that tough, reusable silicone baking parchment, my beloved Bake-O-Glide, it does the job well enough, and as the cake is so dark, you don't see if it catches a little).

❊ Put the fruits, butter, sugar, honey, Tia Maria, orange juice and zests, spice and cocoa powder into a large, wide saucepan and gently bring to the boil, stirring as the butter melts.

❊ Simmer the mixture for 10 minutes, then take off the heat and leave to stand for 30 minutes.

❊ When the 30 minutes are up – it will have cooled a little, but you can leave it for longer if you want – add the beaten eggs, flour, ground almonds, baking powder and bicarbonate of soda, and stir with a wooden spoon or spatula to combine.

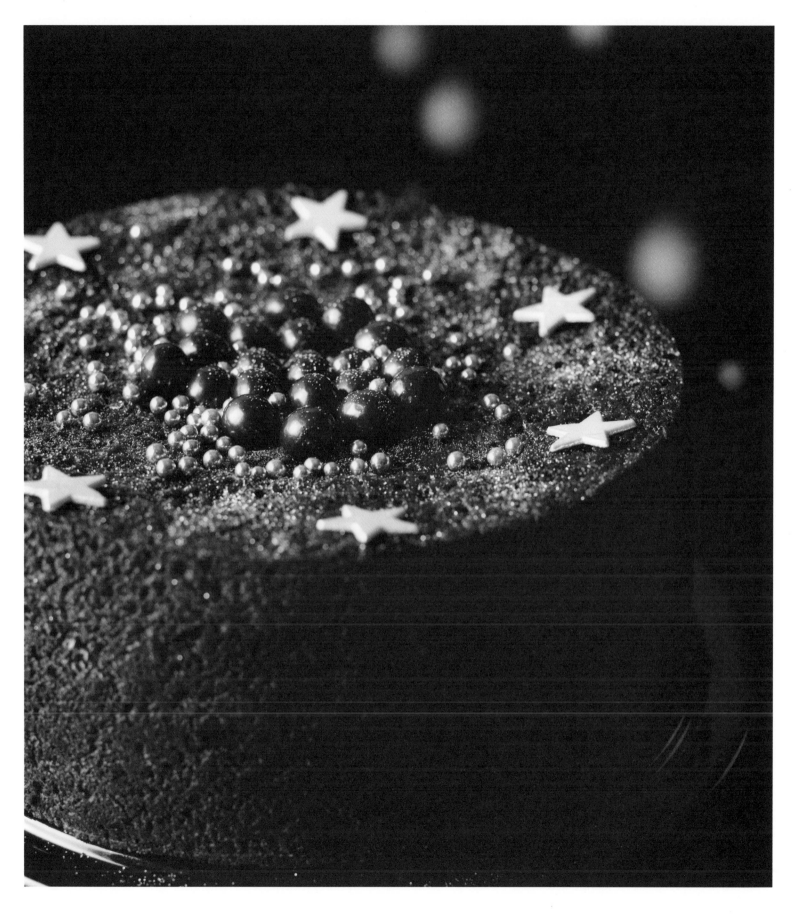

❄ Pour the fruit cake mixture into the prepared cake tin. Place in the oven and bake for 1³/4–2 hours, by which time the top of the cake should be firm but will have a shiny, sticky look. If you insert a cake tester or skewer into it, the cake will still be a little gooey in the middle.

❄ Put the cake, still in its tin, on a wire cooling rack – it will hold its heat and take a while to cool; once cool, take it out of the tin and, if you don't want to eat it immediately (like any fruit cake it has a long life), wrap it in baking parchment or greaseproof paper then in foil and store in a cake or other airtight tin.

❄ To decorate, though this is optional, place the chocolate-covered coffee beans in the centre of the cake and arrange the gold stars around the perimeter of the top. Then sprinkle some gold mini-balls over the whole cake, and the edible glitter over the top, not minding that you will be a-glitter yourself for a while.

CHRISTMAS-SPICED CHOCOLATE CAKE

There are few more popular ways to end a dinner party than with a fallen chocolate cake – the cakes are so called because they are compact and flourless and, when cooling out of the oven, their rich centres drop and dip a little. It is into this dip, not so dramatic as to be called a crater, that you drop or scatter the sticky nut topping.

I serve this with **Cointreau Cream**, made simply by whisking 250ml double cream until softly whipped, whisking in about 45ml of Cointreau (or Triple sec or Grand Marnier, of course) to taste at the end.

❋ Take anything you need out of the fridge to bring it to room temperature. The only truly important thing, however, is that the eggs aren't cold, so if they are, just put them into a bowl (I use the KitchenAid bowl I'm going to whisk them in later) and cover with warm water for 10 minutes.

❋ Preheat the oven to 180°C/gas mark 4. Butter the sides and line the bottom of a 23cm springform tin.

❋ Melt the chocolate and butter together in a heatproof bowl, in a microwave according to the manufacturer's instructions, or suspended over a pan of simmering water, and set aside to cool slightly.

❋ Beat the eggs, sugar and vanilla together until thick, pale and moussy. They should have at least doubled in volume, even tripled. If you're using a free-standing mixer, as I do, this is effortless.

❋ Gently fold in the ground almonds, cinnamon, cloves, clementine/satsuma zest and espresso powder, taking care not to lose the air you have whisked in, then, finally, pour and scrape in the melted, slightly cooled, chocolate and butter, folding gently again.

❋ Pour into the prepared tin and bake in the oven for 35–40 minutes, by which time the top of the cake should be firm, and the underneath still a bit gooey.

❋ Remove from the oven, and sit it on a wire rack, draped with a clean tea towel, to cool completely.

❋ To make the topping for the cake, put the clementine/satsuma juice into a small, preferably non-stick, frying pan with the butter, sugar and cinnamon and melt everything together, then let it sizzle for a minute or so and begin to caramelize before adding the almonds.

Makes 10–12 slices

FOR THE CAKE:
150g dark chocolate, chopped
150g soft butter
6 eggs
250g caster sugar
1 teaspoon vanilla extract
100g ground almonds
1 teaspoon ground cinnamon
pinch of ground cloves
zest of 1 clementine/satsuma
4 teaspoons instant espresso powder

FOR THE TOPPING:
juice of zested clementine/satsuma (above)
15g butter
1 x 15ml tablespoon caster sugar
1/4 teaspoon ground cinnamon
50g flaked almonds

GLUTEN-FREE CAKE

MAKE AHEAD TIP:
Make the chocolate cake up to 3 days ahead and store in an airtight container. Make the nut mixture and store, on baking parchment, in small airtight container or wrap in a loose "bag" of foil.

FREEZE AHEAD TIP:
Make and freeze the chocolate cake up to 1 month ahead. Thaw overnight in a cool room.

❈ Stir everything together, and occasionally tip the pan to keep it all moving; what you want is for all the liquid to disappear and the nuts to look shiny and be coated thinly in a fragrant, orange-scented toffee.

❈ Remove to a plate and cool.

❈ Unspring the cake and transfer to a cake stand or plate; I am brave enough to take it off its base sometimes, but don't if you're scared. Remember this cake, however intense and elegant within, has a rather ramshackle rustic appearance on the outside.

❈ Scatter with the almonds, mainly letting them pile up in the centre of the cake, but drop a few here and there all over the top, and serve with the Cointreau Cream (see p.183) if wished.

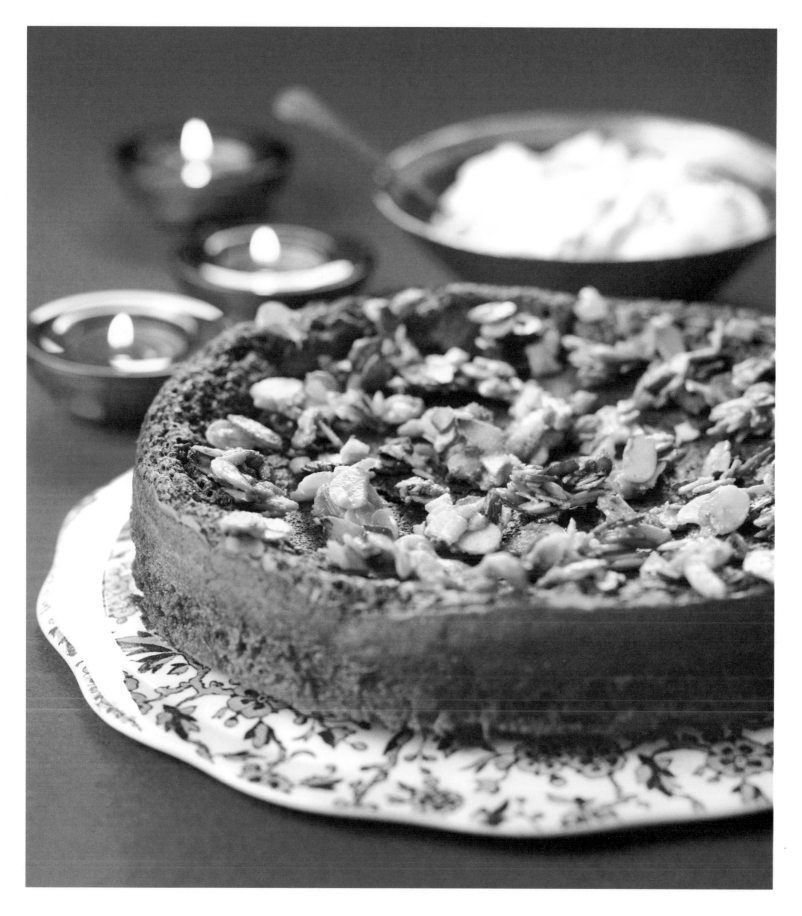

STAR-TOPPED MINCE PIES

Makes 36

240g plain flour
60g vegetable shortening, such as Trex
60g cold butter
juice of 1 orange
pinch of salt
approx. 350g mincemeat
icing sugar for dusting

MAKE AHEAD TIP:
Make the mince pies up to 1 week ahead and leave
to cool. Store in an airtight container layered up
between sheets of greaseproof paper. Pop into a
warm oven for 3–4 minutes before serving, dusted
with icing sugar.

FREEZE AHEAD TIP:
Make and pack the pies as above and freeze for up
to 3 months. Thaw overnight on a cooling rack and
reheat as above.

This is the way I make my mince pies, and there is no changing me or them: they are small, to be popped straight into the mouth in one go; the pastry is plain, the better to contrast with the rich, fruited filling; and they have not full casings but little stars as lids, which makes them look beautiful and taste flutteringly light.

By all means use good shop-bought mincemeat if you want, but I'm hoping you might give my new Cranberry-Studded Mincemeat a go (see p.189): it tastes both rich and boozy and fresh and fruity at the same time; and it makes for a slightly different mince pie, but in a welcome rather than challenging way.

With mince pies, I must have butter of some sort: I'll take brandy butter (my mother's), rum butter or a brown-sugar bourbon butter (see p.190 for butter recipes). Mince pies are to be savoured – not just as one of the last truly seasonal foods in England, but also as a home-grown culinary triumph, provoking one delighted Frenchman to exclaim in a letter, as quoted proudly by Agnes Jekyll in her *Kitchen Essays*: "ce que j'adore dans la cuisine anglaise ce sont vos petits mince-pi".

✽ Get out a tray of miniature tart tins, each indent 4.5cm in diameter, along with a 5.5cm fluted, round biscuit cutter and a 4cm star cutter.

✽ Measure the flour into a shallow bowl or dish and, with a teaspoon, dollop little mounds of vegetable shortening into the bowl, add the butter, diced small, shake to cover it, then put in the freezer for 20 minutes. This is what will make the pastry so tender and flaky later.

✽ Mix together the orange juice and salt in a separate, small bowl, cover and leave in the fridge to chill.

✽ After the 20 minutes, empty the flour and fat into the bowl of your **food processor** and blitz until you've got a pale pile of porridge-like crumbs. Pour the salted juice down the funnel, pulsing until it looks as if the dough is about to cohere; you want to stop just before it does (even if some orange juice is left). If all your juice is used up and you need more liquid, add some iced water.

✽ **If you prefer to use a freestanding mixer** to make the pastry, cut the fats into the flour with the flat paddle, leaving the bowl in the fridge to chill down for the 20-minute flour-and-fat-freezer session. Add liquid as above. I often find the pastry uses more liquid in the mixer than the processor.

✽ Turn the mixture out of the processor or mixing bowl onto a pastry board or work surface and, using your hands, combine to a dough. Then form into 3

discs (you'll need to make these in 3 batches, unless you've got enough tart tins to make all 36 pies at once).

❄ Wrap each disc in clingfilm and put in the fridge to rest for 20 minutes. Preheat the oven to 220°C/gas mark 7.

❄ Roll out the discs, one at a time, as thinly as you can without exaggerating; in other words, you want a light pastry case, but one sturdy enough to support the dense mincemeat. This is easy-going dough, so you don't have to pander to it: just get rolling and patch up as you need.

❄ Out of each rolled-out disc cut out circles a little wider than the indentations in the tart tins; I use a fluted cookie cutter for this. Press these circles gently into the moulds and dollop in a scant teaspoon of mincemeat.

❄ Then cut out your stars with your little star cutter – re-rolling the pastry as necessary – and place the tops lightly on the mincemeat.

❄ Put in the oven and bake for 10–15 minutes: keep an eye on them as they really don't take long and ovens do vary.

❄ Remove from the oven, prising out the little pies straight away and letting the empty tin cool down before you start putting in the pastry for the next batch. Carry on until they're all done.

❄ Dust over some icing sugar by pushing it through a tea strainer, and serve the pies with one of the butters on p.190.

ABOVE:

Cranberry-studded Mincemeat

CRANBERRY-STUDDED MINCEMEAT

I used to be old-school about mincemeat, preferring the sort that is really no more than dried fruits stirred up with some brandy, grated apple and suet and stuffed into a jar. It's certainly easy, since no cooking is involved, but Hettie (who's had more than a walk-on part in every one of my books since *How to Eat*), introduced me to the notion of a suet-free mincemeat, a recipe I used gratefully in *How to be a Domestic Goddess*, and which I've adapted here to make it garnet-glinting and tartly fruity with cranberries.

I know this doesn't make a huge amount, but it is enough to fill a good 50 of my little mince pies. It also happens to be the work – if you call tipping things into a pan and then scraping them out again, work – of moments, so if you need more (and it would be beautiful, in a jar, as a present), it's not going to take much out of you.

I love the louche, old-fashioned mixture of port and brandy (which used to be administered to children for tummy aches) but if you wish to be a little more austere, replace the ruby port with cranberry juice and add another 2 heaped teaspoons to the amount of brown sugar below.

❋ In a large saucepan, dissolve the sugar in the ruby port over a gentle heat.

❋ Add the cranberries to the saucepan.

❋ Then add the cinnamon, ginger and cloves, with the currants, raisins and dried cranberries and the zest and juice of the clementines.

❋ Simmer for 20 minutes or until everything looks pulpy and has absorbed most of the liquid in the pan. You may need to squish the cranberries a little with the back of a wooden spoon to incorporate them.

❋ Take off the heat and, when it has cooled a little, stir in the brandy, almond and vanilla extracts and honey and beat once more, vociferously, with your wooden spoon to encourage it to turn into a berry-beaded paste.

❋ Spoon the mincemeat into sterilized jars (see p.221).

Makes approx. 600ml – enough for 50 mince pies

60ml ruby port
75g soft dark brown sugar
300g cranberries
1 teaspoon ground cinnamon
1 teaspoon ground ginger
$1/2$ teaspoon ground cloves
75g currants
75g raisins
30g dried cranberries
finely grated zest and juice of
    1 clementine/satsuma
25ml brandy
$1/8$ teaspoon or a few drops almond extract
$1/2$ teaspoon vanilla extract
2 x 15ml tablespoons honey

If you want to revert to a more traditional, still suet-free, mincemeat, replace the fresh cranberries with a small grated cooking apple and take out the dried cranberries, adding 15g each of currants and raisins.

MAKE AHEAD TIP:
Make the mincemeat and spoon into sterilized jars. Seal with jam pot covers or a lid and store in a very cool, dry place for up to 1 month. (An extra splash of brandy on top at this stage helps prevent the mincemeat from going mouldy.)
Note: if using cranberry juice in place of port, store the mincemeat in the fridge for up to 10 days.

FREEZE AHEAD TIP:
Make the mincemeat and spoon into a freezer-proof container or sealable bags. Freeze for up to 3 months. Thaw overnight at room temperature and use immediately.

RUM AND BRANDY BUTTERS

Makes approx. 400ml

225g icing sugar
150g soft butter
50g ground almonds
3 x 15ml tablespoons good dark rum or best
    brandy, or to taste

MAKE AHEAD TIP:
Make the butter, cover tightly and keep in the fridge
for up to 2 weeks.

FREEZE AHEAD TIP:
Spoon the butter into a freezer-proof container or
wrap in foil and freeze for up to 3 months. Thaw
overnight in the fridge and use within 1 week.

I veer between using rum and brandy to flavour this butter, but it remains, essentially, my mother's version, which has – unusually, I've learnt – ground almonds in with the sugar, giving it a gorgeous, grainy, marzipanny richness.

❄ The easiest way to make this is with a processor. It means you don't need to sieve the sugar: simply put the icing sugar in the processor and process to get rid of lumps.

❄ Add the butter and process again to mix well, then scrape down the sides and add the ground almonds and process again.

❄ Now, with the motor running, gradually add the liquer down the funnel, tasting as you go. You may find one spoonful is all you want; you may find that the suggested 3 is far from enough.

BOURBON BUTTER

Makes 300ml

100g very soft butter
200g soft light brown sugar
2–3 x 15ml tablespoons bourbon, or to taste

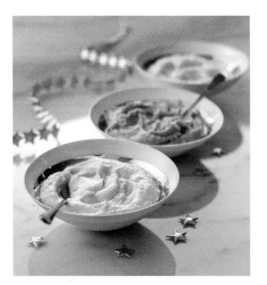

I don't think I've come out of my bourbon phase; it doesn't look as if I'm going to any time soon, either. Still, consider yourself the beneficiary: this is lush.

❄ Cream the butter and sugar either using an electric mixer, a processor or simply by hand. Don't worry if it looks grainy; the liquor will make it all cohere.

❄ Gradually add the bourbon, depending on how much of a hit you want this to have.

YULE LOG

A traditional French *bûche de Noël* always looks just the right side of cutely enchanting, and there is nothing hard to like about its tender, melting chocolatiness. But I warm to it most of all for the rich pagan symbolism: it is no less than a cake-emulation of the log that the Norsemen would drag home through the streets to burn in celebration of the winter solstice and to honour the gods and hope, thus, to cajole from them a good year to come. But always, too, it is about bringing fire and light to cold and darkness; this, too, is the gift of the winter kitchen.

I know the recipe looks finicky, and I can't promise it's a doddle, but it works easily and you will soon find you are rolling chocolate logs without a care. In fact, if you have a lot of people coming round, and you can find a serving dish or board long enough, it might be worth making 2 cakes and sitting them end to end, to look like a really long log. But even if you're making just one log, I advise at least a freestanding mixer or a hand-held electric whisk: I wouldn't contemplate this by hand.

Now, it doesn't look anything like a log when it is just a bald roulade, but once you've spread on the chocolate icing, made approximations of wood-markings on it (I use the sharp end of a corn-on-the-cob holder for this) and all, it does look quite impressive. I don't go as far as the French, and make sugar mushrooms to adorn it: this is not only because I lack the talent, but also because a light snowfall of icing sugar is all this yule log really needs to complete its wintry perfection.

❄ Preheat the oven to 180°C/gas mark 4.

❄ In a large, clean bowl whisk the egg whites until thick and peaking, then, still whisking, sprinkle in 50g of the caster sugar and continue whisking until the whites are holding their peaks but not dry.

❄ In another bowl, whisk the egg yolks and the remaining caster sugar until the mixture is moussy, pale and thick. Add the vanilla extract, sieve the cocoa powder over, then fold both in.

❄ Lighten the yolk mixture with a couple of dollops of the egg whites, folding them in robustly. Then add the remaining whites in thirds, folding them in carefully to avoid losing the air.

❄ Line a Swiss roll tin with baking parchment, leaving a generous overhang at the ends and sides, and folding the parchment into the corners to help the paper stay anchored.

Makes about 12 fat slices

FOR THE CAKE:
6 eggs, separated
150g caster sugar
50g cocoa powder
1 teaspoon vanilla extract
3–5 teaspoons icing sugar to decorate

FOR THE ICING:
175g dark chocolate, chopped
250g icing sugar
225g soft butter
1 x 15ml tablespoon vanilla extract

MAKE AHEAD TIP:
Make the Yule Log up to 1 week ahead and store in an airtight container in a very cool place.

FREEZE AHEAD TIP:
Make the Yule Log and freeze in a rigid container for up to 3 months. Thaw overnight in a cool room and store in an airtight container until needed.

❄ Pour in the cake mixture and bake in the oven for 20 minutes. Let the cake cool a little before turning it out onto another piece of baking parchment. If you dust this piece of parchment with a little icing sugar it may help with preventing stickage, but don't wory too much as any tears or dents will be covered by icing later. Cover loosely with a clean tea towel.

❄ To make the icing, melt the chocolate – either in a heatproof bowl suspended over a pan of simmering water or, my preference, in a microwave following the manufacturer's guidelines – and let it cool.

❄ Put the icing sugar into a processor and blitz to remove lumps, add the butter and process until smooth. Add the cooled, melted chocolate and the tablespoon of vanilla extract and pulse again to make a smooth icing. You can do this by hand, but it does mean you will have to sieve the sugar before creaming it with the butter and stirring in the chocolate and vanilla.

❄ Sit the flat chocolate cake on a large piece of baking parchment. Trim the edges of the Swiss roll. Spread some of the icing thinly over the sponge, going right out to the edges. Start rolling from the long side facing you, taking care to get a tight roll from the beginning, and roll up to the other side. Pressing against the parchment, rather than the tender cake, makes this easier.

❄ Cut one or both ends slightly at a gentle angle, reserving the remnants, and place the Swiss roll on a board or long dish. The remnants, along with the trimmed-off bits earlier, are to make a branch or two; you get the effect by placing a piece of cake at an angle to look like a branch coming off the big log.

❄ Spread the yule log with the remaining icing, covering the cut-off ends as well as any branches. Create a wood-like texture by marking along the length of the log with a skewer or somesuch, remembering to do wibbly circles, as in tree rings, on each end.

❄ You don't have to dust with icing sugar, but I love the freshly fallen snow effect, so push quite a bit through a small sieve, letting some settle in heaps on the plate or board on which the log sits.

EDIBLE CHRISTMAS TREE DECORATIONS

Makes approx. 35–40

FOR THE BISCUITS:

300g plain flour, plus more for dusting
pinch of salt
1 teaspoon baking powder
1 teaspoon ground cinnamon
1/4 teaspoon ground cloves
1–2 teaspoons freshly ground black pepper
100g soft butter
100g soft dark sugar
2 large eggs, beaten with 4 x 15ml tablespoons runny honey

**FOR THE ICING AND TRIMMINGS (see
 Stockists p.267):**

300g instant royal icing, from a packet
edible gold or silver balls or sprinkles
florists' ribbon for hanging

MAKE AHEAD TIP:
Make the biscuits up to 1 week ahead and store in
an airtight container. Ice the biscuits the day before
needed to allow them plenty of time to set.

FREEZE AHEAD TIP:
The raw cookie dough can be made and frozen for
up to 1 month. Thaw in the fridge overnight.
The cooked biscuits can be made and frozen in
sealable bags for up to 6 months.

I couldn't have Christmas without these, or at least, not happily. Rituals are essential to give us meaning, a sense of ceremony, and making these peppery, gingerbready edible decorations is how I have always marked with my children that Christmas has begun.

❉ Combine the flour, salt, baking powder, cinnamon, cloves and pepper in a food processor and, with the motor on, add the butter and sugar, then, slowly, the beaten eggs and honey, though don't use all of this liquid if the pastry has come together before it's used up.

❉ Form 2 fat discs and put one, covered in clingfilm or in a freezer bag, in the fridge while you get started on the other.

❉ Preheat the oven to 170°C/gas mark 3 and line 2 baking sheets with parchment.

❉ Then dust a work surface with flour, roll out the disc, also floured, to about 5mm and cut out your Christmas decorations with cutters of your choice, which could include fir-tree shapes, angels, stars, snowflakes, and so on.

❉ Re-roll and cut out some more, setting aside the residue from this first disc, well covered, while you get on with rolling out the second. When you've got both sets of leftover clumps of dough, roll out and cut out again, and keep doing so till all the dough's used up.

❉ Now take a small icing nozzle and use the pointy end to cut out a hole just below the top of each biscuit (through which ribbon can later be threaded).

❉ Arrange the pastry shapes on the lined baking sheets and cook for about 20 minutes: it's hard to see when they're cooked, but you can feel; if the underside is no longer doughy, they're ready. Transfer to a wire rack and leave to cool.

❉ Make up the instant royal icing, beating it until it's thick enough to be able to cover the biscuits with a just-dripping blanket of white; but don't beat it for as long as the packet says or you'll have icing so thick it will need to be spread with a spatula and you won't get such a neat outline.

❉ Carefully ice the cold decorations, using a teaspoon (the tip for dripping, the back for smoothing), and scatter sparkles or sprinkles as you like. When the icing is set, thread ribbon through the holes and hang on your tree.

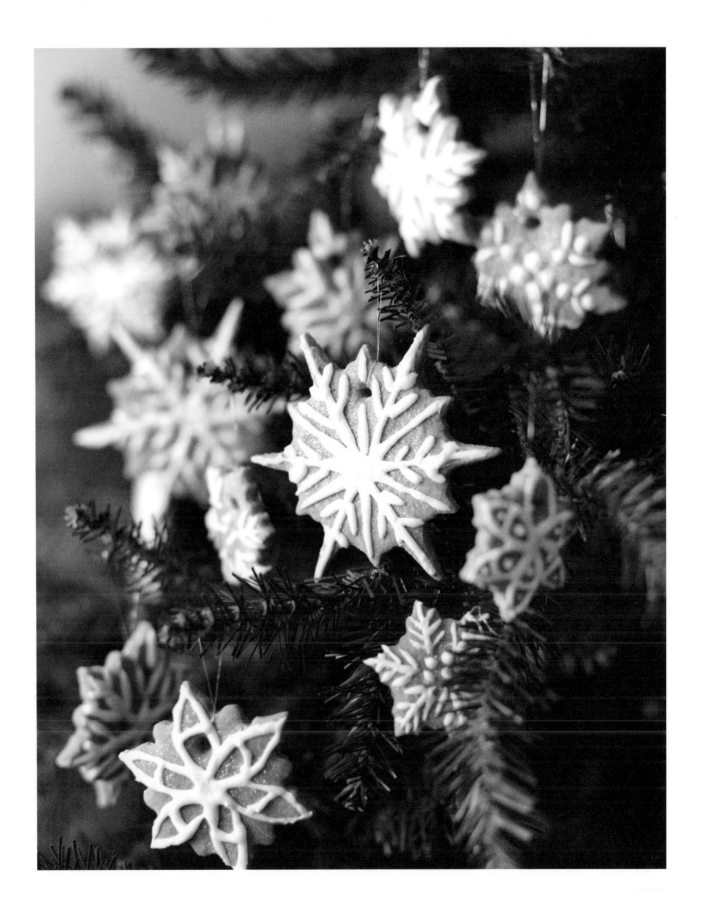

PANFORTE

I spent enough of my life in Italy when I was young to feel almost as strongly attached to Italian culinary traditions as I do to my own, home-grown ones. I couldn't have Christmas without a panettone in the house, though I am happy to buy one. Panforte, that other seasonal sweetmeat, is another matter: it's easy to produce, and I love the nougat-chewiness of a homemade version; it tastes rather like a clove-flavoured Curly Wurly. Or at least my take on it does – not strictly authentic but recognizably panforte even to Italians.

The original uses candied citron and orange peels; I found some Seggiano chocolate-covered clementines in a cupboard and, snipped up with scissors, they are extravagantly perfect in the already cocoa-darkened panforte. See Stockists p.267 or use peel; a little crystallized ginger along with the candied peel would work well here, too.

What you're making is not exactly a cake, although it's baked in a cake tin, but rather a fruit and nut compacted dark nougat patty. It is wonderful with coffee and with sharp white cheese.

❄ Preheat your oven to 170°C/gas mark 3. Line the bottom and sides of a single sandwich tin (20cm) with Bake-O-Glide or baking parchment.

❄ Mix together the nuts, dried fruits and snipped-up chocolate-covered candied clementines (or peel) in a heatproof bowl.

❄ Add the cloves, cinnamon, nutmeg, flour, white pepper and cocoa powder.

❄ Put the sugar, honey and butter into a saucepan and melt together gently.

❄ Take off the heat and pour into the dry ingredients in the heatproof bowl. Stir slowly and patiently to mix everything together well.

❄ Tip into the sandwich tin and, using wet hands or wearing vinyl disposable gloves, pat and press down on the top to get as smooth a surface as you possibly can.

❄ Bake in the oven for 40 minutes; the top of the cake will be bubbling when it's ready.

❄ Let the cake cool completely in the tin, then remove all the lining and push the icing sugar thickly through a small sieve over the top of the cake before removing to an airtight tin.

Makes approx. 20 very thin slices, perhaps even more

125g natural almonds, with skins

100g blanched almonds

125g whole shelled hazelnuts

75g soft dried figs, roughly scissored into 2cm x 1cm pieces

1 x 200g packet chocolate-covered candied clementines (see Stockists p.267) or mixed orange and lemon or citron peel, roughly scissored as above

1/2 teaspoon ground cloves

1 teaspoon ground cinnamon

good grating of fresh nutmeg

50g plain flour

good grating of white pepper

1 x 15ml tablespoon cocoa powder

150g sugar

150g honey

30g butter

1 x 15ml tablespoon icing sugar

MAKE AHEAD TIP:
Make the Panforte up to 3 weeks ahead and keep in an airtight tin.

Cointreau Cream (see p.183) if wished.

Cointreau Cream (see p.183) if wished.

Makes about 12 slices

225g soft butter, plus more for greasing (or
use flavourless oil)

300g caster sugar

6 eggs

350g plain flour

1/2 teaspoon bicarbonate of soda

250ml (250g) plain fat-free yogurt

4 teaspoons vanilla extract

1–2 x 15ml tablespoons icing sugar

MAKE AHEAD TIP:
Make the cake, turn out and leave to cool. Wrap in
clingfilm and foil and store in an airtight container
for up to 2 days.

FREEZE AHEAD TIP:
Make, wrap and freeze the cake for up to 3
months. Thaw overnight in a cool room.

SPRUCED-UP VANILLA CAKE

This is a sleight of hand, or a trick of equipment rather than an act of brilliance. True, the cake does look incredibly complicated and seasonally impressive as it comes to the table, but that is all down to the shape of the tin. It's an expense to get a tin that can't be used all year round, but it really is a beautifully Christmassy creation, and a doddle to make.

For the "spruced up" of the cake refers to the Holiday Fir tin I bake it in (see Stockists p.267); at other times of the year, I call this Eggy Vanilla Cake and cook it in a 2.5-litre bundt tin, as you can now, too. Whatever the shape, and with either the Antioxidant Salad on p.254 or the deep blushing pink Rhubarb and Strawberry Compote on p.104, it is one of my proudest creations. And the thing is, it doesn't need just to be brought out as a festive flourish for a supper party, but can be satisfyingly baked and left to preside grandly over the kitchen, commanding anyone to have a slice, damply plain, or toasted, by way of a seasonal treat.

To turn this into **Spruced-Up Spice Cake**, even more seasonal and just as good, but with less appeal to children, halve the vanilla and add 2 teaspoons each of ground cinnamon and ginger and a half teaspoon of ground cloves.

❉ Preheat the oven to 180°C/gas mark 4 and put a baking sheet in at the same time. Butter or oil your large, regular or fir-tree shaped bundt tin (2.5 litres capacity) very, very thoroughly. (I use oil-sodden kitchen paper.)

❉ Either put all the ingredients except the icing sugar into the processor and blitz together; or mix by hand or in a freestanding mixer as follows:
– Cream together the butter and sugar in a mixing bowl until light and fluffy.
– Add the eggs one at a time, whisking each one in with a tablespoon of flour.
– Fold in the rest of the flour, and add the bicarbonate of soda, the yogurt and vanilla extract.

❉ Pour and spoon the mixture into your greased tin and spread about evenly.

❉ Place the tin on the preheated baking sheet in the oven and cook for 45–60 minutes until well risen and golden. After 45 minutes, push a skewer into the centre of the cake. If it comes out clean, the cake is cooked. Let it sit out of the oven for 15 minutes.

❉ Gently pull away the edges of the cake from the tin with your fingers, then turn out the cake, hoping for the best.

❉ Once cool, dust with the icing sugar pushed through a small sieve, to decorate: think fresh snowfall on the alps.

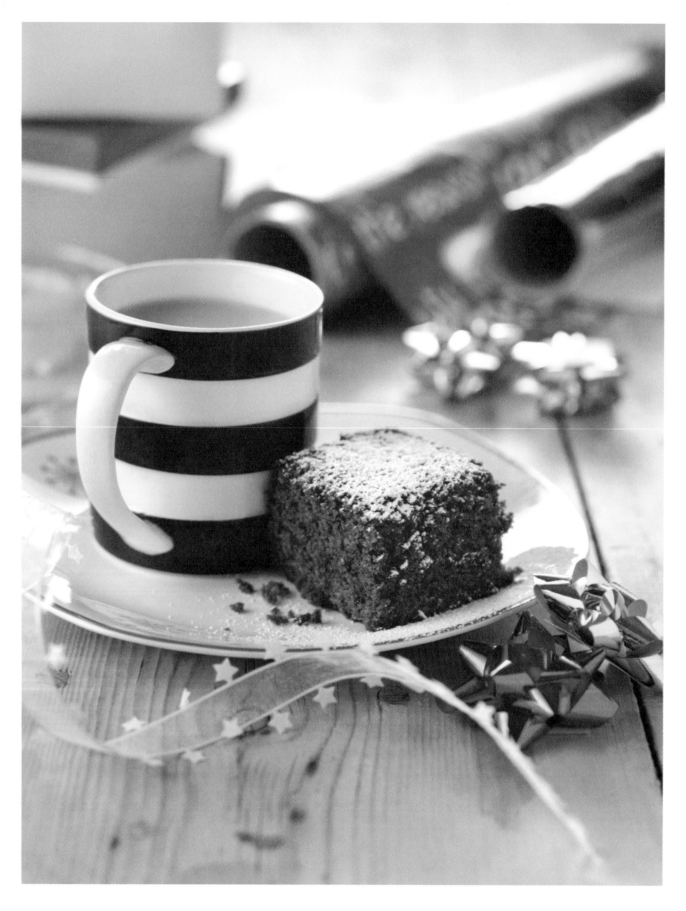

STICKY GINGERBREAD

I can't disentangle the smell of gingerbread from the smell of Christmas: I can think of no better welcome as people come through the door of the kitchen than the waft of it freshly baking in the oven. It is relaxingly simple to prepare, is good at any hour and keeps wonderfully.

I'm happy with it unfrosted, just left plain or perhaps snowily dusted with icing sugar, but if you want you can (as I do if it is for a bake sale) make a **sharply contrasting icing** by sieving 175g icing sugar and mixing it till thick and spreadable with a tablespoon of lemon juice and one of warm water. Spread this over the cold slab of gingerbread, and leave to set before cutting.

But it is, perhaps, the simplicity of the gingerbread, sticky with syrup and dark muscovado sugar, that makes me love it most. A square of it with a nice cup of tea would make even wrapping-up seem less vile, though I'd recommend having a pack of wipes nearby.

❅ Preheat the oven to 170°C/gas mark 3 and line a roasting tin or ovenproof dish (approx. 30cm x 20cm x 5cm) with Bake-O-Glide, foil or baking parchment (if using foil, grease it too).

❅ In a saucepan, melt the butter over a lowish heat along with the sugar, syrup, treacle, fresh and ground gingers, cinnamon and cloves.

❅ Take off the heat, and add the milk, eggs and dissolved bicarbonate of soda in its water.

❅ Measure the flour into a bowl and pour in the liquid ingredients, beating until well mixed. It will be a very liquid batter, so don't worry. This is part of what makes it sticky later.

❅ Pour it into the prepared tin and bake for 45–60 minutes until risen and firm on top. Try not to overcook, as it is nicer a little stickier, and anyway will carry on cooking as it cools.

❅ Transfer the tin to a wire rack and let the gingerbread cool in the tin before cutting into 20 squares, or however you wish to slice it.

Makes 20 squares

150g butter
200g golden syrup
200g black treacle or molasses
125g dark muscovado sugar
2 teaspoons finely grated ginger
1 teaspoon ground ginger
1 teaspoon ground cinnamon
¹/₄ teaspoon ground cloves
1 teaspoon bicarbonate of soda, dissolved in
    2 x 15ml tablespoons warm water
250ml full-fat milk
2 eggs, beaten to mix
300g plain flour

MAKE AHEAD TIP:
Make the gingerbread up to 2 weeks ahead, wrap loosely in baking parchment and store in an airtight tin. Cut into squares as required.

FREEZE AHEAD TIP:
Make the gingerbread, wrap in baking parchment and a layer of foil then freeze for up to 3 months. Thaw at room temperature for 3–4 hours and cut into squares.

SCARLET-SPECKLED LOAF CAKE

Makes 10–12 slices

1 large uncooked beetroot, approx. 200g

250g soft butter

finely grated zest and juice of $^1/_2$ lemon

200g caster sugar

4 eggs

150g dried cranberries

$^1/_2$ teaspoon ground nutmeg

300g plain flour

1 teaspoon baking powder

Simple loaf cakes are grossly underrated in the unspoken hierarchy that exists in baking. They don't have the show-off credentials of a frosted layer cake or glazed torte, but they are unassumingly, unfailingly good. Hettie, my assistant and so much more, calls them the pumps rather than the high heels of the cake world.

This one here is not exactly plain, however, but more of a festively hued fruit loaf – the kind you eat thickly sliced for tea, maybe with some cream cheese spread over it. I had the idea straightforwardly enough. If you can make a cake from grated carrots – and I've made one with grated courgettes, too – why not from grated beetroot? Well, it works, and although its colour is distinctive, the taste is not emphatic, though the lesser amount of lemon does sing through with refreshing clarity; I doubt anyone could guess the cake had beetroot in it. I advise not advertizing the fact: too many people who would adore the cake in reality, might let their prejudices hold sway, as prejudices will.

❈ Preheat the oven to 180°C/gas mark 4.

❈ Butter and line a 900g loaf tin with baking parchment or greased foil, or use a shop-bought paper insert (my preference) to drop into the tin.

❈ Peel the beetroot, and grate it using the finer grating blade of a food processor. It's as well to wear vinyl or rubber gloves for this, or you'll have a touch of the Lady Macbeths.

❈ In a large bowl, cream together the butter, lemon zest and caster sugar, then beat in the eggs, one at a time.

❈ Stir in the beetroot, cranberries, lemon juice and nutmeg. Then, finally, stir in the flour and baking powder and spoon the mixture into the loaf tin, spreading it out evenly.

❈ Bake in the oven for 1 hour, or until a cake tester or skewer inserted into the cake comes out clean. Let it cool in the tin, before turning it out onto a wire rack.

MAKE AHEAD TIP:
Make the loaf up to 3 days ahead, wrap loosely in baking parchment and store in an airtight tin.

FREEZE AHEAD TIP:
Make the loaf, wrap in baking parchment and a layer of foil, then freeze for up to 3 months. Thaw at room temperature.

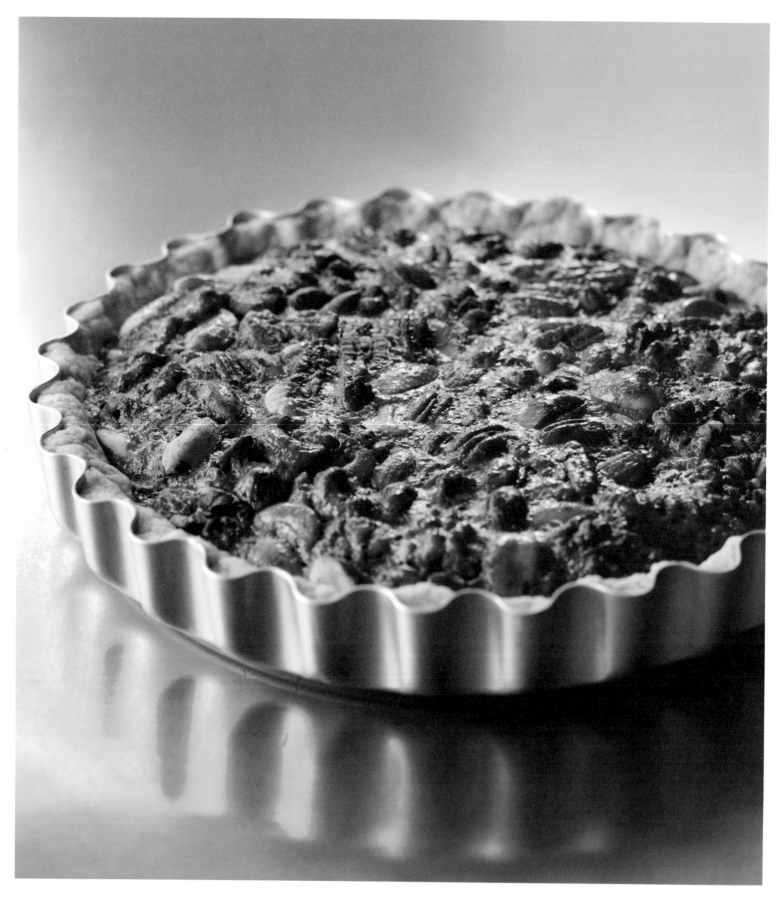

PECAN-PLUS PIE

This is somewhat of an Anglo-American enterprise. I have taken a pecan pie, and added other nuts, simply because for me, an English Christmas means bowls of mixed nuts and the memory of my grandfather being able to crack them, pressing two against each other, in his bare hands.

I don't crack them myself here even with a nutcracker, I'm afraid. But I do make sure I buy good fresh (check the dates on the packet) natural ones – that's to say unsalted and free of additives – that come together in a pack comprising Brazils, almonds, hazelnuts, pecans and walnuts.

If you eat this while it's still warm, then it's hard to put up a good argument against having a scoop of vanilla ice cream with it; when cold, I like it with a little cream, whipped or poured.

There is something so gloriously festive about this gleaming, golden, nut-laden pie, I wouldn't even rule it out for Christmas Day itself. The pastry couldn't be simpler: it's very plain, as the filling is so rich, and you don't roll it out, but press it down into the tin; I aim to ease.

Makes approx. 12 slices

225g plain flour
1/2 teaspoon salt
125ml flavourless vegetable oil
60ml full-fat milk
150g golden syrup
100g soft butter
200g soft light brown sugar
1 teaspoon vanilla extract
350g mixed nuts
3 eggs

❉ Preheat your oven to 180°C/gas mark 4. In a large bowl, mix the flour, salt, oil and milk to form a rough dough.

❉ Tip out into a 25cm wide, just under 4cm deep, flan dish, and press the dough patiently over the base and the sides of the dish, slightly coming up over the top if possible. Put in the freezer.

❉ Melt the syrup, butter and brown sugar over a lowish heat in a saucepan.

❉ Add the vanilla, stir, then take off the heat and let it stand for 10 minutes.

❉ Take the pastry-lined flan dish out of the freezer, and arrange the nuts on it.

❉ Whisk the eggs into the slightly cooled sugary syrup until it looks like a caramel mixture, then pour it over the nuts.

❉ Bake in the oven for 40 minutes, or until the filling has set and the pastry is golden.

MAKE AHEAD TIP:
Make the pie up to 2 days ahead and keep in an airtight container.

CHRISTMAS CHOCOLATE BISCUITS

Makes approx. 24

250g soft butter
150g caster sugar
40g cocoa powder
300g plain flour
1/2 teaspoon bicarbonate of soda
1 teaspoon baking powder

FOR THE FESTIVE TOPPING:
2 x 15ml tablespoons cocoa powder
175g icing sugar
60ml boiling water, from a kettle
1 teaspoon vanilla extract
Christmas sprinkles (see Stockists p.267)

I love these dark, fat patties of chocolate shortbread exuberantly topped with festive sprinkles. There's something so cheering about the sight of them, but they have more in their favour than looks: they are a doddle to make, and meltingly gorgeous to eat.

❋ Preheat the oven to 170°C/gas mark 3 and line a baking sheet with Bake-O-Glide or baking parchment.

❋ Cream the butter and sugar in a bowl and, when you have a light, soft, whipped mixture, beat in the 40g cocoa powder (sieving if it is lumpy) and, when that's mixed in, beat in the flour with the bicarb and baking powder. Or just put everything in the processor and blitz, if you prefer.

❋ This mixture is very soft and sticky and I find it easiest to form the biscuits wearing my CSI (disposable vinyl) gloves, so pinch off pieces about the size of a large walnut, roll them into balls, then slightly flatten into fat discs as you place them, well spaced, on your baking sheet; you should get about 12 on at a time.

❋ Bake each batch for 15 minutes; even though the biscuits won't feel as if they've had enough time, they will continue to cook as they cool. They will look slightly cracked on top, and it's this cosy, homespun look I love.

❋ Remove the baking sheet to a cold surface and let it sit for 15 minutes before transferring the biscuits to a wire rack, with a sheet of newspaper under it (to catch drips while topping them).

❋ To make the topping, put the cocoa powder, icing sugar, water and vanilla extract into a small saucepan and whisk over a low heat until everything's smoothly combined. Take off the heat for 10 minutes.

❋ When the biscuits are cool, drizzle each one with a tablespoonful of chocolate glaze – to glue the sprinkles on in a minute – using the back of the spoon to help spread the mixture, though an uneven dribbly look is part of their charm. After you've iced 6 biscuits, scatter with some of the Christmas sprinkles, and continue thus until all the biscuits are topped. If you ice them all before sprinkling, you will find the cocoa "glue" has dried and the sprinkles won't stick on.

MAKE AHEAD TIP:
Bake the biscuits up to 5 days ahead. Cool and store in an airtight container between sheets of parchment paper.

FREEZE AHEAD TIP:
Freeze the cooled biscuits in sealable bags or rigid containers for up to 3 months. Thaw at room temperature.

CRANBERRY AND WHITE CHOCOLATE COOKIES

Makes 30

150g plain flour
$1/2$ teaspoon baking powder
$1/2$ teaspoon salt
75g rolled oats (not instant)
125g soft butter
75g dark brown sugar
100g caster sugar
1 egg
1 teaspoon vanilla extract
75g dried cranberries
50g pecans, roughly chopped
150g white chocolate chips

This is yet another recipe to make use of dried cranberries, and it is not an accident. I can't help feeling that their inclusion in a cake, muffin or cookie confers instant Christmassiness, despite their all-year-round availability.

I also love their spicy tartness, which balances perfectly with the intense sweetness of the white chocolate morsels, though you can use darker, meaner chips, if you want. Still, even if you are not usually a white chocolate eater, you will, I think, find these persuasive, perhaps even having to eat a second one straight away just to make perfectly sure.

❊ Preheat the oven to 180°C/gas mark 4 and line a baking sheet with Bake-O-Glide or baking parchment.

❊ Measure the flour, baking powder, salt and rolled oats into a bowl.

❊ Put the butter and sugars into another bowl and beat together until creamy – this is obviously easier with an electric mixer of some kind, but otherwise you just need to put some muscle into it otherwise – then beat in the egg and vanilla extract.

❊ Beat in the flour, baking powder, salt and oat mixture, then fold in the cranberries, chopped pecans and chocolate chips.

❊ Roll tablespoonfuls of dough into balls with your hands, then place them on your prepared baking sheet and squish the dough balls down with a fork. (You may need 2 baking sheets or be prepared to make these in 2 batches.)

❊ Cook for 15 minutes; when ready, the cookies will be tinged a pale gold, but be too soft to lift immediately off the sheet, so leave the sheet on a cool surface and let the cookies harden for about 5 minutes. Remove with a spatula, or similar, to cool fully on a wire rack.

MAKE AHEAD TIP:
Bake the cookies up to 5 days ahead. Cool and store in an airtight container between sheets of parchment paper.

FREEZE AHEAD TIP:
Bake and then freeze the cooled cookies in sealable bags or rigid containers for up to 3 months. Thaw at room temperature.

CHRISTMAS CORNFLAKE WREATHS

Makes 22

100g soft butter
200g miniature marshmallows
1/2 teaspoon almond extract
1/2 teaspoon vanilla extract
125g cornflakes
50g sesame seeds (optional)
Christmas sprinkles to decorate

I try to rein myself in, but not always successfully, and here's evidence of my bolting from the constraints of good taste. That's not to say these don't taste good: they are crunchy and chewy and (very) sweet, and the almond and vanilla come through strongly. As you might expect, children especially, though not exclusively, adore them. And, what's more, they can help you make them or even, after a certain age, make these wreaths themselves – so well worth bearing in mind for the school Christmas Fair. My office children, Zoe and Anzelle, made the ones here.

❋ Put a piece of greaseproof paper, baking parchment or Bake-O-Glide on a surface for the wreaths to sit and set on later.

❋ In a generous-sized pan, over a gentle heat, melt the butter then add the marshmallows, stirring until both are smoothly combined.

❋ Take the pan off the heat, and stir in the almond and vanilla extracts.

❋ Add the cornflakes, and sesame seeds (if you like them), gently crushing the cornflakes as you go and mixing well so that all are covered in creamy goo.

❋ Pull out a clump of sticky cornflakes the size of a small satsuma, squish it down into a disc on the baking parchment, then make a hole in the middle to form a wreath of about 6cm in diameter. After you've made 3 wreaths, scatter with your Christmas sprinkles; if you leave it any longer, they won't adhere. Continue until all your cornflake mixture is finished.

❋ Leave – for at least 2 hours – to cool and firm up out of harm and small hands' way.

MAKE AHEAD TIP:
Make the wreaths up to 1 week ahead. Store in an airtight container between sheets of baking parchment or greaseproof paper.

FREEZE AHEAD TIP:
Make the wreaths and freeze in a rigid container for up to 3 months. Thaw in a cool room.

212 JOY TO THE WORLD

GOLD-DUST COOKIES

I freely acknowledge there is a place for the jauntily vulgar at Christmas, as is evidenced by – not least – the previous recipe, but sometimes quietly smouldering elegance can do the trick, too. These gold-dust cookies certainly have that: they are simple, ginger-seasoned (if I'm making them for the children I use vanilla instead) butter biscuits cut into pretty shapes – I am a sucker for stars – and, when baked and cooled, brushed with edible gold dust or glitter flakes. You need a specialist supplier for this (see Stockists p.267) but the actual gilding is easy, and since the cookies are not otherwise iced, you can get them done and dusted in no time. They're beautiful as a present, offered up after dinner with coffee or to keep in your festive cookie jar or biscuit tin for any eventuality.

Makes about 30, depending on size

90g soft butter
100g caster sugar
1 large egg
1 teaspoon ground ginger (or vanilla extract)
200g plain flour, plus more for sprinkling
1/2 teaspoon baking powder
1/2 teaspoon fine salt
edible gold dust or glitter flakes (see Stockists p.267)

❉ Preheat the oven to 180°C/gas mark 4 and line a baking sheet or two with baking parchment or Bake-O-Glide.

❉ Cream the butter and sugar together until whipped soft and pale, then beat in the egg, followed by the ginger (or vanilla), flour, baking powder and salt and continue mixing until it all comes together to make a soft dough.

❉ Form into 2 discs, wrap each one in clingfilm and let it rest in the fridge for 20–30 minutes.

❉ Sprinkle a suitable surface with flour, place a disc of dough on it and sprinkle a little more flour on top. Then roll it out to a thickness of about 5mm.

❉ Cut into shapes, dipping the cutter into flour as you go, and place the biscuits a little apart on the lined baking sheet/s. Keep the scraps of the first disc, to mix with the scraps of the second and roll and cut, re-roll and cut, until you've used up the mixture. This is a wonderfully pliable dough, which makes it an unstressful joy to work with.

❉ Bake in the oven for 8–12 minutes: this depends on their shape, how many sheets are in the oven at the same time, and whether on the upper or lower shelf, though you can swap them around after about 5 minutes. When they're ready, expect them to be tinged a pronounced pale gold around the edges; they'll be softish still in the middle, but will harden on cooling.

❉ Take the sheets out of the oven, remove the cookies, with a flat, preferably flexible, spatula to a wire rack and leave to cool.

❉ Using a small (unused) paintbrush or eyeshadow brush, dip in the edible gold dust – I use Pearl – or glitter flakes, and give each cookie its gilded coating.

MAKE AHEAD TIP:
Bake the cookies up to 5 days ahead. Cool and store in an airtight container between sheets of parchment paper.

FREEZE AHEAD TIP:
Bake and then freeze the cooled cookies in sealable bags or rigid containers for up to 3 months. Thaw at room temperature.

CHRISTMAS MORNING MUFFINS

Makes 12

250g plain flour

2¹/₂ teaspoons baking powder

¹/₂ teaspoon bicarbonate of soda

100g caster sugar

1 teaspoon ground cinnamon

good grating of fresh nutmeg (or ¹/₄ teaspoon ground nutmeg)

2 clementines/satsumas

approx. 125ml full-fat milk

75ml vegetable oil (or melted butter left to cool slightly)

1 egg

175g dried cranberries

FOR THE TOPPING:

3 teaspoons demerara sugar

MAKE AHEAD TIP:
Bake the muffins up to 3 days ahead. Cool and pack in an airtight container between layers of parchment paper. Pop into a warm oven for 5 minutes just before serving.

FREEZE AHEAD TIP:
Make and then freeze the muffins in a rigid container for up to 3 months. Thaw at room temperature. Pop into a warm oven for 5 minutes just before serving.

I have never quite understood how people can go in for vast, rich breakfasts on Christmas morning. I am hardly a modest eater by anyone's standards, but even I can't quite accommodate a platterful of buttery scrambled eggs with smoked salmon before the gargantuan Christmas feast. And I speak as cook and eater on this one.

I do, however, see the need to make breakfast special in some way, and these muffins do that. What's more, if you measure out the dry ingredients the night before and put the muffin cases in the muffin tin, you don't need to do anything more labour intensive on Christmas morning itself than preheat your oven, whisk up a few runny ingredients in a jug and stir them into the waiting bowl. Then dollop the batter into the prepared muffin cases and all's sweet – and smelling of cinnamony, orange-scented Christmas.

A last, heartfelt, note: Christmas, as I've said often, is about ritual and tradition; we inherit some, we invent others. But even those we invent are not sacrosanct. These muffins were my way, years back, of establishing a Christmas routine as a grown-up, and I have no desire to change things – essentially – now. But I've improved the recipe, and give you its new, evolved form here. In the kitchen, as in life, it is possible to play with tradition, without turning away from the past.

❄ Preheat the oven to 200°C/gas mark 6. Line a 12-bun muffin tin with muffin papers or (as I have here) silicone inserts.

❄ Measure the flour, baking powder, bicarbonate of soda, caster sugar, cinnamon and nutmeg into a large bowl; grate the zest of the clementine/satsuma over, and combine. If you are doing this in advance, leave the zesting till Christmas morning.

❄ Squeeze the juice of the clementines/satsumas into a measuring jug, and pour in the milk until it comes up to the 200ml mark.

❄ Add the oil (or slightly cooled, melted butter) and egg, and lightly beat until just combined.

❄ Pour this liquid mixture into the bowl of dried ingredients and stir until everything is more or less combined, remembering that a well-beaten mixture makes for heavy muffins: in other words a lumpy batter is a good thing here.

❄ Fold in the cranberries, then spoon the batter into the muffin cases and sprinkle the demerara sugar on top.

❋ Bake in the oven for 20 minutes, by which time the air should be thick with
the promise of good things and the good things themselves golden brown and
ready to be eaten, either plain or broken up and smeared, as you go, with
unsalted butter and marmalade.

CHRISTMAS CUPCAKES

Makes 12

FOR THE CUPCAKES:
125g soft butter
125g sugar
2 eggs
125g flour
1/2 teaspoon bicarbonate of soda
2 teaspoons baking powder
2 teaspoons vanilla extract
2–3 x 15ml tablespoons full-fat milk

FOR DECORATION (see Stockists p.267):
1/2 x 500g packet instant royal icing
Christmassy sprinkles
red and green readymade roll-out icing or
    sugarpaste (optional)
seasonal sugar decorations (optional)

MAKE AHEAD TIP:
Make the cupcakes the day before and store in an
airtight container.

FREEZE AHEAD TIP:
Make and freeze the cupcakes for up to 3 months.
Thaw on a wire rack. Use on the same day.

These are what I make – biggest batch to date 96 in one morning – when required to provide something for the cake stall at the school Christmas Fair. I double the recipe, put 2 trays of cupcakes in the oven at a time and then blitz on and on (4 double batches all told) until my whole kitchen table is covered. When they're cool, I ice and decorate – all white, but some scattered with sprinkles, some with holly and berries made from bought fondant icing, some with sugar poinsettia (expensive but enchanting) and other seasonal delights – and a more beautiful sight is hard to imagine.

But a simple, single batch of 12 is all you need under normal Christmassy conditions. The thing about sponge is that it is best the day it's made, although if covered thickly and completely with the royal icing, you might buy yourself an extra day.

❊ Take everything you need out of the fridge in time to come to room temperature – this makes a huge difference to the lightness of the cupcakes later – and preheat the oven to 200°C/gas mark 6. Fill a muffin tin with paper cases.

❊ Put all the ingredients for the cupcakes except the milk into a food processor and blitz until smooth.

❊ Pulse while adding the milk down the funnel – try one tablespoonful at a time – to make a smooth dropping consistency.

❊ Divide the mixture in your prepared muffin tin, and bake in the oven for 15–20 minutes. They should have risen and be golden on top.

❊ Let them cool a little in their tins on a rack, and then carefully take them out of the tin to cool in their papers, still on the wire rack.

❊ To ice, make up the royal icing as directed on the packet and, using a tablespoon, dollop over the cupcakes, so that each one is thickly covered.

❊ Adorn with sprinkles (don't let the icing dry before scattering) or sugar decorations, or roll out the fondant icing or sugarpaste and cut out Christmassy shapes of your choice to go on top.

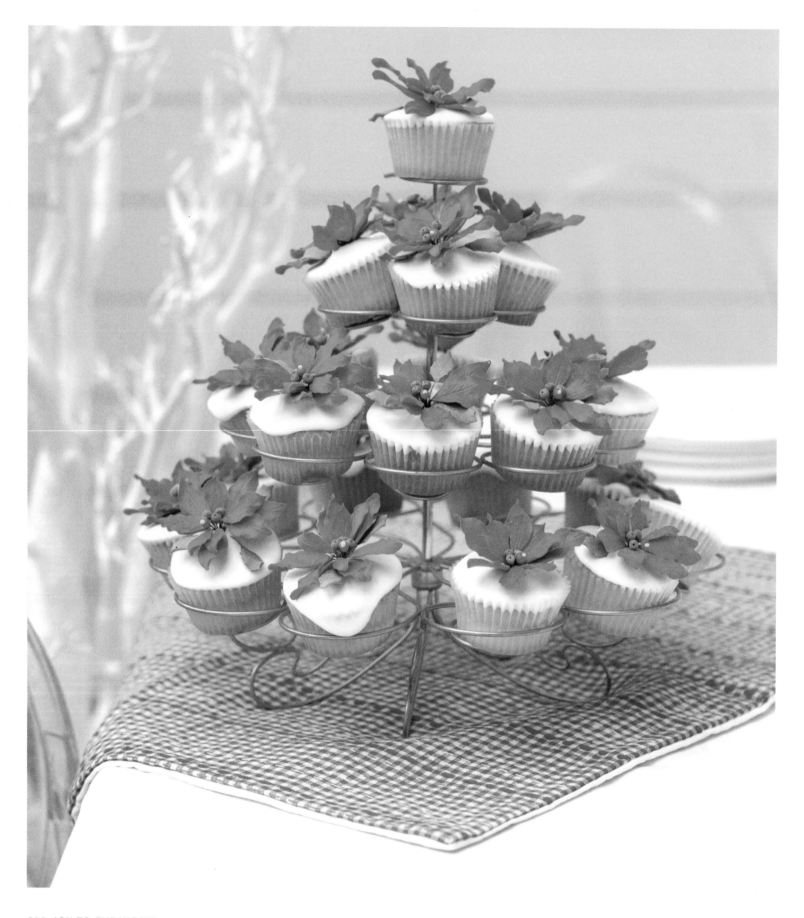

ALL WRAPPED UP
EDIBLE PRESENTS AND PARTY PRESERVES

I AM AWARE THAT it sounds almost affectedly home-spun to advocate the return of handmade presents, but my fervour here makes me indifferent to any accusation of winsomely retro fancy. There is a wonderful German adjective, *rechthaberisch* – to denote someone who always thinks they're right – that describes me, at least on this issue, with delicious Teutonic accuracy. I am beyond doubt; no contemporarily faddish self-questioning or equivocation can diminish my zeal. I know I'm right. It's not that I feel such an overwhelming drive to be stirring pots, and clipping lids and getting labels ready – though I do – but that the other choices, the Christmas-present game as it is currently played out, seems vulgar, grotesque, idiotic by comparison.

Of course, this is not essentially new: people have been tut-tutting about the crass commercialization of Christmas ever since I was a child and, I'm willing to believe, long before that. I don't doubt it has been getting steadily worse, but then, after a certain age it seems that most things do. And perhaps at this time of year, nostalgia bites in a little too sharply. Christmas can't ever match up to our childhood memories of it. Even now – and I am a person without a sentimental bone in her body – I can remember the ecstatic excitement of waking up in the early hours of dawn with the leg-deadening weight of my Christmas stocking at the end of my bed. And it's also true that if I filled my children's stockings with what my childhood stockings were stuffed with – a book or two, several tangerines, a pomegranate and a lucky dip sweetie bag, hair clips and transfers – they would probably not take it in good part. But still, I am too committed a consumer to feel able to complain about rampant commercialism with a clear conscience or good heart.

Nevertheless, even for me, there comes a moment, a long, protracted, sanity-busting moment, when it all seems just too much. And it is too much: too much money, too much shopping, too much wrapping, too much to worry about, and just too out of control. Wrapping paper costs more than presents used to. And there are so many presents to get. I don't say that because I'm mean or because I have anything against the exchange of gifts. Actually, giving presents is one of the few pure pleasures in life. I relish and savour it, and delight in getting it right. But that requires thought, honest selection and time for a proper unpanicked, focused search. Can you tell me that any of this is possible at Christmas? No, I didn't think so. It's too easy to feel the mania and the raging impatience come over you in the bustle of the shops, and then you end up with presents that cost too much and aren't even right. According to my history teacher at school, Churchill once apologized for the length of a memorandum, saying that if he'd had more time, he'd have made it shorter. Present buying is a bit like that: it takes time to find the right thing, and when you don't have that, you just spend more to lesser effect.

I can't help feeling, too, that it made a little more sense when you gave presents only to people you knew well. But the proliferation of presents can seem like the Arms Race, doomed to be self-perpetuating, and cripplingly expensive.

I'd like to feel that what I'm giving meant something. This chapter carries, in more senses than one, the essential message of this book, because for me Christmas is created and celebrated in the kitchen. You don't have to take the slightly emetic food-is-love line to know that giving a present of something you've made with your own hands, in your own time, is what Christmas is or should be about.

Not that the time required of you is excessive. Far from it: none of the recipes is complicated or takes very long; another of the joys of the edible present approach is that it's less stressful; you can buy ingredients in the normal course of your grocery shopping; and a pretty jar, a handwritten label and maybe a rosette or a ribbon are all you need in the way of wrapping (see Stockists p.267). Don't forget, though, to write any storage instructions on the label, and a note of how long your present will keep for.

You don't even have to cook: spiced salt, vanilla sugar, flavoured vodka or vinegar are among the options for those who want to start in the shallow end. But as I've said, all the recipes I suggest below are simple. If you don't want to buy jars and bottles, if your drive to make presents is part of a general relish for virtuous recycling, then know that the jars and bottles you no doubt have in your kitchen already will do just as well. If, however, you want to buy containers expressively for this project, again turn to p.267 for Stockists.

Although the recipes that follow are intended to form a shortlist of easy, pleasing presents, there are two caveats here. The first is that I don't advise giving away all of them: a store of chutneys and a relish or two are pantry preserves you should keep on hand yourself, even if you don't have a pantry. Cold cuts and suppers made from leftovers soar to gastro-greatness with judicious addition of something tangy out of a jar. Indeed, there are some who hold that Christmas is nothing without its condiments; I suspect they're right.

Second, please don't be confined by this chapter. Throughout the book are recipes that can be packaged up as presents without even any amendment. The Chocolate Peanut-Butter Cups and Christmas Rocky Road from The More the Merrier (pp.25 and 28) can be popped into boxes, or slipped into cellophane bags, and tied with ribbon. If it's before Christmas, give friends a jar of Redder Than Red Cranberry Sauce (p.119), knowing that you're contributing towards their feast day celebrations. Consider, too, the Sticky Maple Pecans (without the attendant pancakes) and the Cranberry, Almond and Honey Granola from A Christmas Brunch (pp.253 and 257).

And while a Christmas cake makes a generous present, there's nothing wrong with making a few presents out of each batch of baking. Certainly, unless it's for a whole family, then a smaller, individually sized cake, can be perfect. You can get four 10cm cakes out of the quantities specified for the smallest diameter of the Traditional Christmas Cake on p.172, and they will need 40–50 minutes in a 150°C/gas mark 2 oven.

Indeed, a lot of the recipes from Joy to the World (as the title, I hope, indicates) beg to be included in a list of possible presents (see pp.194–215). Think Star-Topped Mince Pies, Panforte – a few slender wedges in a cellophane bag would do it – the Edible Christmas Tree Decorations or Sticky Gingerbread, which you can simply cut into squares and box or bag up. I like, too, to bake mini gingerbread loaves in brown-card loaf cases; one batch of regular recipe fills three medium bakers' moulds (which is what they were called where I got them, and see Stockists p.267), 16cm x 8cm x 5cm and two small bakers' moulds, measuring a cute 10cm x 5cm x 4cm. I know that mathematically it shouldn't work out this way, but it just does. I put them all together in the 170°C/gas mark 3 oven, taking the baby loaves out after 20 minutes and leaving the other ones in for another 20, making it 40 minutes altogether.

The cookies from the same chapter – Cranberry and White Chocolate Cookies, Christmas Chocolate Biscuits, Christmas Cornflake Wreaths and Gold-Dust Cookies – are obvious contenders too, and it's not as if you need dedicate a whole batch of each per present: a few, charmingly wrapped, say everything you want.

But that's the point: whatever you make is going to be a better present than almost any you might buy. Even a batchful of Christmas Cupcakes, which last no longer than the day you give them, brings happiness that endures long after they are eaten up.

And, really, wouldn't you rather be in your kitchen instead of the shopping mall at Christmas?

STERILIZING JARS

Jars (and see Stockists on p.267 if you want something special) and bottles should be sterilized before having foodstuff put in them, but I have to say that I regard a dishwasher-clean jar or bottle (providing it comes fresh from the machine, with not so much as a finger touching the inside) as a sterilized one. If you wish to be more meticulous, you can sterilize by washing your jars well in soapy water, then rinsing them and letting them dry in a cool (140°C/gas mark 1) oven. If you're putting warm chutneys or jellies into them, all jars must be used warm.

VANILLA SUGAR

I start with an idea, rather than a recipe, as I want to emphasize (even to the point of hectoring repetition) that you don't have to be a master culinary craftsperson in order to make an edible Christmas present. You don't, as you will see, even need to cook.

This is probably the most basic of homemade edible gifts, but it is no less lovely, and will be none the less appreciated, for all that. I love the snow-whiteness of the sugar in the jar, just as it is, but I have nothing against tying on festive ribbons and bows: the season gives licence for exuberance.

To denote what's in the jar, however, I feel a no-nonsense brown luggage label or parcel tag looks best, and it has the advantage of giving you space to suggest uses for the vanilla sugar – which are that it brings an exotic yet nursery-comforting scent to mugs of coffee or hot chocolate, warm milk, cakes, cookies, pies and muffins and anything else that takes your or the recipient's festive fancy. Be sure to make clear, too, that the sugar can be replaced as it is used, keeping the jar as a permanent source of aromatic sweetness.

I think it's best to make the sugar up – and it's hardly arduous to tip some sugar into a jar and snip in a vanilla pod – at least a week before you're giving it, but you could do it months ahead. I keep a jar permanently in my kitchen.

Makes enough to fill 1 x 500ml jar

500g caster sugar
1 vanilla pod

1 x 500ml sealable jar, or whatever permutation of sizes you prefer

---

❄ Sterilize your jar, following the instructions on p.221, and leave to cool.

❄ Pour the sugar into the cooled jar.

❄ With the point of a small, sharp knife, cut into the vanilla pod lengthways, so its black and densely aromatic seeds are revealed, then cut this spliced and splayed stick into 3 short lengths and drop them into the sugar, embedding most of them well.

❄ Seal the jar and leave in a cool, dark place for at least a week before giving to some lucky person.

MAKE AHEAD TIP:
Vanilla sugar can be stored in a cool, dark place for about 1 year. If you make it 1 month before using or giving, add a label to say it can be kept for a further year and topped up as the sugar is used. After 1 year, replace the vanilla pod.

CHRISTMAS-SPICED SALT

Makes enough to fill 1 x 500ml jar

250g good-quality sea salt or Maldon salt
2 teaspoons red peppercorns
2 teaspoons crushed dried red chillies
4 star anise

1 x 500ml sealable jar

You could call this the savoury version of the Vanilla Sugar on the previous page: an idea, simply achieved, with the ingredients gathered in the course of your normal supermarket shop. Not all supermarkets stock red peppercorns, it's true, but plenty do, and a scour around a local deli should easily yield a supply (or if you're a mail order queen like me, turn to p.267 for Stockists).

But do make sure you get red peppercorns, as it's the little red cheeks peeking through the salt, like holly berries in the snow, that make this so Christmassy.

And maybe scrawl on a piece of red card that this salt is good sprinkled on steak or roast chicken or to add a little oomph to the table and plate whenever desired.

❄ Sterilize your jar, following the instructions on p.221, and leave to cool.

❄ Put the salt into a bowl with the peppercorns, dried chillies and star anise.

❄ Toss everything about, then carefully tip into your cooled, prepared jar and seal tightly.

MAKE AHEAD TIP:
Spiced salt can be stored in a cool, dark place for about 1 year. If you make it 1 month before using or giving, add a label to say it can be kept for a further year and topped up as the salt is used.

STEEPED CHRISTMAS FRUITS

Many of you will know that this is not a new enthusiasm, but an undimmed one, which I think speaks more for it anyway. The first of the options, the Mixed Fruits steeped in Pedro Ximénez – that Spanish sherry tasting of raisin and muscovado sugar – truly is Christmas pudding in a jar; as you open it, the thick scent of treacle-dark sherry and rich fruit hits you. I love it, as I do the other fruits here, the golden sultanas suspended in and swollen with the deeper golden Grand Marnier and the dark-red dried cherries in the equally dark-red syrupy, clove-scented cherry brandy – spooned over vanilla ice cream to make an instant pud. But I'm not just finding an excuse to satisfy my own greed, unapologetic though I am about such an instinct: these are my seasonal no-wrap standbys. There are some people I wouldn't dare not give a jar to at Christmas, but then these liquor-steeped fruits make the perfect present: simple to make; luxurious to receive.

❄ Sterilize your jar (or jars), following the instructions on p.221, and leave to cool.

❄ Add the dried fruit to its cooled, prepared jar and then pour in the liqueur, which should just cover the fruit if it is a jar that isn't too roomy for it. Clamp on the lid, or seal tightly, and leave to stand in a cool, dark place.

❄ It is preferable to keep these for at least 4 days before giving away, but you could, if in a hurry, give them away instantly. However, as the fruit stands in the liqueur, it will absorb it and swell; after 4 days of steeping, you may want to top up with about 100ml more liqueur.

Each batch makes enough to fill 1 x 500ml jar

FOR THE MIXED FRUITS IN PEDRO XIMÉNEZ:

250g mixed luxury dried fruits (raisins, sultanas, currants and glacé cherries)

250ml Pedro Ximénez, plus 100ml for topping up if needed (see Stockists p.267)

1 x 500ml sealable jar (or 2 x 250ml jars)

FOR THE GOLDEN SULTANAS IN GRAND MARNIER:

250g golden (or regular) sultanas (see Stockists p.267)

250ml Grand Marnier, plus 100ml for topping up if needed

1 x 500ml sealable jar (or 2 x 250ml jars)

FOR THE DRIED CHERRIES IN CHERRY BRANDY:

250g dried cherries

250ml red cherry brandy (not kirsch), such as Gabriel Boudier brand, plus 100ml for topping up if needed

1 x 500ml sealable jar (or 2 x 250ml jars)

MAKE AHEAD TIP:
Make the steeped fruits up to 1 month before eating or giving, and keep the alcohol level topped up. Store in a cool, dark place and use within 1 year. Once opened, keep in the fridge and use within 1 month.

MARINATED FETA

600g drained feta, cut into 1cm cubes, or 3 x
    390g cartons of ready-cubed feta in brine
1 teaspoon crushed chillies
1 teaspoon dried mint
1 teaspoon dried oregano
500ml regular (not extra virgin) olive oil

2 x 250ml and 2 x 125ml sealable jars

There's something rather lovely about giving the sunny taste of the Greek hillside as a Christmas present. And I can't help relishing that, despite the Aegean sunshine conjured up by the promise of salty feta in its herb-sprinkled oil, the sight of the white cubes, speckled with the dark green of the mint and oregano and the red of the crushed chillies does, in fact, look Christmassy in the extreme.

This is another bung-in, rather than cook-up, present. And, to make your life even easier, you could buy the feta that comes ready cubed in little tubs of brine. But if you do so, be aware that about half of the tub's weight is made of the liquid the feta's sitting in.

❊ Sterilize your jars, following the instructions on p.221, and leave to cool.

❊ Put the cubed feta into a bowl and add the chillies, mint and oregano, gently tossing the cubes about to get even coverage, keeping in mind that you don't want to bash the feta about too much.

❊ Fill the cooled, prepared jars loosely with the herb- and chilli-sprinkled cubes to just below the rim, and pour oil over to cover. Seal the jars and keep in the fridge. Don't forget to scribble storing notes on the label.

MAKE AHEAD TIP:
Prepare the marinated feta up to 1 week before eating or giving, and store in the fridge. Use within 1 month, keeping the cheese topped up with olive oil.

OLIVES 'N' PICKLED THINGS

This is, I suppose, a hybrid of a recipe, if putting pickled vegetables and spices in a jar counts as an actual recipe. I wanted to make a jar of the sort of pickles you might be given over a glass of Bandol rosé or pastis if you're in the south of France, but which would be just as nice with a hunk of good, English bread and cheese or a post-Christmas meal for anyone lucky enough to get it in their stocking.

The nigella seeds, borrowed from Indian cooking, are here to add their sour oniony taste, their sooty black colouring (*nigella* denoting little and black) and for obvious egomaniacal gratification; the rice vinegar, which is plucked from my Southeast Asian shelf, is here for no other reason than that it is as clear as water and I didn't want even the pale straw colour of cider or white wine vinegars to interfere with the sombre preserved beauty of the pickles. A distilled malt vinegar would work on this principle, but might be a bit rough on the palate.

100g black pitted olives

125g cornichons (baby gherkins, about the size of a child's little finger)

3 x 15ml tablespoons capers

75g cocktail or pearl onions

1 teaspoon cumin seeds

1 teaspoon whole coriander seeds

1 teaspoon nigella seeds

3 fresh long red chillies

175ml rice vinegar

1 x 750ml sealable jar (or 3 x 250ml jars), with vinegar-proof lid, such as Kilner jar or re-usable pickle jar

❉ Sterilize your jar (or jars), following the instructions on p.221, and leave to cool.

❉ Drain the olives, cornichons, capers and cocktail (or pearl) onions of any liquid they may be in.

❉ Tip them into your cooled, sterilized jar (or jars), and spoon in the cumin, coriander and nigella seeds.

❉ Halve and deseed 2 of the chillies, tucking the 4 halves into the jar.

❉ Now deseed and finely chop the remaining chilli, sprinkling the Christmas-red confetti into the jar as well.

❉ Top up the jar with the rice vinegar, so that everything is covered, then screw on the lid.

MAKE AHEAD TIP:
Make the pickles up to 1 month before eating or giving. Store in a cool, dark place for up to 3 months. Once opened, store in the fridge and use within 1 month, keeping the pickles topped up with vinegar.

WINTER-SPICED VODKA

Makes 500ml

1 teaspoon whole coriander seeds

3 cardamom pods, bruised

$^1/_2$ teaspoon cumin seed

1 cinnamon stick

1 dried red chilli

500ml vodka

1 x 500ml sealable bottle

It's true, a shot of vodka is warming enough, but this makes a real present out of doing little more than opening a bottle and some spice jars. I love how beautiful it looks, with the dried chilli, the cinnamon stick, the seeds and pods captured in the vodka, and imbuing it with fireside warmth and glowing pale amber colour.

You may suggest, as you hand it over, that it be knocked back in shots, used to make a festively spiced martini or, with the addition of some tomato juice, a sprinkle of salt and a dash of Worcestershire sauce, a particularly memorable Christmassy Bloody Mary.

❊ Sterilize your bottle (see p.221) and leave to cool.

❊ Pop all the spices into your cooled, prepared bottle.

❊ Preferably using a miniature funnel (see p.267 for Stockists of such arcane kitchenalia, as well as of bottles and jars, and so forth), pour in the vodka, seal the bottle and put it to steep, in a cool, dark cupboard, or anywhere away from the light.

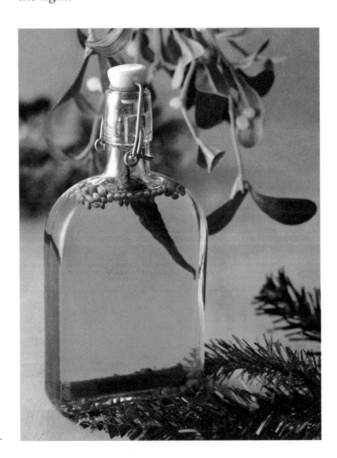

MAKE AHEAD TIP:
Make the spiced vodka up to 1 month before drinking or giving. Store in a cool, dark place and use within 1 year.

POMEGRANATE VODKA

I concede: there is no occasion in your or anyone's life when Pomegranate Vodka will be a pressing need. But that is why it makes such a wonderful present. It's out of the ordinary, but eminently usable, in an indulgent, uplifting kind of a way.

For me, pomegranate is the quintessential Christmas fruit, bringing back memories of a time when it appeared only at Christmas, bulging in my stocking, and I'd spend captivated hours winkling the seeds out with a pin and a kirby grip. And I say this even though I find packets of the seeds, freshly popped out for me, in the supermarket pretty well all year round now.

You don't have to be as lazy as I am: by all means buy the whole fruit and deseed it yourself, but make sure you drain them (and you can drink the juice) before putting in the vodka bottle.

I defy anyone to look at the pretty pale-pink vodka and not to smile: it is indisputably happy-making. The steeping pomegranate seeds don't, it's true, make as emphatic a difference to the taste as to the colour, but that floral sour-sweet fragrance does make itself delicately, mysteriously felt. I don't think anyone drinking this would be able to say exactly what the flavour was, but it's plainly not straight vodka: perhaps it's more accurate to think of it as scented rather than flavoured with pomegranate. But, whatever, you can tell the lucky recipient that it lends itself, iced, to petal-coloured shots, or fragrant martini-mixing or even the building of long, pink drinks.

❋ Sterilize your jar (see p.221) and leave to cool.

❋ Add the pomegranate seeds to the cooled, prepared jar, followed by the vodka. Seal and give the jar a safe shake before putting it in a cool, dark cupboard, or anywhere out of the light.

❋ Leave it for 4 days, shaking it any time you remember to, before sieving it into a measuring jug. Sterilize your 70cl bottle (or indeed the original vodka bottle with the label freshly soaked off), pour in the steeped vodka and put the lid on tightly before storing.

Makes 700ml/70cl

150g pomegranate seeds
1 x 70cl bottle of vodka

1 large sealable jar, approx. 1 litre for steeping
1 x 70cl sealable bottle for presenting

MAKE AHEAD TIP:
Make the fragrant vodka. Store the bottle in a cool, dark place and use within 1 year.

HONEYED FIG VINEGAR

Makes 1 litre

1 litre white wine vinegar
250g soft dried figs, chopped fairly fine
75g runny honey
2 teaspoons dried thyme
1 teaspoon white peppercorns

1 large sealable jar, approx. 2 litres, with
    vinegar-proof lid, such as Kilner jar or
    re-usable pickle jar
2 x 500ml sealable bottles

I have to confess, I have never been one for flavoured or fruity vinegars, which became such a cliché of the late Eighties – when I first started going to restaurants, and even reviewing them – that I developed something of an aversion.

But in the right circumstances I can reconsider. And am humbly happy to do so now: the mellowness and warm depth that the honey and figs bring to the vinegar make this perfect, with nothing more than a little oil and salt added, for dressing a seasonal salad; and in terms of flavour and present presence, so to speak, you really do get a lot of bang for your buck.

❋ Sterilize your jar (see p.221) and leave to cool.

❋ Pour the vinegar into the cooled, sterilized jar, then add the figs, honey, thyme and peppercorns, seal tightly and give a good shake.

❋ Put the fig-steeping vinegar into a cupboard, or anywhere out of the light, and leave for 4 days. It will begin to look like some strange specimen jar, the sort of freak-show medical curiosities collected by the tzars and now stored in that spooky museum in St Petersburg, the name of which I'm too traumatized to remember. But try not to let this put you off.

❋ Sieve into a large measuring or batter jug, taking care that no dusty spikes of thyme get through the net.

❋ Now, sterilize your 2 bottles, let them cool, then pour the vinegar in. Seal tightly and set aside in a cool, dark place until you present them.

MAKE AHEAD TIP:
Make the fig vinegar. Store the bottles in a cool,
dark place and use within 1 year.

CHRISTMAS CHUTNEY

Chutney is not the most obviously festive, seasonally indulgent, must-have food-stuff, but it is the cornerstone of my Christmas pantry. I begin to hyperventilate, now as I write, even at the idea of not having a stock of it. My need is threefold: cold cuts and Christmas Day leftovers are impossible to contemplate without chutney (and the Christmas ham first-time-out must have it as well); it is what I make, annually, and with very, very little effort for the children's school Christmas Fairs; and since it is easy to prepare a lot at one time, you can get a tidy number of presents seen to out of one under-an-hour stint in the kitchen, too.

Four of my favourite chutneys are recorded here, but this first, unsubtly named Christmas Chutney, is the one – in jars decorated as they are here, with squidgy, cut-out snowflake ribbon – that I box up and heave over to the Christmas Fair, along with as many cupcakes as I can muster.

Of course, any of the chutneys in this chapter would do, and gloriously, but this one is just so full of Christmassiness, crammed as it is with dates, cranberries and clementines, and spiced with cloves and cinnamon.

❄ Sterilize your jars (see instructions on p.221). You get about 2.2 litres from this recipe, so you can either fill 9 x 250ml jars or go (as I do) for a variety of jars of differing sizes, amounting, give or take, to the total volume.

❄ Put the apples, onion, cranberries and dates into a large pan.

❄ Zest the clementines/satsumas over the top, then squeeze in the juice and scrape in the pulp.

❄ Add the sugar, ground cloves, ginger, cinnamon and cayenne pepper, then pour the vinegar over and sprinkle in the salt.

❄ Now all you have to do is give a good stir, turn on the heat, bring to a boil, then turn down the heat and let it bubble cheerfully, uncovered, for about an hour or until you have a pulpy mass.

❄ Spoon into your warm, prepared jars and seal.

Makes approx. 2.2 litres

750g cooking apples, peeled, cored and chopped small

1 medium onion, peeled and roughly chopped

500g fresh or frozen cranberries, thawed if frozen

250g soft pitted dates, each date cut into 3

zest, pulp and juice of 2 clementines/satsumas

400g caster sugar

$1/2$ teaspoon ground cloves

1 teaspoon ground ginger

$1^1/2$ teaspoons ground cinnamon

$1/4$ teaspoon cayenne pepper

500ml white wine vinegar

2 teaspoons Maldon salt or 1 teaspoon table salt

9 x 250ml sealable jars, with vinegar-proof lid, such as Kilner jar or re-usable pickle jar

MAKE AHEAD TIP:
Make the chutney up to 2 months before using or giving (the longer it has to "mature" the better). Store in a cool, dark place for up to 1 year. Once opened, store in the fridge and use within 1 month.

RICH FRUIT CHUTNEY

Makes 1.5 litres

250g dried apricots

250g pitted dried dates

250g dried pears

250g dried cranberries

125g light muscovado sugar

300ml cider vinegar

300ml water

1 teaspoon Maldon salt or ¹/₂ teaspoon
    table salt

zest of 1 lemon, finely grated

¹/₄ teaspoon ground cloves

¹/₂ teaspoon ground allspice

1 teaspoon ground cinnamon

1 teaspoon ground ginger

3 x 500ml sealable jars (or 6 x 250ml jars),
    with vinegar-proof lid, such as Kilner jar
    or re-usable pickle jar

MAKE AHEAD TIP:

Make the chutney up to 2 months before using or
giving (the longer it has to "mature" the better).
Store in a dark, cool place for up to 1 year. Once
opened, store in the fridge and use within 1 month.

This could be described as a soft-set, savoury take on Christmas pudding. But as someone who has always liked a slab of un-iced fruitcake with a slice of sharp cheese, I see that as a good thing. What gives the richness, and the reminder of the pud, is that this chutney is made with dried fruits. What you end up with is a rich, dark, fruity, deeply-spiced chutney with a slightly more luxurious taste and texture than you might expect. This, of course, makes it an ideal present.

It also happens to be the easiest of the chutneys to make (not that it would be possible to find one that's difficult) because you don't have to peel or chop anything: all the dried fruit goes, as is, into the pan, and then, only when cooked, is gently processed to turn it into a sticky, spoonable preserve.

❄ Sterilize your jars (see p.221). The amount of chutney you're making here is enough to fill 3 x 500ml jars (as I've done) or 6 half that size, or, indeed, any permutation in the middle.

❄ Put all the ingredients into a decent-sized saucepan and bring to the boil.

❄ Once it has begun to bubble in earnest, turn down the heat, partially cover the pan (unlike the other chutneys, this one has no fresh fruit to give off liquid as it cooks) and simmer for 15–20 minutes or until all the fruit is soft.

❄ Take the pan off the heat for about 10 minutes to let it cool a little, before scraping it into a processor fitted with the double-bladed knife.

❄ Process for approx. 3 seconds, then open the lid to scrape down the chutney before pulsing again in short bursts. You want this chopped but not like untextured pulp or mush.

❄ Fill your warm, prepared jars and seal.

BEETROOT AND GINGER CHUTNEY

Some people of my generation were put off prunes at school; I developed an antipathy to beetroot. For those of us who grew up eating it at its worst, beetroot can conjure up an almost putrid sweetness and corrosive vinegariness. But to borrow, almost, a famous phrase: the past is another country; they cook things differently there.

So now I find myself on the verge of becoming a born-again beetroot lover: I admire the beauty (and the taste) of them raw; I look for ways to celebrate them in my cooking. This chutney, which marries the earthy sweetness of the beet with the pepperiness of fresh ginger – the sourness of the apple, like a useful go-between, providing balance – is a triumph of prejudice overcome.

You need give nothing but a small jar of this gorgeous stuff as a present, but if you wanted to pair it with anything to amplify the gift, may I suggest a snowy log of sharp but creamy goat's cheese.

❋ Sterilize your jars (following instructions on p.221).

❋ Take a large saucepan and tip in the beetroot and apple – the beetroot takes a lot longer than the apple to cook, so the latter doesn't have to be chopped as small. Add the red onion.

❋ Grate in the fresh ginger, tumble in the chopped crystallized ginger and sprinkle the brown sugar, salt and ground allspice over.

❋ Pour the vinegar over and stir to mix.

❋ Turn on the heat, bring to the boil, then turn down the heat and let the pan simmer steadily for approx. 1 hour, stirring every now and again, until the beetroot pieces are tender. The apple will have turned to mush long before this.

❋ Spoon into your warm, prepared jars and seal.

Makes approx. 1.5 litres

500g fresh beetroot, peeled and finely chopped

1kg cooking apples, peeled, quartered, cored and roughly chopped

275g (1 large or 2 small) red onion, peeled and finely chopped

1 x 2.5cm piece fresh ginger

75g crystallized stem ginger, each cube fairly finely chopped

350g soft light brown sugar

2 teaspoons Maldon salt or 1 teaspoon table salt

1 teaspoon ground allspice

750ml red wine vinegar

6 x 250ml sealable jars, with vinegar-proof lid, such as Kilner jar or re-usable pickle jar

MAKE AHEAD TIP:
Make the chutney up to 2 weeks before using or giving. Store in a cool, dark place for up to 6 months. Once opened, store in the fridge and use within 1 month.

CRANBERRY AND APPLE CHUTNEY

Apple is – generally – the basis of a chutney, as it's the sourness and pectin-rich nature of a Bramley, or indeed all cooking apples, that gives chutney its soft set and its sour-sweet tang. The Rich Fruit Chutney, on p.236, is an exception, but deliberately so. Apple can be used, therefore, as a binding vehicle for other ingredients but it can, indeed, be the only fruit. The cranberries that dot this chutney are dried, so they stand in for sultanas, providing punctuation rather than adding flesh, as the fresh ones do in the Christmas Chutney on p.235.

I add dried cranberries in preference to any other dried fruit, simply because their redness, their celebratory seasonality, makes this feel more Christmassy; the whole of the chutney's cheery hue does its festive bit, too.

❋ Sterilize your jars (see p.221).

❋ Take a medium-sized (not too big) saucepan and chuck into it all the ingredients. Stir with a wooden spoon and then put the pan on the heat.

❋ Bring to the boil, then turn down the heat a little to let the pan cook, uncovered, on a fast simmer for about 45 minutes, or until the chutney has thickened slightly and the fruit is soft.

❋ Spoon into your warm, prepared jars and seal them.

Makes about 1 litre

750g cooking apples, peeled, quartered, cored and chopped small
250g dried cranberries
1 onion, peeled and finely chopped
350ml cider vinegar
200g caster sugar
1 teaspoon ground ginger
1 teaspoon ground turmeric
1 teaspoon ground cumin
1 teaspoon ground coriander
2 teaspoons Maldon salt or 1 teaspoon table salt

4 x 250ml sealable jars, with vinegar-proof lid, such as Kilner jar or re-usable pickle jar

MAKE AHEAD TIP:
Make the chutney up to 2 months before using or giving (the longer it has to "mature" the better). Store in a dark, cool place for up to 1 year. Once opened, store in the fridge and use within 1 month.

CHILLI JAM

Although I call this chilli jam, I don't mean that it's the sort of thing you'd spread on your toast at breakfast (though smeared inside a bacon sandwich, it could be a real help one hungover morning) but rather a chilli jelly – chelly? – that glows a fiery, flecked red and is fabulous with cold meats or a cheese plate. And just a small pot of it makes a gorgeous present.

In the traditional run of things, jellies are incredibly hard work to make, or at least I find them so. If I tell you that jelly-making tends to involve tying jelly bags or muslin to the leg of an upended stool and straining stuff through the fine cloth into a bowl sitting in the underside of the stool's seat for at least 12 hours, you'll get the picture.

But don't worry. I don't strain – in either sense of the word – myself, but leave the orange-glowing, red jelly cheerfully freckled with the bits of chilli and sweet pepper, and, instead of getting my jellied set from preparing, cooking and sieving bucketloads of high pectin fruit, I simply cook the chillies in vinegar and pectin-added sugar, an essential ingredient I buy from the supermarket where it is labelled "jam sugar". It could scarcely be easier.

I make the "chelly" with equal weights of hot and sweet peppers, but if you wanted a bit more fire in your jelly, you could up the amount of chilli peppers and reduce the amount of bell pepper. But this proportion provides enough tingle for those who like it hot, but without burning more sensitive palates.

Makes approx. 1.5 litres

150g long fresh red chillies, each deseeded and cut into about 4 pieces
150g red pepper, cored, deseeded and cut into rough chunks
1kg jam sugar
600ml cider vinegar

6 x 250ml sealable jars, with vinegar-proof lid, such as Kilner jar or re-usable pickle jar

❋ Sterilize your jars (see p.221) and leave to cool.

❋ Put the cut-up chillies into a food processor and pulse until they are finely chopped. Add the chunks of red pepper and pulse again until you have a vibrantly red-flecked processor bowl.

❋ Dissolve the sugar in the vinegar in a wide, medium-sized pan over a low heat without stirring.

❋ Scrape the chilli–pepper mixture out of the bowl and add to the pan. Bring the pan to the boil, then leave it at a rollicking boil for 10 minutes.

❋ Take the pan off the heat and allow it to cool. The liquid will become more syrupy, then from syrup to viscous and from viscous to jelly-like as it cools.

❋ After about 40 minutes, or once the red flecks are more or less evenly dispersed in the jelly (as the liquid firms up, the bits of chilli and pepper start being suspended in it rather than floating on it), ladle into your jars. If you want to stir gently at this stage, it will do no harm. Then seal tightly.

I put a saucer into the freezer before I start, and after 10 minutes take the pan off the heat and splodge jam onto it. If it wrinkles when pushed with a finger, it's ready. If you prefer to use a jam thermometer, it'll be ready when the red line hits the word 'jam', around the 105°C mark.

MAKE AHEAD TIP:
Make the jam up to 1 month before using or giving. Store in a cool, dark place for up to 1 year. Once opened, store in the fridge and use within 1 month.

CHRISTMAS KETCHUP

Makes about 2 litres

1kg fresh or frozen cranberries, thawed if frozen

2 long cinnamon sticks, or 4 short ones

3 star anise

1 x 5cm piece fresh ginger (unpeeled), sliced into thin coins

1 fresh long red chilli, deseeded and finely chopped

1 orange

1 teaspoon ground cloves

500ml cider vinegar

500ml water

500g packed light brown sugar

2 teaspoons salt

1 x 400g can chopped tomatoes

100g caster sugar

4 x 500ml sealable bottles

MAKE AHEAD TIP:
Make the ketchup up to 1 month before using or giving. Store in a cool, dark place for up to 6 months. Once opened, store in the fridge and use within 4–6 weeks.

I've made a lot of chutneys in my life, but very few ketchups. I love homemade brown sauce (and the one I made in *Domestic Goddess* really came about as a way of rectifying a rhubarb chutney I'd attempted and overcooked), but I think that red sauce – tomato ketchup – is so loved in its industrial form, that I have never been able to face the sneer and snub of my children were I to offer my own version. This is a red sauce, but a deep, garnet red, a ketchup that's made primarily with cranberries and just begs to be added to the Christmas-leftover table. It's also – for what it's worth, and I think a tip in the right direction is always good for a slight detour – fantastic dribbled over some seared scallops, or mixed with mayonnaise to make a dip or dressing for cold pink prawns. It's a strangely gratifyingly, versatile little number.

You will need a Mouli or food mill for this ketchup; you could always push it through a sieve, but a food mill is easier and faster (and it's not an expensive piece of equipment).

❋ Sterilize your bottles (see p.221), and make sure you've got a funnel.

❋ Put the cranberries into a wide, medium-sized saucepan, and add the cinnamon sticks, star anise, ginger and chilli.

❋ Finely zest the orange over cranberries and spices, then squeeze out the juice from the orange and pour that in.

❋ Add the ground cloves, cider vinegar, water, brown sugar, salt and chopped tomatoes.

❋ Stir well with a wooden spoon, then put on the heat and bring to the boil.

❋ Once it's started boiling, turn down the heat to let it simmer, uncovered, with steady gusto, for 30 minutes, then take the pan off the heat and let the contents cool a little.

❋ Work the mixture through a Mouli, or other food mill, into a fresh pan. Or mouli it into a batter jug and then into the washed-out pan.

❋ Add the white sugar to the smooth ketchup, stir well, then reheat till it comes back to the boil and let it boil vigorously for about 10 minutes or until it becomes thick and glossy. Stir occasionally to ensure an even heat.

❋ Pour, through a funnel, into your warm, prepared bottles and seal well.

CORN CHOW-CHOW

Just in case you're wondering, this bears no resemblance to the sugary, vinegary corn relish you find in burger joints. Or perhaps that's not quite accurate: it bears a resemblance, but tastes so much better.

The term chow-chow comes from the Pennsylvanian Dutch (those Low German speakers who settled in America) but the relish has its counterpart, too, in American cooking of the South. I've slightly made it my own by using hot English mustard rather than the milder one that would be used Stateside.

It isn't as set as the shop-bought stuff, but I prefer it this way, and I find the tumbling beads of corn, sweet, sharp and glossed in its dressing, utterly addictive; moreover, its sunny yellowness is an uplifting sight on a winter's day.

I use frozen sweetcorn, since you need plenty and it makes more sense than canned, but if you forget to thaw it, just sit it in a large sieve over a bowl and pour boiling water from the kettle over it.

❋ Sterilize your jars, following the instructions on p.221. (I favour a 350ml wide-necked bottle, so I use 5 of those plus 1 x 250ml jar, but 8 of the smaller jars might be wiser.)

❋ Take the sweetcorn out of the freezer and let it begin to thaw in a sieve over a bowl. If you need to speed the process, pour boiling water over it.

❋ Put the mustard, honey, vinegar, salt and sugar into a saucepan, and place it on a low heat, stirring with a wooden spoon to help everything dissolve.

❋ Stop stirring, and turn up the heat so that the mixture comes to the boil, then let it boil for 5 minutes.

❋ Check the corn is thawed and drained, tip it into a bowl, and add the spring onions and diced peppers.

❋ Once your liquid has boiled for 5 minutes, take it off the heat and pour through a sieve (so you get a smooth syrup) onto the corn, spring onion and pepper mixture.

❋ Ladle equal amounts of corn mixture and liquid into your warm, prepared jars. The syrup should cover the chow-chow; or rather, no corn should sit above the syrup but it doesn't matter if the syrup comes up over the corn a bit.

❋ Seal the jars or screw on the lids, and store in the fridge.

Makes 2 litres

900g frozen sweetcorn, thawed

8 teaspoons hot English mustard, from a jar

300g honey

500ml cider vinegar

3 teaspoons celery salt

50g caster sugar

8 spring onions, sliced into 5mm rounds

4 red peppers, deseeded and cut into 1cm dice

8 x 250ml sealable jars, with vinegar-proof lid, such as Kilner jar or re-usable pickle jar

MAKE AHEAD TIP:
Make the chow-chow and store in the fridge for up to 2 months before using or giving. Once opened, use within 1 month.

PEANUT BRITTLE WITH ART AND SOUL

Makes approx. 400g

200g caster sugar
60ml water
150g golden syrup
150g salted peanuts
1^1/$_2$ teaspoons vanilla extract
25g soft butter
1^1/$_4$ teaspoons bicarbonate of soda

This title isn't a boast, but a name to denote provenance. It's a recipe given to me, at my greedy request, by the cook-and-a-half, Art Smith. True, I've slightly simplified it, but only because I don't have his deserved confidence, so I make my batch smaller, and leave out the difficult technical bits.

But even so, what this makes is fabulous: you really have to steel yourself to give it away.

❉ Get out a large sheet of Bake-O-Glide and place on a baking sheet (or put some foil on the sheet and butter it). Sit it by the stove, waiting to receive the brittle once it's ready to pour.

❉ Put the sugar, water and syrup into a pan, stir and then bring to the boil gently. Then turn up the heat and let it boil for 5 minutes or until a rich deep amber. Do not stir while it is boiling and keep a close eye on the mixture as it boils.

❉ Take the pan off the heat and, with a wooden spoon, stir in the nuts, followed by the vanilla, butter and bicarbonate of soda. You will have a golden, frothy, hot and gooey mixture.

❉ Pour this briskly onto the waiting parchment or foil, using your wooden spoon to coax and pull it to make a nut-studded sheet, puddle-shaped though it may be, rather than a heap.

❉ Leave it to cool, then break into pieces and store in an airtight container or box; or bag up to give at once as presents. You'll get about 400g in total, and it's up to you how much you want to put in each packet, really. I find it easier to do several small batches like this, rather than multiplying quantities as I cook.

MAKE AHEAD TIP:
Make the brittle up to 1 week before eating or giving. Store in airtight bags or containers in a dry, non-humid environment. Once opened, eat within 7 to 10 days.

CHRISTMAS PUDDINI BONBONS

I know there aren't many sweet things in this chapter – strictly speaking only two – but that is mainly because, as I suggested in the introduction, there are lots of sweet treats, just waiting to be wrapped and beribboned (see pp.194–215). And the truth is, apart from baking, making sweets is a lot harder than making savoury edible presents. These bonbons, however, are almost alarmingly easy. I was inspired by a picture I saw in *The Australian Women's Weekly*, fell in love with their cuteness and had to have a go myself. This isn't quite their recipe, but the idea – and the decoration – is the same, which is to say, these are delectable little truffley bonbons made by mixing up cold Christmas pudding, liquor, syrup and melted chocolate, rolling them into small balls, then melting white chocolate over them and arranging small pieces of red and green glacé cherries on top to make them look like miniature Christmas puddings themselves.

I made this just after last Christmas, using some leftover pudding, foil-wrapped and waiting to be gratifyingly recycled (though you could buy a mini one, microwave it and leave it to get cold) and adding a slug of my beloved Pedro Ximénez – since that was the alcohol I'd originally put into the pudding – and an ooze of golden syrup before compacting it with melted dark chocolate, but you could just as easily add rum or brandy and, as the original recipe also does, 40g icing sugar.

The hard part – in the sense that you need superhuman patience, rather than any special skills – is dripping over the melted white chocolate and snipping the cherries and arranging them to evoke a sprig of berried holly. I am not really cut out for this work, and you will curse my name as you do it, but, afterwards, you will be thrilled with what you've done.

And, although they look like baby Christmas puddings, they taste like meltingly rich, spiced chocolate truffles. These babies have got everything going for them.

❋ Line a baking sheet (that will fit in the fridge) with clingfilm, baking parchment, foil or Bake-O-Glide, and set it to one side while you make the bonbons.

❋ Melt the dark chocolate in a heatproof bowl suspended above a pan of simmering water, or in the microwave according to the manufacturer's guidelines.

❋ Crumble the cold Christmas pudding into a bowl, add the Pedro Ximénez sherry and golden syrup and stir briskly till all is incorporated.

❋ Pour in the melted dark chocolate and stir again: this will make the mixture much more cohesive.

❋ To make this step easier, put on a pair of those disposable vinyl gloves sold in

Makes about 30

125g best-quality dark chocolate, finely chopped

350g leftover, or freshly cooked and cooled, Christmas pudding

60ml Pedro Ximénez sherry (see Stockists p.267)

2 x 15ml tablespoons golden syrup

FOR DECORATION:
100g white chocolate, finely chopped

6 red glacé cherries

6 green glacé cherries, or 6 short lengths angelica

MAKE AHEAD TIP:
Make the bonbons up to 2 weeks before eating or giving. Pack in boxes and store in a very cool place. If made 2 weeks ahead, add a label to say "keep cool and eat within 1 or 2 days".

hardware stores and supermarkets, pinch out small lumps of mixture and roll so that you have little rounds about the size of a chocolate truffle. You should get about 30 out of this mixture; fight the impatient urge to make these balls larger as you go.

❄ Cover with clingfilm and slot into the fridge to firm up.

❄ To decorate, melt the white chocolate either in a heatproof bowl suspended over a pan of simmering water, or in the microwave according to the manufacturer's guidelines, then let it cool for about 5 minutes, to make it easier to work with, while you chop the red cherries into small pieces (to evoke berries), and snip the green cherries (or angelica) into miniature lengths, to represent leaves.

❄ Using a teaspoon, drip a little of the melted but slightly cooled white chocolate on each bonbon, then arrange the infuriatingly sticky pieces of cherry on top.

❄ Place in boxes to give away – if you use small boxes that will fit 6 bonbons each, you will get 5 adorable presents out of this – or on a plate to hand round with coffee, instead of dessert, after a post-Christmas dinner.

A CHRISTMAS BRUNCH FOR 6–8

MUCH AS I LOVE COOKING, and derive perhaps more pleasure from feeding people than is altogether decent, at this time of year it can make sense to think of how to curtail kitchen activity. I don't wish to sound lacking in seasonal cheer or sociability, but I know from experience that if you overstretch yourself, it's hell for everyone: you suffer, growing more resentful by the meal; your family ditto, as they bear the brunt of your probably self-imposed martyrdom. Sometimes – and I know I shouldn't project on to all of you my flaws, inherited with almost ironic precision down the maternal line – the domestic overload is an unavoidable feature of the festivities. But a little mealtime merging can lessen the load. And this is where brunch comes in.

Not, I hasten to add, that I intend my Christmas brunch to be for the big day itself. I have no desire to bust a gut – infelicitous as that sounds – on Christmas Day: there's enough cooking and eating as it is, without adding more of either. But around that time, whether you have family staying or friends visiting, brunch can be the answer. This isn't just about streamlining the schedule: the essential uneverydayness of this hybrid of a meal makes it feel like a holiday hoolie from the off.

Cooking a good breakfast for people really requires you to be a short-order chef; my brunch is designed to free you from stoveside captivity or last-minute frenzy. Yes, there are eggs, but the strata – which is a cross between a savoury bread-and-butter pudding and a toasted sandwich – is assembled the night before, left in the fridge to steep and merely popped in the oven to bake mid-morning. The pumpkin in the pancakes means they can be made ahead of time and kept warm, or reheated, without drying out or going limp. I have been known to make the Antioxidant Fruit Salad with ready-cubed mango; and the Christmassy Cranberry, Almond and Honey Granola, well, that can be done ages ahead, in quantity, to be stored in a jar and brought out whenever needed.

Not that anything needs adding, but if at any time there's some Spruced-Up Vanilla Cake (see p.198) knocking around, slice and toast it and present people with golden triangles of what tastes like French toast, but requires no soaking or frying.

But the final step here is really my first: that's to say, if there's a better kick-start than is provided by the Espresso Martini overleaf, I've yet to discover it. I don't even drink coffee in the normal run of events, and yet I can knock this back. You could, of course, partner it with a matching jug of Marteani or cut a little slack for those who want to start the day less boldly by mixing up – see p.3 for the recipe – a pitcherful of Poinsettia, a festively red and knock-backable drink made of fizzy wine, orange liqueur and cranberry juice.

ESPRESSO MARTINI

Makes 1 litre

250ml espresso or very strong coffee, left to cool

250ml Kahlúa or other coffee liqueur

250ml vodka, chilled

250ml toffee vodka (see note below) or butterscotch schnapps

ice cubes to serve

I love the Cornish toffee vodka called, compellingly, Todka (see Stockists p.267).

MAKE AHEAD TIP:
Make the espresso the day before, cool, cover and chill. Next day, mix all the ingredients together up to 4 hours ahead. Cover and leave in a cool place.

It's not too much of an exaggeration to say that this magnificent creation – a full fabulous jugful of it – is the rock on which this whole brunch rests.

I am unashamed to boast about it, as it is a filch rather than a fully-fledged offspring of mine. That's to say, I once had a sip of the espresso martini at Locanda Locatelli in London, and I knew, just knew, I had to make it mine. I own, too, that my version isn't quite as virtuoso as theirs. Order one there, and it comes whizzed to perfection, with that pale frothy head of foam – the authentic *crema* – and a trio of coffee beans on top. I just mix the ingredients together, but it tastes no less fabulous.

The only thing to bear in mind is that you should make your espresso the night before so it's properly cold, chilled if possible, before you start.

❋ To make a pitcher, mix the ingredients together and serve over ice.

❋ To make just 1 drink, remember that this martini is made up of equal parts, so 1 x 25ml measure of each component is enough, with a pile-up of ice, for a gratifying martini-glassful.

MARTEANI

Makes 1 litre

250ml strong Earl Grey tea, left to cool

250ml Cointreau, gin, or Triple sec

250ml vodka, chilled

As already mooted, this is an obvious partner for the coffee-cocktail, above. As with that, remember to get the crucial component – here tea, rather than the espresso above – brewed the night before so it's cold and ready to be mixed into a cool drink for your brunch.

❋ To make a pitcher, mix the ingredients together and serve over ice.

❋ To make just one drink, replace the 250ml amounts with a 25ml shot each.

TRIPLE CHEESE AND ONION STRATA

A strata is, in effect, a savoury bread pudding and this one is a particularly shining model of its kind. It's the easiest way to make an egg dish for breakfast when you've got a tableful of people, as it's composed in advance and you don't need to stand at the stove like a harassed, short-order cook.

I tend to let the bread stale in the day, and put the strata together before I go to bed, removing it from the fridge and cooking in the oven the next morning, which makes for a very unstressful way of having people over.

I kept this meatless on purpose, as a veggie-pleasing brunch dish is always a consideration, but of course a panful of sizzling bacon served alongside would keep me most awfully happy.

1 baguette or French stick (both elbow-ends discarded), cut into 1cm slices and allowed to go stale (this is about 225g of stale bread slices, in case you want to substitute other loaves or types of bread)

6 spring onions, roughly sliced

1 ball mozzarella, roughly chopped

50g flaked Parmesan (I like to make this in the processor, so it's easier to use flaked Parmesan, but if you're grating, do use proper block Parmesan.)

100g cheddar, broken into pieces

100ml sour cream

6 eggs

small bunch of chives to garnish

❋ Arrange the stale baguette slices in a dish measuring approx. 24cm square.

❋ Put the spring onions, mozzarella, Parmesan and cheddar into a food processor.

❋ Add the sour cream and eggs, then process to make an eggy-cheese sauce. Pour this over the stale bread, cover with clingfilm, and leave it to soak overnight. If you want to do this by hand, simply whisk together the eggs and sour cream, then finely chop the spring onions and mozzarella and add them to the eggs. Grate in the cheddar and Parmesan and stir to combine before pouring over the bread pieces.

❋ In the morning, preheat your oven to 180°C/gas mark 4. Take the strata out of the fridge and uncover it.

❋ Bake for 30 minutes, though the strata may need longer in the oven if it is really f-f-f-fridge c-c-c-cold when it goes in.

❋ Once it's out of the oven, scissor the chives finely over the strata and spoon onto serving plates.

MAKE AHEAD TIP:
Assemble the strata the evening before. Cover with clingfilm and leave to soak overnight in the fridge. Next day, take the strata out of the fridge and uncover. Allow to come to room temperature while you preheat the oven. Cook as directed.

PUMPKIN PANCAKES WITH STICKY MAPLE PECANS

Although these pancakes are perfect for a brunch with a party feel, to be honest, I feel they can be eaten at any time. Add a little ice cream or crème fraîche and you have a pretty fantastic supper-party pudding, too.

What I like about them particularly is that without too much of an initial shopping expedition you can be sure you have the wherewithal to make these as and when: maple syrup and canned pumpkin purée are stashed in the store cupboard; buttermilk has a pretty long life in the fridge, or you could simply add a teaspoon of vinegar to ordinary milk and let it stand, souring, for 5 minutes or so before proceeding.

And these are special. Pumpkin pancakes are to ordinary breakfast pancakes as a duvet is to a blanket. The sweet puréed flesh blends with the sour tang of buttermilk to make a pancake that is fleshy and downy and supersoft. You could, of course, eat these any way you so wish, but topped with pecans that have been tossed in a hot pan with maple syrup and doused with more maple syrup, is the best way I can think of.

It's probably easiest to make these before people appear and just stash them, covered loosely with foil and interleaved with greaseproof paper, in a low oven (say 120°C/gas mark $1/2$), for 45 minutes to an hour.

❄ Whisk together the eggs and buttermilk until frothy, then add the pumpkin purée and whisk again.

❄ Beat in the flour, sugar, baking powder, bicarbonate of soda and salt, whisking until you have a smooth batter. Or just put everything into the blender, together, and liquidize.

❄ Heat a heavy-based frying pan or flat griddle, and pour in the oil. Wipe away any excess with kitchen paper, taking care not to burn your fingers, so that the pan is very lightly oiled. Any more than that, and the pancakes will burn.

❄ Using an espresso cup, pour small amounts of batter into the pan or onto the hot griddle, gently coaxing them into 7–8cm diameter circles.

❄ When bubbles form on the top of the pancakes, flip them over. (You'll have to do this in batches, depending on the size of your pan or griddle. I get 4–5 on my griddle comfortably at any one time.)

❄ Cook for another $1^1/2$–2 minutes, then transfer them to a plate, and keep warm with a layer of foil over the pancakes.

❄ This amount of batter does make a lot, but the pancakes are not very big,

Makes approx. 30

FOR THE PUMPKIN PANCAKES

2 eggs

375ml buttermilk (see margin note below)

1 x 400g can pumpkin purée

250g plain flour

3 x 15ml tablespoons caster sugar

1 teaspoon baking powder

$1/2$ teaspoon bicarbonate of soda

$1/2$ teaspoon Maldon salt or $1/4$ teaspoon table salt

1 teaspoon vegetable oil

FOR THE STICKY MAPLE PECANS

175g pecans

2 x 15ml tablespoons maple syrup, plus more for pouring over pancakes

You can make milk into buttermilk by souring it with vinegar, but you can also substitute a runny natural yogurt here, such as Activia.

MAKE AHEAD TIP:
Make the pancakes the day before and stack on a heatproof plate. Cover with a "tent" of foil and keep in a cool place. To reheat, keep them on the plate under the foil and pop in a warm oven, about 170°C/gas mark 3, for 20 minutes.

FREEZE AHEAD TIP:
Make the pancakes and cool as above. Stack them interleaved with greaseproof paper. Wrap securely in foil and freeze for up to 1 month. Thaw overnight at room temperature. Reheat as above.

OPPOSITE:
Espresso Martini, Triple Cheese and Onion Strata, Pumpkin Pancakes with Sticky Maple Pecans

and will keep well under foil until you have finished making all of them. And they're so good for when you've got people staying that it seems a pity to make fewer (and you can always freeze any leftover pancakes).

STICKY MAPLE PECANS

❋ Toast the pecans in a large, hot, dry frying pan.

❋ When the pecans are warm and smelling nutty, spoon the maple syrup over, stir to coat them and keep sautéeing them in the pan until they are stickily, glossily coated.

❋ Take the pan off the heat, and as you serve the pancakes, sprinkle each plate with a few sticky pecans and pour some maple syrup over the top.

ANTIOXIDANT FRUIT SALAD

750g mango cubes (I buy 2 tubs of ready-diced mango, each just 400g in weight, but if you're using whole mango, you'd probably need 3 large or 4–5 small ones)
300g blueberries
150g pomegranate seeds (I buy pomegranate seeds in packs of just this weight; otherwise, we're probably talking 2–3 pomegranates here.)
4 teaspoons lime juice

This combination of mango, pomegranate and blueberries – named not entirely ironically to take account of fashionable medico-dietary concerns – is probably my favourite fruit salad of all time. It is sensational, at any time, and I often serve it alongside the Spruced-Up Vanilla Cake on p.198 as a dinner party dessert. But it is a crucial part of this or, I rather think, any brunch. I'm certainly not suggesting you make everything altogether every time, but I'd never leave this out.

If you're using a whole mango, to dice, stand the mango on its end in front of you and, using a sharp knife, score vertically through the skin all round. It should then be easy to peel off the skin from one half. Now, cut through the peeled half of the mango, right to the stone, in lines down, about 1cm apart; do the same across. Then, take your knife and press it down, sliding it right against the stone so you feel it scrape the stone, thus letting the dice you've scored through tumble out. Do the same – messily – with the other side. If I can do this, it really doesn't require any great dexterity, trust me.

✽ Put the mango cubes into a bowl and tumble the blueberries and pomegranate seeds in after them.

✽ Squeeze the lime juice over the fruit, mix everything together gently, and taste to see if you want to add more lime juice before serving.

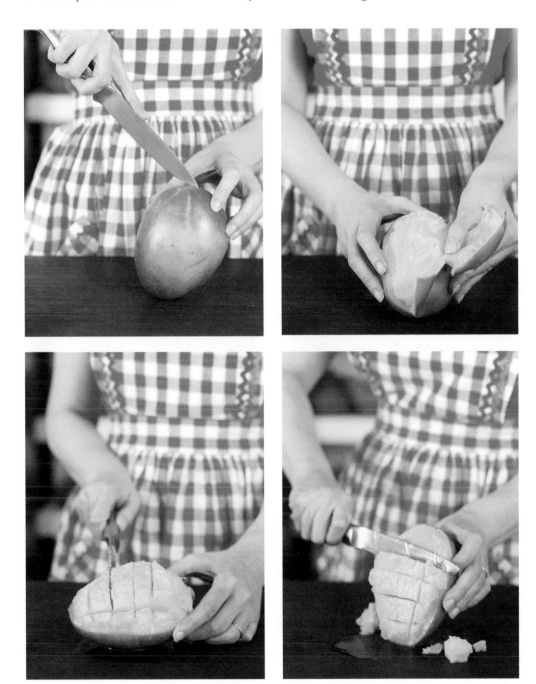

MAKE AHEAD TIP:
If using whole mangoes, prepare the mango cubes the day before and put into a non-metallic bowl. Squeeze the lime juice over, cover and chill. When ready to serve, add the blueberries and pomegranate seeds.

CRANBERRY, ALMOND AND HONEY GRANOLA

Granola is really nothing more than extra-crunchy muesli. And this seasonal variant provides texture and a gorgeous cinnamony honeyed taste, best savoured – both taste and texture – with a luscious dollop of yogurt. By all means, though, eat it with milk like regular breakfast cereal if you prefer. I am permissive in these matters; besides, I concede that the granola-flavoured milk at the end of a bowlful is always a treat worth looking forward to.

❄ Put everything except the dried cranberries into a large mixing bowl and mix well. Two spatulas are probably the best tools for the job here – or use your own two hands, wearing CSI (vinyl disposable) gloves.

❄ Spread this mixture on a lined baking sheet and bake in a 170°C/gas mark 3 oven, turning over the mixture with a spatula about halfway through baking and redistributing the granola evenly during the baking process. The object is to get the granola evenly golden without toasting too much in any one place. If you have a convection or fan oven, you may need to turn it to a lower heat as well as keeping a sharp eye on it.

❄ This should be ready – golden enough and dried out like a crunchy breakfast cereal rather than the sticky mess that went into the oven – in anything from 40–50 minutes.

❄ Remove from the oven and let cool, taking it off the hot baking sheet, before mixing with the dried cranberries. Store in an airtight container.

Makes enough to fill a 1.2-litre tin or jar

225g rolled oats (not instant)
60g sunflower seeds
60g white sesame seeds
2 teaspoons ground cinnamon
150g (125ml) runny honey
50g soft light brown sugar
60g whole natural almonds
60g blanched almonds
1/2 teaspoon Maldon salt or pinch of table salt
1 tablespoon rapeseed or sunflower oil
150g dried cranberries

MAKE AHEAD TIP:
Make the granola, cool and store in an airtight container for up to 1 month.

A BEVY OF HOT DRINKS

THERE ARE FEW THINGS BETTER THAN COMING in from the cold and wrapping your hands around a cup of warm cheer. All these drinks do the trick, raising your spirit levels in every sense, and imbuing all and sundry with festive feeling.

MULLED CIDER

Makes 1.2 litres, enough for about 6 servings

1 litre dry cider
60ml dark rum
250ml apple and ginger tea, made up from herbal teabag
40g soft dark brown sugar
2 clementines/satsumas
4 whole cloves
2 sticks cinnamon
2 fresh bay leaves
2 cardamom pods, bruised

I find Dr Stuart's apple and ginger tea (see Stockists p.267) perfect here, but there are so many herbal teas to choose from now, so take your pick.

MAKE AHEAD TIP:
Make the cider, strain and cool. Remove the cloves at this point otherwise the flavour will become too overpowering as the drinks sits. Cover and keep in a cool, dark place for up to 2 days until needed. When ready to serve, return the mulled cider to the saucepan and reheat gently without boiling.

Much as I adore the *vin chaud* on p.261, I think there is room to expand the repertoire of warm punches to get a Christmas party started, or to warm body and soul after a brisk walk or a bout of carol singing (not that I could ever inflict my voice on anyone). This mulled cider is mellow and fruity and, despite the rum sploshed in as well, mild to the taste and all too drinkable. Just make sure you don't swig while it's still mouth-burningly hot.

❋ Pour the cider, rum and herbal tea into a wide saucepan, add the sugar and put over a low heat to mull.

❋ Halve the clementines or satsumas, stick a clove into each half, and add them to the pan.

❋ Break the cinnamon sticks in half, and tip into the pan. Add the bay leaves and bruised cardamom pods, and let everything infuse as the pan comes almost to the boil.

❋ Once the pan is near to boiling, turn down the heat, so that it just keeps warm, and ladle into heatproof glasses with handles to serve.

❋ To make this into **a non-alcoholic warmer**, replace the cider and rum with 1 litre of apple juice and 60ml freshly squeezed lemon juice. You probably won't need the sugar, but taste when warm to see if you want a little and then add as you like.

Hot Honeyed Vodka (back left and front right); Mulled Cider (centre); Vin Chaud (back right and front left)

VIN CHAUD

Yes, this is simply the French for mulled wine, but this is how I like to think of it, as drunk from paper cups at the beautiful Christmas market in Brussels or in Francophone alpine regions – I love snow-peaked mountains, so long as I don't have to ski down them.

❄ Pour the wine into a large saucepan and add the remaining ingredients.

❄ Bring to an almost boil, *don't* actually let it boil, then turn down the heat and let it simmer gently.

❄ The mulled wine is ready when the sugar has dissolved, though you can leave the pan on a very low heat so that your *vin chaud* stays *chaud*. This is best served in small cups or heatproof glasses with handles.

❄ To make an approximate, **non-alcoholic version**, replace the 75cl bottle of wine with 500ml pomegranate juice and 500ml cranberry juice, and dispense with the cognac.

Serves 6–8

1 x 75cl bottle good robust red wine, such as Beaujolais

4 cinnamon sticks

1 x 13cm curl orange zest, shaved off the orange with a vegetable peeler

75g sugar

1 star anise

5 whole cloves

80ml cognac

MAKE AHEAD TIP:
Make the *vin chaud*, strain and cool. Remove the cloves at this point otherwise the flavour will become too overpowering as the drinks sits. Cover and keep in a cool, dark place for 1 day until needed. When ready to serve, return it to the saucepan and reheat gently without boiling.

HOT HONEYED VODKA

This is a warmed-up version of *Krupnik*, the Polish honey vodka – and none the worse for that. Indeed, you can make this and drink whatever's left (in that unlikely instance) cold. It's all good.

❄ Put the sugar into a large, heavy-based saucepan with the cold water and dissolve over a low heat.

❄ When the sugar has dissolved and started bubbling, leave to bubble for a few seconds until it turns a pale caramel colour. Carefully pour in the boiling water, standing well back as you do so, as it will splutter.

❄ Add the allspice berries, cinnamon stick, cloves and lemon zest (shaved off with a vegetable peeler) and bring to the boil – *never* stir – and let it bubble for 5 minutes.

Makes 1.25 litres, enough for about 25 double-shot glasses

400g sugar

2 x 15ml tablespoons cold water

1 litre boiling water, from a kettle

10 allspice berries

1 cinnamon stick

2 whole cloves

1 lemon, zest and juice

300g honey

500ml vodka

❅ Add the honey, stir, and keep stirring until the honey has dissolved into the spiced caramel.

❅ Bring to the boil again, then take off the heat and add the vodka, stirring well, and the juice of the peeled lemon.

❅ Strain into a jug and pour into waiting shot glasses; it should be invigoratingly warm, rather than burningly hot, so that it can be knocked back with relish. *Na zdrowie!*

HOT SCHNOCOLATE

Makes enough for 2 cups

500ml full-fat milk

100g best-quality dark chocolate, chopped small

4 teaspoons sugar

1 x 25ml measure peppermint schnapps (see Stockists p.267)

FOR SERVING:

125ml whipping or double cream

3 peppermint candy canes (see Stockists p.267), or minty boiled sweets

Well, how could I resist? A friend gave me this gorgeously named concoction – hot chocolate with peppermint schnapps in it, of course – a Christmas or so ago, and I have had to appropriate it. She couldn't remember where she got the name or the idea, so whoever created it, thank you. The recipe below, however, is mine, from distant, delicious memory.

❅ Whip the cream and put aside. Put the milk and chopped chocolate into a pan and slowly warm, until the chocolate has melted.

❅ Add the sugar, stir well, and bring to almost boiling point, though *at no time* must it boil.

❅ Off the heat, stir in the peppermint schnapps, and leave while you crush one of the candy canes or your boiled sweets: you just need enough beautiful pink splinters to adorn the top of the hot schnocolates; leave aside for one moment, though.

❅ Pour the hot schnocolate into 2 mugs and top with the whipped cream, sprinkle the crushed candy cane (or sweets) on top and, if wished, put a whole candy cane into each before drinking one and handing out the second to a lucky other.

❅ If you want this to be a **non-alchoholic, but still pepperminty hot chocolate,** replace the schnapps with a drop or two of natural peppermint flavouring, which is generally how the best-tasting peppermint essence is labelled.

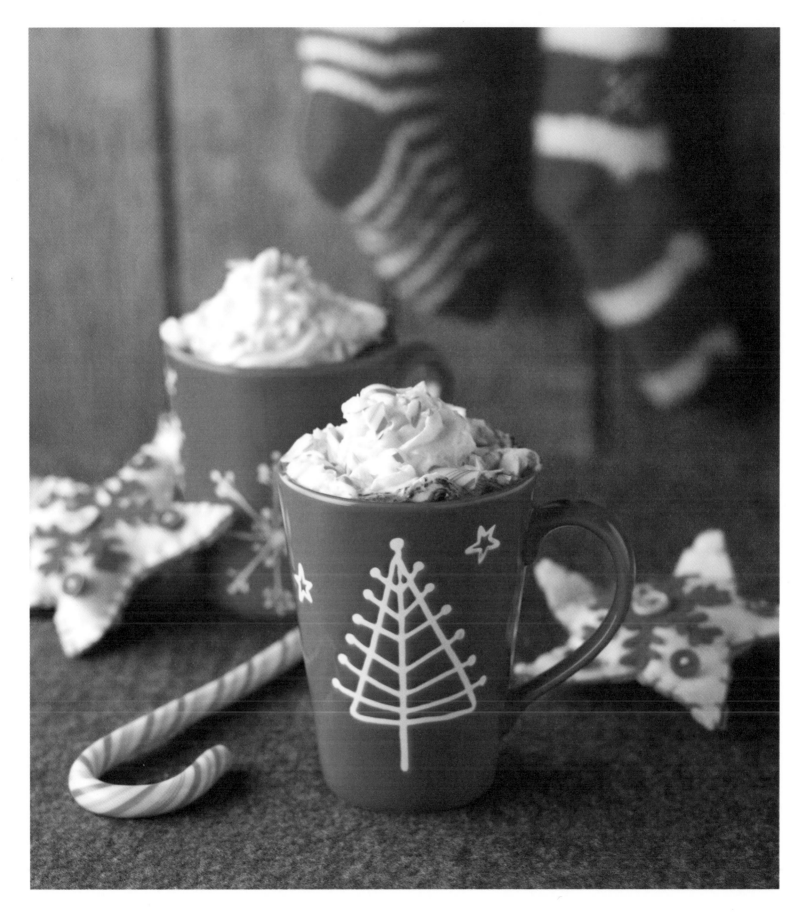

DR LAWSON PRESCRIBES ...

EVEN BOWING UNDER THE WEIGHT of this season of over-indulgence, I will never be a nil by mouth kind of a person. I go with the Ancient Greeks on this: let food be your medicine. So here is a brace of recipes to help you through the festivities.

CUBAN CURE BLACK BEAN SOUP

Serves 2

150g chorizo sausage (not the salami sort)

2 spring onions

¹/₂ teaspoon ground cumin

1 x 425g can black beans, drained

1 fresh tomato

500ml chicken broth/stock (I do not intend
    for you to make your own stock for this; I
    use the stuff in concentrated form which
    you simply add to water)

juice of 1 lime, or to taste (feel free to squirt
    in lime from a plastic bottle)

2–4 x 15ml tablespoons chopped coriander

This is the perfect antidote to an evening soured by too much office-party wine. A clanging head finds solace in fire and fat, and this bean stew of a soup provides both, with ease and speed.

❋ Cut the chorizo sausage into slices about the size of one-pound coins (2cm diameter). Then cut each coin in half or quarters, as you wish.

❋ Cook the chorizo pieces in a dry pan for about 5 minutes, or until they give up their orange oil and crisp up a little. Remove them with a slotted spatula to a bowl or plate.

❋ Cut off the green parts of the spring onions and reserve for slicing later, then finely slice the white part and add this to the pan slicked with orange oil, along with the ground cumin, stirring everything together for a couple of minutes over a gentle heat.

❋ Tip the black beans into the pan and roughly chop the tomato, adding the pieces – peel, pips and all – along with the chicken stock. Stir the pan and let it simmer, uncovered, for 10 minutes.

❋ Ladle the soup into 2 bowls; add the reserved chorizo pieces, then give each bowl a good squirt of lime juice and sprinkle with the finely sliced green part of the spring onions and some chopped coriander.

MAKE AHEAD TIP:
Make the soup up to 3 days ahead. Cool, cover and store in the fridge. When ready to serve, return the soup to the saucepan and bring slowly to the boil. Reduce the heat and simmer very gently for 5 minutes until piping hot. Ladle the soup into bowls and finish as directed.

A PANACEA FOR SEASONAL AND SELF-INFLICTED ILLS

I love any sort of chicken soup, known in its original form as "Jewish penicillin". This version is rather different: hot with ginger, which is warming, soothing and exotically aromatic. It's been recently "proved" – whatever that means – that chicken soup really does inhibit infections and clear the tubes, so those Jewish matrons weren't actually wrong… Not that they ever thought they were.

Fantastically sour, fragrant Seville oranges often come into season at Christmastime, but if they are late, or not in season where you are, a clementine or satsuma (or similar) mixed with lime approximates the taste and sour punch you want. And provides the same very necessary vitamin C.

Chicken wings, I find, make for the best chicken soup, and a gratifyingly economical one. You can eat this soup plain, or spiked with any or all of the suggestions, right.

❉ Put the chicken wings, carrot, onion and cinnamon stick into a large saucepan. (I never bother to peel onions for stock as I feel the skin adds to the deep gold of your eventual stock.)

❉ Pour in the water, stir in the salt, and add the piece of ginger left whole.

❉ Finally add the juice of the Seville orange (or the mixed clementine or satsuma and lime juices).

❉ Bring to the boil, then turn down and let simmer for $1^1/2$–2 hours, until the liquid has reduced by about half. Taste to see if the chickeniness has come through: when it has, the stock is reduced enough and ready.

❉ Strain into a wide-necked measuring jug or bowl and leave to cool (you should have about 1.5 litres) and when cold, chill in the fridge overnight to let all the fat rise to the surface, so it becomes a solid layer you can easily remove.

❉ When you want salvation in the form of this soup, scrape off the fat, and wipe over the surface with kitchen paper to degrease efficiently, then ladle as much as you want to cook at each time into a saucepan and bring to the boil.

❉ Drink from a mug if you want this clear; or spoon from a bowl, first adding some beansprouts and, after ladling in, scatter with chilli, spring onions and coriander as you wish.

Makes 4–6 bowls or mugs

1.5kg chicken wings (you can use a couple of chicken carcasses or a fresh, uncooked small chicken instead)

1 carrot, peeled and halved

1 onion (unpeeled), cut in half

1 cinnamon stick

3 litres water

1 x 15ml tablespoon Maldon salt or $^1/2$ tablespoon table salt

approx. 1 x 7cm knob ginger, peeled

juice of 1 Seville orange (or juice of 1 clementine or satsuma mixed with juice of $^1/2$–1 lime to taste)

FOR SERVING (OPTIONAL):
handful of beansprouts

1 small red chilli, deseeded and cut into fine wheels

2 spring onions, finely sliced

chopped coriander

MAKE AHEAD TIP:
Make the chicken stock up to 3 days ahead. Cool, cover and store in the fridge. When ready to serve, remove the fat, ladle into a saucepan and bring slowly to the boil. Finish as directed.

FREEZE AHEAD TIP:
Cool and freeze the chicken stock, in handy portions, for up to 3 months. Thaw overnight in the fridge, then reheat as above and finish as directed.

STOCKISTS

Not all the ingredients or items below will be hard for you to find, but some could be, so – being an internet shopping addict myself – I feel it only right to give a short list of online suppliers to help you source something I've mentioned in the text but that might elude you on the high street. For a wider range of stockists, see **www.nigella.com**.

DRINKS

Crème de lychee, Pama, Todka, Bramley and Gage quince liqueur, Tuaca, butterscotch and peppermint schnapps and many other cocktail ingredients and glasses; Monin syrups; lychee purée
www.thedrinkshop.com

Cornish Camel Valley sparkling wine and Bramley and Gage quince liqueur, Todka
www.kernowharvest.co.uk

Pedro Ximénez sherry
www.jeroboams.co.uk

Dr Stuart's apple and ginger tea
www.goodnessdirect.co.uk

CAKE DECORATING AND SPECIALIST BAKING EQUIPMENT

Fir-tree cake tin, and cake papers, edible gold stars, gold lustres, disco glitters, gold leaf, ready-to-roll icing, crystallized rose petals and various Christmas sprinkles and cutters, gift bags and boxes
www.jane-asher.co.uk

Large variety of Christmas sprinkles, decorations, cutters, and related paraphernalia
www.splatcooking.com

Sugar poinsettias for decorating Christmas cupcakes and other Christmassy icing items
www.thecakeplace.co.uk

Candied and crystallized fruits and flowers
www.confiserieflorian.com

Chocolate covered clementines, golden sultanas, mini marshmallows, chocolate-covered coffee beans
www.panzers.co.uk

CULINARY AMERICANA

Mini marshmallows, peppermint candy canes, canned black beans, canned pumpkin purée
www.americansweets.co.uk

Canned black beans, canned pumpkins, mini marshmallows
www.panzers.co.uk

MEAT AND POULTRY

Geese and wide selection of meat cuts
www.donaldrussell.com

Turkey (with turkey/meat thermometer thrown in)
www.kelly-turkeys.com

All meat and poultry and wide variety of other foodstuffs
www.natoora.co.uk

OTHER FOODS

Mellow Yellow rapeseed oil
www.farrington-oils.co.uk

The Food Doctor original seed mix
www.thefooddoctor.com

SPICES

Red peppercorns, white peppercorns, and huge variety of other produce and ingredients
www.oakleaf-european.co.uk

Nigella seeds and other seasonings
www.seasonedpioneers.co.uk

OTHER ITEMS

Meat thermometer, decorative cocktail sticks, jam and preserving jars and bottles, gift bags, cardboard cake cases and a rich supply of other kitchen paraphernalia
www.lakeland.co.uk

Trees, baubles, fairy lights, wrapping paper and all things Christmassy
www.christmastimeuk.com

ACKNOWLEDGEMENTS

This is the first time, since I began with *How to Eat* in 1998, that I have published a book two years running. I don't feel it's something I should make a habit of, but nor can I regret it. Writing and making a book is something I love above all else and, besides, self-denial has never been my strong suit. I just feel grateful that I have work I enjoy so much. But such gratitude is really owed to the raft of people whose hard work allows me to enjoy myself, and whose support and encouragement are crucial. Thanks – heartfelt and enduring – to (in alphabetical order) Olivia Antolik, Jan Bowmer, Louise Dennys, Moyra Fraser, Mary Gibson, Vivienne Gill, Poppy Hampson, Caz Hildebrand (the *sine qua non* of any enterprise I embark on), Julie Martin, Lis Parsons, the inspirational and pitch-perfect Gail Rebuck and Alison Samuel, the most elegant and erudite of editors: without all these, it wouldn't be as much fun; indeed, it wouldn't even be possible.

The same is true of those whose names follow (again, alphabetically) and who make up what I think of as my work family, and who, teasingly I think, call themselves Team Nigella: Kate Bull, Mark Hutchinson, Rose Murray, Hettie Potter, Ed Victor, Zoe Wales and Anzelle Wasserman. I know how fortunate I am to be thus surrounded by those I love and trust.

Over the last year my home has looked like a cross between Santa's Grotto and Miss Havisham's apartments. Much of this agreeable clutter I provided myself, but as much again was gratefully harvested especially for this project and I owe thanks to those who have so generously helped furnish the pictures in this book, even if simultaneously feeding my addiction for seasonalia, in particular Aspen & Brown, B&Q, Best Season, Big Tomato Company, Cath Kidston, Ceramica Blue, Cherubim, ChristmastimeUK and the ever helpful Alfred Rose and his elves, The Conran Shop, The General Trading Company, Heals, Jane Asher Party Cakes & Sugarcraft and the fabulous David Trumper, John Lewis Partnership, Krebs International Glass, Laura Ashley, Marks & Spencer, Merchant Gourmet, Nordicware, Ocean Spray, Papstar, Peter Harvey, Star Trading, Steelite International, Sur la Table (notably Olivia and her staff at the Dallas branch), VV Rouleaux, Wedgwood and Wild Card.

This book is subtitled "Food, Family, Friends, Festivities", and it remains only for me to say that the food and festivities would mean nothing without those other two components; it is to my family and my friends that my deepest gratitude are owed, not just–as the Dogs Trust admonitory poster used to say– for Christmas, but for life.

INDEX

ONE OF THE *OBSERVER FOOD MONTHLY*'S
TEN CHEFS OF THE DECADE

**'QUEEN OF THE KITCHEN · NATIONAL TREASURE ·
PUTS US IN TOUCH WITH OUR INNER DOMESTIC GODDESS'**
OBSERVER

Nigella Lawson is the author of nine bestselling
cookery books which, together with her TV series
and Quick Collection apps, have made hers
a household name around the world.

'I am unapologetic about being a home cook rather than a chef.

Real cooking, the sort that goes on in homes, does not have to be tricksy or difficult. A dish of chicken poached with leeks and carrots definitely isn't fancy. But it tastes good, and feels essentially nourishing, to both body and soul, to cook and eat.

I want you to feel that I'm there with you, in the kitchen, as you cook. My books are the conversations we might be having.'

Nigella Lawson